BRITAIN
a Portrait

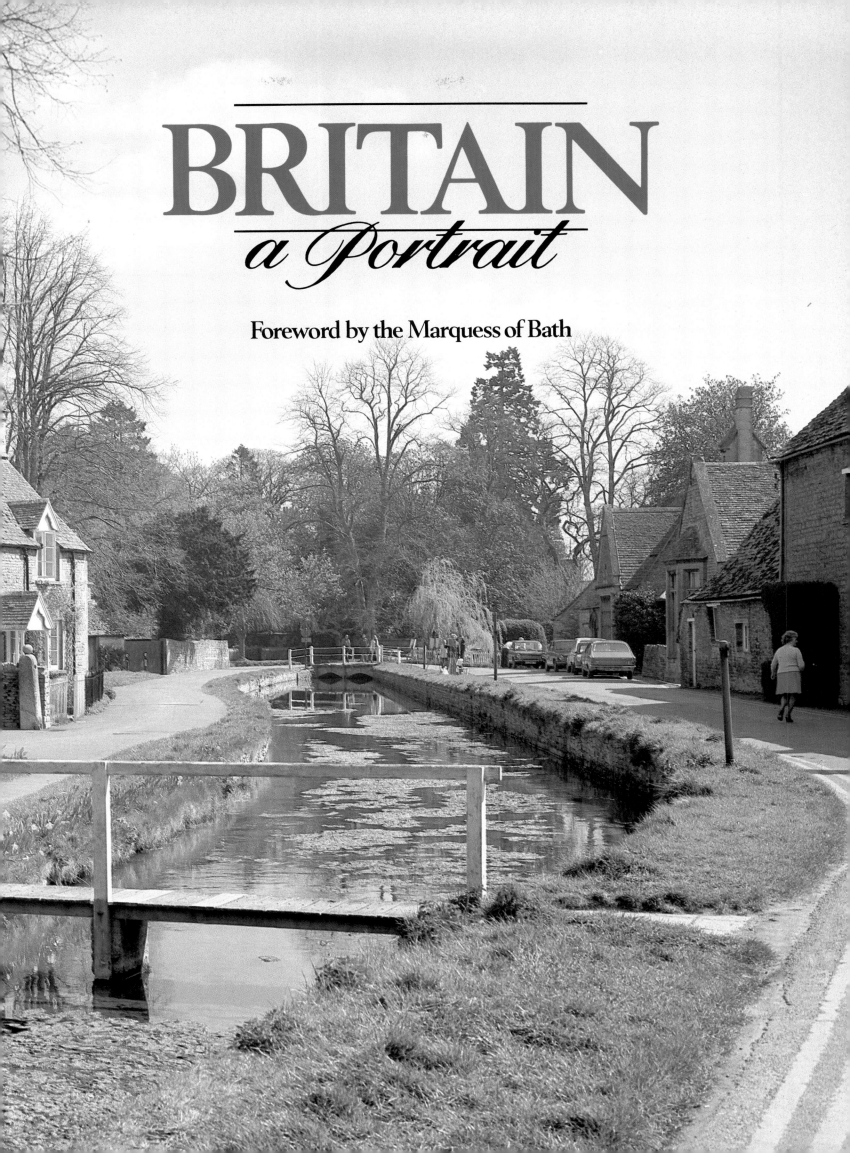

BRITAIN
a Portrait

Foreword by the Marquess of Bath

CONTENTS

Britain A Portrait was first published in 1984
by Octopus Books Limited
59 Grosvenor Street, London W1

This special abridged edition published in 1985

© 1984, 1985 Hennerwood Publications Limited

ISBN 0 86273 238 7

Printed and bound in Hong Kong

Some of the material in this book originally appeared in
The Love of Britain series published by Octopus Books Limited.
These sections have been revised and updated.
New material by Joyce Robins.

FOREWORD BY
THE MARQUESS OF BATH

In these troubled times of international and industrial unrest, there is one factor that has remained unchanged by time and devastating wars – the pride of the British people in their heritage; yet now I fear that even this is in danger, as daily we read of Houses and Estates having to be sold through lack of sufficient funds. For even as I write many of this country's treasures are being dispersed around the world, and lost to our nation. I feel it is the duty of the media in general to rekindle and encourage this fire of pride in the British peoples, so that our heritage can stand proud for many centuries to come. This is why it gives me immense pleasure to have been asked to write a foreword to this excellent portrait of Britain's outstanding beauty.

I suppose that I can count myself lucky, for I have the total support of my wife, Virginia, and other members of my family and a remarkable staff, all of whom are utterly dedicated to the preservation of Longleat and its outstanding surroundings. I, personally, cannot imagine what I would have done with my life if I had not been so fortuitous to have inherited such a magnificent property. My only regret is that it occurred through the death of my elder brother in the Great War. My efforts, as those of others, would be worthless without responsible publications such as this.

If you happen to read the foreword before you consider purchasing this volume, whether you are a visitor to our shores, or an inhabitant, please understand my pride in home and country, and forgive me for what you may well decide is boasting. Pride is numbered as one of the 'Seven Deadly Sins'. It is a sin of which I am totally guilty, and without shame I will suffer the consequences that go with it. This publication has, however, eased my mind that I am not alone in suffering from this sin, for within its pages you will find the glory that is forever ours, to be shared with all nationalities that admire a beautiful and varied scenery, quality and creative genius. Geniuses such as 'Capability' Brown, Vanbrugh, Wren and Repton, who were inspired to create lasting monuments in an island that inspired them.

Authors and poets have written, and hopefully will continue to write, eulogies to our land; a land that created them, and indirectly fashioned their success, yet, ironically, occasionally rejected them. The Wordsworths of this country saw Britain in its finest simplicity – a gift that I, regretfully, am incapable of being able to put into words. Forgive me, therefore, if I borrow for a moment a verse from one of our greats, Rudyard Kipling, who managed to combine his pride with humour.

> If England were what England seems
> An' not the England of our dreams
> But only putty, brass an' paint
> 'Ow quick we'd drop 'er. But she ain't.

It is therefore with great enthusiasm that I wish this book the credit that I feel is due to it. Thumb through its pages, but, please, treat it with respect, for what you will find between its leaves is our national heritage – an entity to be appreciated and not destroyed.

I proudly remain Britain's most ardent and faithful supporter.

(signed) Bath

page 1: Buttermere and High Stile, Cumbria
pages 2-3: Lower Slaughter, Gloucestershire
left: Longleat House

INTRODUCTION

In world terms the British Isles are tiny. Great Britain, which is merely the political term used for the three countries of England, Scotland and Wales, covers an area barely one-third that of the state of Texas. Now Texas may not be as big as some Texans believe but during the First World War when the United States announced that two million soldiers were to be shipped across the Atlantic to England, there was widespread disbelief that there could possibly be room for so many additional people in 'that little dot on the map'. Little dots on world maps usually turn out to be a lot bigger when you reach them and Britain has, in fact, over 4,000 square metres (about one acre) of dry land for every one of its nearing sixty million inhabitants. So no visitor to Britain – and some twelve million arrive each year – need fear to find standing room only. In addition, for those who do not mind getting their feet wet, there are some 240,000 hectares (600,000 acres) of inland water – canals, lakes and rivers.

Even so, Britain is a very compact unit. The distance from Land's End in the far south-west to John o'Groats in the far north-east is a little under 965 km (600 miles) as the 'Concorde' flies and the greatest east-west dimension is about 563 km (350 miles). Thus no place is ever very far distant from any other place – a fact which really makes it relatively easy to see a great deal of the country in a very short time.

Happily for those people who love the countryside the population spread in Britain is very uneven. One third of the people live in urban areas which occupy only about three per cent of the land. To many people's astonishment there are, particularly in Wales and much of Scotland, great tracts of uninhabited and almost unvisited country, and in England itself it is not uncommon to hear of search parties looking for walkers reported missing in the wild open spaces of Dartmoor, the Lake District or the Yorkshire moors. Even around London and other big cities there are still places so rural and peaceful that foxes, deer and badgers abound and often surprise townspeople by wandering through their gardens or even, sometimes, raiding their refuse bins.

On the whole Britain's scenery does not attempt to compete in grandeur with such outsize marvels as the Grand Canyon or the Himalayas. Her speciality (though the Scottish highlands, Snowdonia and the Cumbrian lakes instantly refute it) is the man-made scene: the ordered landscape, the compact view, the happy juxtaposition of church and village green, cottage and tree, wood and hillside, house and park.

Man fashioned much of the countryside of Britain

Above: *The old cottages and medieval abbey walls of Shaftesbury's cobbled Gold Hill overlook the Blackmore Vale.*

when he carved fields out of forests, drained swamps and planted the hedgerows. He first began to put his stamp on the landscape 5000 years ago, when the first farmers cleared land for their crops. The grasslands of Salisbury Plain, the Yorkshire Wolds and the South Downs are legacies from these primitive farmers.

Prehistoric man left other legacies: the mysterious stone monuments like Avebury and Stonehenge in Wiltshire and Callanish on the Isle of Lewis, the Iron Age hill forts such as Maiden Castle and Hambledon Hill in Dorset. He established the first trading routes across Britain, the most famous of them the Icknield Way.

Each milestone in British history left its mark on the countryside. Four centuries of Roman occupation left 9,654 km (6,000 miles) of roads, many of them, like Watling Street across Kent and Fosse Way from Devon to London, still used today, and the Roman provincial cities grew into county towns like Gloucester, Chester and Cirencester. After 1066, the Normans built a chain of imposing castles to control their newly conquered territory. Many, like Ludlow in Shropshire, still stand as imposing monuments to their power.

It was only in Tudor times that Britain began to take on the look which gives it special charm: the neatly hedged fields, the great country houses with their deer parks and landscaped grounds. Henry VIII's onslaught on the monasteries meant that land was available in plenty for the aristocracy to build the palatial houses which are today's stately homes. Often they stripped the abandoned monasteries and abbeys for their construction materials. Fountains Hall in North Yorkshire used stone from nearby Fountains Abbey and Longleat in Wiltshire

incorporated the ruins of an Augustinian Priory.

Man-made, too, were the parks and pleasure-grounds which surround the great houses of the 'landed gentry' and which are such an agreeable feature of the British scene. The two most famous names in landscape gardening both belong to the 18th century – Lancelot 'Capability' Brown and Humphry Repton. Both had an intense and instinctive feeling for the quality of English landscape: Brown the practical gardener turned artist; Repton the imaginative artist turned gardener. Economic pressures are constantly eroding these big estates and hundreds of country houses, many of real architectural merit, have been pulled down since 1945 because their owners could not afford to maintain them. Some of the more enterprising owners of the larger estates, like the

Above: *A travelling blacksmith shoes a mighty shire horse.*

Above: *Little Moreton Hall is a fine example of Cheshire's decorative black and white timbering.*

Above: *Dorset's Corfe Castle remains an impressive ruin.*

seems right that every citizen should have access to it: there is virtually no private foreshore in Britain.

Britain is singularly rich in ecclesiastical architecture and her cathedrals, mostly the concept of Norman architects, excel in size, and arguably in magnificence, many of those in Europe, while even non-Christians are singularly proud of the churches which are such a feature of every town and village. In them can be traced every architectural influence from pre-Saxon to the present day. The churches of Merrie England were village centres for singing, dancing and drama and the tradition lives on in bell-ringing. Churches were built as an expression of community pride, so they are often far larger than needed for the size of the parish, let alone the congregation: for instance, money from the thriving wool trade gave rise to the great churches of Lavenham in Suffolk and Chipping Campden in the Cotswolds.

The villages of Britain have changed with the times; they no longer aim to be mainly self-supporting, living off the land. Some have to cope with an influx of tourism, some are hide-aways for commuters or weekenders. Yet all over the British Isles there are unspoiled villages taking their character from the area from which they grew: the cob and thatch of Devon, the colour-washed stone of Cornwall, the half timbers of the West Midlands, the blue slate of Wales, the coloured sandstone of Lothian and Tayside.

Alehouses have been recorded in Britain for 2000 years and the names of country pubs are often links with the past: 'The Bull', 'The Bear' and 'The Cock' are reminders of the brutal sports of baiting bulls and bears and cock-fighting and those dating from mediaeval times often take their names from those given to abbey hospices. 'The Cross Keys' is the emblem of St Peter, 'The Lamb and Flag' was the symbol of the Knights Templar pledged to protect pilgrims to the Holy Land. The symbols of the craft guilds still survive as inn signs: 'The Axe and Compass' for the carpenters, 'The Ram' for the cloth-workers and 'The Boot' for the cobblers.

Countryside crafts grew to meet local needs with the materials near at hand and with increasing mechaniza-

Marquess of Bath at Longleat, the Earl of March at Goodwood and the Duke of Bedford at Woburn, have turned them into money-earning businesses catering for a wide spectrum of tourists and holidaymakers. Other estates have come into the hands of the National Trust and other charitable organizations dedicated to preserving Britain's treasures for the benefit of the people for all time.

Since Britain is an island and nowhere is more than 80 miles from the sea, the sea and the sea coast occupy an exceptional position in the affections and in the recreational life of her people. There can be few Britons who have never seen the sea or spent a holiday at the seaside – and what an inviting seaside it is. The waters around Britain may not be as warm as the Mediterranean (though because of the influence of the Gulf stream they never get really cold) but her beaches, bays, inlets, cliffs and rocky headlands are incomparable and rival anything that Europe can muster, while her energetic tidal system scours the coasts clean twice a day. If guaranteed warmth and sunshine could be added to the scenic splendours of the west coast of Scotland it would quickly become the world's most sought-after playground. In all, Britain has 9,654 km (6000 miles) of coastline, again much of it preserved by the National Trust or by local authorities. The sea, Britain's most formidable defence in the past, may now have lost that role, but at least it

Above: *An Oxford Morris 'side' dancing outside the Sheldonian Theatre.*

tion and mass production the old skills began to die out, but there is still a desire for handmade quality and the 1970s brought a revival of interest in crafts. Many old forges are in use making decorative wrought iron, as well as repairing agricultural machinery, an occasional village baker has survived the age of factory bread and draws grateful customers from far and wide and thatchers, each of whom leaves his own distinctive mark on a thatched roof, are in great demand. Weaving, spinning and dyeing are thriving crafts and no area is without its potters, working with clays which differ in colour, texture and content according to the locality. One factor which has a continuous influence on everything in Britain is the climate. It greens the fields, weathers the stone, shapes the hills and ripens the crops. Every Briton claims an inalienable right to complain about the weather. King Charles I, who is credited with the remark that the English summer is made up of three fine days followed by a thunderstorm, was merely giving royal approval to the right that his subjects demanded. They complain not because the weather is necessarily bad but because it is changeable and unpredictable. The Meteorological Office does its best and its forecasts are usually right – somewhere. As weather conditions in Britain are so localized their forecast may be wrong in one place but perfectly right a few miles away. Compared with many countries Britain's climate is benign: there are rarely extremes of heat or cold, hurricanes are unknown, rainfall is low in the south and east, moderate in the west and north and, contrary to Hollywood's belief that

Above: *Keen cricketers of every age and ability play on Britain's village greens.*

London is perpetually enshrouded, fog is experienced on fewer than five days a year on average. In the summer, daylight can be 18 hours long.

In spite of her political and economic problems, in spite of planning errors that have allowed industry to mar large areas of countryside, in spite of housing, roads, railways, pylons, power stations, car parks and television aerials, Britain remains a happy, green and very pleasant land full of pleasure-giving sights, sounds and scenery; a country that engenders much love and devotion especially among those who may have left her shores. There can be no country in the world which so many misty-eyed exiles fondly refer to as 'home'.

Above: *'Dawn, a secret, shy and cold' breaks over some of Britain's most fertile farming land, in Oxfordshire.*

SCOTLAND

On the map or from the air Scotland resembles an uncompleted jigsaw puzzle, a puzzle whose northernmost pieces overlap the latitude of Greenland and the southernmost latitude of Omsk. Its climate and botany, however, reflect little of the extremes of those places.

Scotland is about the size of Belgium and the Netherlands together, with about one-fifth of their combined populations. The country is divided broadly into Highlands, a group of massifs, moors, ravines and torrents, and Lowlands, which are not in fact low but are mainly a series of smooth hills and pastures intersected by river valleys and belts of manufacturing towns. On the eastern seaboard, cliffs and headlands stand guard over river estuaries (firths) and angular bays. The west coast is split into ragged promontories and inland seas (sea lochs) which overlook a panorama of 700 islands. Three groups of islands, Orkney and Shetland in the north and the Outer Hebrides in the northwest, are rich in Norse memories.

As the beating of Atlantic rollers formed the seascape, so the harsh weathering of native rock and the passage of glaciers shaped the landscape: the attractive pinks and greys of sandstone and granite hills, Scott's 'darksome glens and gleaming lochs', and the crag-and-tail formations on which were built the superb fortresses of Stirling and Edinburgh. These impressive formations occurred where ice-rivers hit impregnable rock. The ice divided and flowed round the rock, leaving behind a diminishing trail of rubble.

The Scots have a fierce love for their country. Sir Walter Scott, supreme propagandist for the nation, and a host of patriotic writers since his time have stressed the superiority of all things Scottish: the scenery, Scottish determination and courage, and Scottish law, education and football. Sceptical non-Scots should beware; these extravagant claims are frequently all too true. Scotland's scenery is spectacular, though its greatest river is but a rivulet and the highest mountain but a hill on the world scale.

Some irresistible element infuses everything Scotland offers us. There may be other countries whose fighting men wear skirts, whose music comes from a bag of wind, whose peasant diet includes offal and onions, and whose deepwater lakes have their mythical monsters. But for most, the kilt, bagpipes, haggis and Loch Ness monster evoke the spirit of Scotland.

Industrialization has changed some of the scenes which Scott made famous. Scotland has its urban sprawls and, in the once-idyllic north-east, a growing oil industry. However, over broad tracts of mainland and on every island the visitor may still travel on peaceful, well-made roads and networks of hill and forest trails.

Romantics trace Scotland's historical beginnings to Scota, daughter of a Biblical pharaoh. To successive expansionist powers – the Romans, the Norsemen and the Anglo-Saxons – Scotland was little more than a trouble-spot. Until the 14th century the organization of its monarchy was primitive and the one real dynasty, the Stuarts, brought little but anguish until union with England in 1707 settled most quarrels. Jacobite rebellions in 1715 and 1745 account for some picturesque legends in modern Scotland, but its subsequent history was generally speaking that of Great Britain.

The Scots are proud and parochial and resolutely opposed to any movement which threatens their independence. In rural communities there is a strong attachment to old values and moral standards. Religious bigotry is not unknown, but class distinctions in Scotland are less emphatic than in England. The characteristics one associates with the typical Scot are fortitude and obduracy, thrift and a keen business instinct; and a love of Scotland.

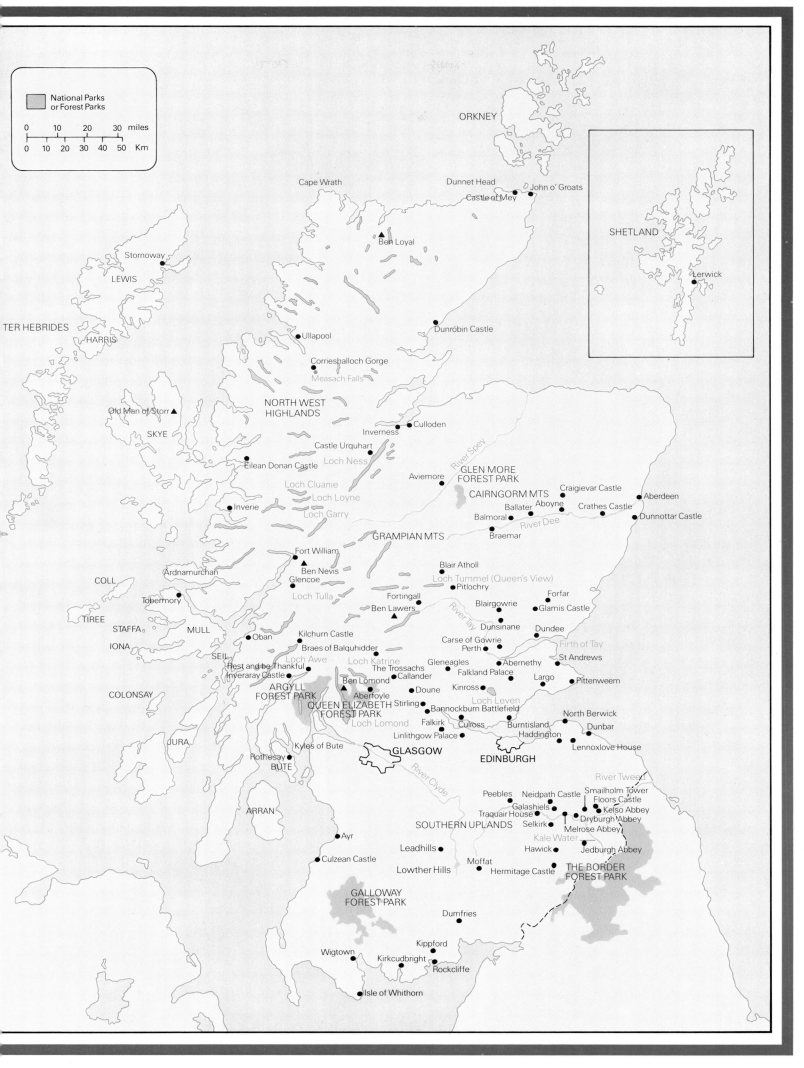

ORKNEY

SHETLAND

Lerwick

National Parks
or Forest Parks

0   10   20   30 miles
0   10 20 30 40 50 Km

Cape Wrath
Dunnet Head
Castle of Mey
John o' Groats

Ben Loyal ▲

Stornoway

LEWIS

TER HEBRIDES

HARRIS

Ullapool
Dunrobin Castle

Corrieshalloch Gorge
Measach Falls

Old Man of Storr ▲

NORTH WEST
HIGHLANDS

SKYE

Culloden
Inverness

Castle Urquhart
Loch Ness

Eilean Donan Castle

Aviemore
GLEN MORE
FOREST PARK

River Spey

Loch Cluanie
CAIRNGORM MTS
Craigievar Castle
Aberdeen

Loch Loyne

Inverie

Loch Garry

GRAMPIAN MTS
Ballater Aboyne
Balmoral
Crathes Castle
Dunnottar Castle

River Dee

Braemar

COLL

Fort William
Ben Nevis ▲
Ardnamurchan
Glencoe

Blair Atholl
Loch Tummel (Queen's View)
Pitlochry

Loch Tulla

TOBERMORY
Tobermory

Fortingall
Ben Lawers ▲

River Tay

Blairgowrie
Forfar
Glamis Castle

TIREE

STAFFA

MULL

Oban
Kilchurn Castle
Braes of Balquhidder

Loch Awe

Dunsinane
Dundee

Carse of Gowrie
Perth

IONA

SEIL

Loch Katrine
The Trossachs
Gleneagles
Abernethy
St Andrews

Rest and be Thankful
Inveraray Castle

Ben Lomond ▲
Callander
Doune
Falkland Palace
Largo

COLONSAY

ARGYLL
FOREST PARK

Kinross
Pittenweem

QUEEN ELIZABETH
FOREST PARK
Aberfoyle
Stirling
Loch Leven

Bannockburn Battlefield

Loch Lomond
Falkirk
Culross
North Berwick
Burntisland
Haddington
Dunbar

JURA

Kyles of Bute
Linlithgow Palace
Lennoxlove House

Rothesay
BUTE

GLASGOW
EDINBURGH

River Clyde

River Tweed

ARRAN

Peebles
Neidpath Castle
Smailholm Tower
Floors Castle
Galashiels
Kelso Abbey
Traquair House
Dryburgh Abbey
Selkirk
Melrose Abbey

SOUTHERN UPLANDS
Kale Water
Jedburgh Abbey

Ayr

Leadhills
Hawick
THE BORDER
FOREST PARK

Culzean Castle
Moffat
Lowther Hills
Hermitage Castle

GALLOWAY
FOREST PARK

Dumfries

Kippford

Wigtown
Kirkcudbright
Rockcliffe

Isle of Whithorn

11

THE HIGHLANDS & ISLANDS

The great surprise for visitors is the changing scenery of northern Scotland. It can pass from heather, bracken and springy turf to granite rock and bog, to serrated peak, snow-water lake and petrified forest, to the red Torridon sandstone of Wester Ross and the flowery land of Lochs Maree and Ewe. The black rocks of the Coolins on Skye, and of the Outer Hebrides, lie like basking whales on the horizon. Sea inlets grow ever deeper and more fjord-like. Cliffs on which the quartzite gleams above crescents of firm sand lead round Sutherland to Caithness, a windswept moorland country of Norse place-names.

The northern archipelagos, two groups of about 200 isles (40 inhabited), are also linked historically and geographically with Scandinavia. A resident of Haroldswick in Shetland, applying for a travel allowance and required to state the nearest railway station, wrote quite correctly 'Bergen' (Norway).

'Shetland for scenery, Orkney for antiquities' the saying goes, and both for bird-watching. Snowy owls, phalaropes, waders and divers, wheatears, shearwaters and Arctic terns, skuas, auks and kittiwakes nest in immense colonies on the stack rocks. A score of promising oil and natural gas fields, and two big terminals, Sullom Voe in Shetland and Flotta in Orkney, on which the pipelines converge, bring immigrant hordes of human beings. But they are an insignificant handful compared with the migratory swarms of many species of birds.

Golden eagles and equally spectacular ospreys can be seen in the west and central Highlands in protected habitats. The deer population is said to be denser than anywhere else in the world and it increases, despite the growing interest in stalking. Belgian, French and German businessmen pay up to £200 a day to participate in this pursuit.

Western islanders and Highlandmen speak Gaelic, a language akin to Erse, Welsh and Manx. There is no universally agreed grammar. The current dictionary dates from 1845 and not all the 90,000 Gaelic speakers in Scotland understand each other. Haunting love songs, chiefly associated with the Harris wool spinners and weavers in Hebridean crofts, are Gaelic's contribution to the nation's cultural heritage. Highland region and the Islands are rich in ancestral memories and their art and architecture are of a primitive nature.

The Shetland and Orkney islands are experiencing radical changes in their life patterns as a result of the exploitation of North Sea oil, but the two groups of islanders are fundamentally different. In the words of Moray McLaren, the Orcadian is a farmer with a boat while the Shetlander is a fisherman with a piece of land. To the west the islands group themselves into the Outer and Inner Hebrides, names that have gained romantic overtones from the lilting music of sad Gaelic songs and from the legends of Bonnie Prince Charlie. The Inner islands, of which Skye is the largest, are almost as mountainous as the mainland but parts of Uist and Lewis are relatively level and the scenery is bleak but striking. Benbecula is less bare and neglected-looking than the islands of the north.

Back on the mainland there is one part of Highland country that is notably 'un-highland', the Thurso-Wick-John o' Groats triangle. Inland from the rocky spectacular coast there are extensive tracts of uninhabited and uninhabitable peat bogs. Here, between John o' Groats and the Dunnet Head, the Queen Mother has her favourite castle-home of Mey, which she bought in 1952. Formerly known as Barrogill Castle, it was built in the sixteenth century and belonged to the Earls of Caithness. John o' Groats (named after John de Groot, a Dutchman who ran the Orkney ferry) is popularly thought of as the northernmost point of mainland Scotland, a distinction which rightly belongs to Dunnet Head, which is 3.2 km (two miles) nearer to the North Pole. From Dunnet Head's precipitous cliffs 90 m (300 ft) high, a lighthouse throws

Right: *Eilean Donan Castle in the western Highlands is much in demand with outdoor-fashion photographers and makers of Bonnie Prince Charlie films. The Prince was never there but the castle did have the distinction of being bombarded by a Royal Navy frigate during an abortive Spanish-Jacobite invasion in 1719. Eilean Donan and Loch Duich are close to journey's end on one of the Roads to the Isles which Doctor Johnson and Boswell travelled in 1773. Clach Johnson, a boulder in Glen Shiel a short distance east, is sometimes presented as the spot where Johnson decided to write his classic literary work of Scottish travel,* A Journey to the Western Isles.

Below: *In the 19th century the ancient castle of Dunrobin, near Dornoch, was turned into a Victorian extravaganza by the Duke of Sutherland, with more rooms than any hotel in Scotland. He was so fascinated by trains that he ran his own railway, fully equipped and staffed, in the park. Beinn a' Braghie rises 305m (1000 ft) above Dunrobin Glen. To reach the statue of the first Duke on its summit was a test of vehicle power in pioneering motoring days.*

Previous page: *A flotilla of islets, anchored for eternity. Highland scenery achieves its greatest splendour and tranquillity at Badcall Bay in north-west Sutherland. Beyond lies Lewis and, beyond that, America.*

Below right: *Crofters' cottages, such as these at Gearranan on the island of Lewis, are in danger of disappearing from the Scottish scene, now that young people find life in Stornoway more attractive. Even the older people of Lewis often need to augment the small income from their crofts by hand-weaving the famous tweed that takes its name from the contiguous island, Harris.*

Below: *The Highland cattle of Scotland are rarely bred elsewhere because they are slow to mature and their milk yield is low, but they are very hardy and their milk is rich. In colour they range from straw-yellow through several shades of red to almost black. They are an exceptionally docile breed.*

its steady beam across the turbulent waters of the Pentland Firth to Hoy, Flotta (at the entrance to Scapa Flow) and Mainland Orkney.

The core of the Highlands lies to the west between Ardnamurchan and Cape Wrath where mountain and loch endlessly alternate to make scenery unmatched anywhere else on earth. And looking seawards from Ardnamurchan Point there is a view of islands that includes those schoolboy favourites Rhum, Eigg and Muck as well as Coll, Tiree and, on a fine day, the Outer Hebrides. The passage north across Wester Ross involves taking either the beautiful if adventurous coast road by Loch Torridon and Loch Maree to Gairloch or crossing half the country to join the road from Inverness to Ullapool. This latter road, just before coming to Loch Broom, passes close to the Corrieshalloch Gorge where the Falls of Measach plunge 60 m (200 ft) into the echoing depths. Ullapool is the natural centre for this area. It is a small fishing port on a promontory jutting out from Loch Broom.

North of Ullapool the roads, which are rapidly being widened and resurfaced to cope with the increased traffic that North Sea oil and tourism are generating, are often single tracks with passing points marked by a diamond-shaped sign on a pole.

Left: *Stornoway, the main town and port of the Isle of Lewis, has a population of some 5000 mainly engaged in fishing and tweed-weaving. Herrings are being packed for export in this picture but there is also a big trade in lobsters. Tourism is making great progress in the island which has spectacular sandy beaches.*

Right: *Ben Loyal, with its four granite peaks, looms over the barren moorland that surrounds Loch Loyal. One of the most northerly mountains of Scotland, it rises to a height of 762 m (2506 ft) out of a truly primeval landscape formed by some of the oldest rock in Britain.*

Above: *Rising through the mists behind Loch Leathan on the east coast of Skye, the Old Man of Storr challenges climbers who find The Storr (719 m/2358 ft) too easy. It is a 49 m (160 ft) natural obelisk of black trap-rock first climbed in 1955. It can be seen from the road running north from Portree.*

Left: *Scotland can offer some of the most magnificent beaches in the world as this photo of Traigh Seilebost in the Outer Hebrides proves. The surrounding scenery is breathtaking with mountains, lochs and a profusion of wild flowers. It may seem surprising that more people do not take advantage of the splendid isolation that would give each islander 27 acres to himself if the land were equally divided. However the fact that one may expect a gale on average every six days and rain equally frequently makes the island more popular with the deer stalkers and fishermen who constitute its main visitors than with the average sun seeker.*

Below: *Very old inhabitants call them the 'long island', but to modern geography they are the Outer Hebrides. This is a kite-shaped group of islands 193 km (120 miles) long from Lewis and Harris, the cloth-weaving isles, down through the tapering tail of the Uists, Benbecula and Barra, to the fluttering fragments of Vatersay, Sandray, Berneray and others. Here lies the north-west frontier of civilized Europe. This is where the millionaire Lord Leverhulme, coming into possession of Lewis in 1918, poured a fortune into various schemes to improve the economy and retired defeated by local apathy.*
Sheep have to be cleared off the runway to permit the aircraft from Glasgow to land. The Politician, *with a huge cargo of whisky, went aground on the Eriskay rocks in 1941 and gave Compton Mackenzie the idea for the popular novel and movie* Whisky Galore.
'Black houses' survive on the smaller isles. These are cottages of undressed boulders, sometimes built half underground and sheeted down with a dense straw thatch. Modifications to the outline, such as windows, chimneys and a paved floor, make this South Uist cottage very attractive.

Right: *Barra, the windswept island, lies in the mainstream of the Gaelic language, folksong and legend. Kishmul Castle, built about 1430 by Barra's overlords, the MacNeils, is said to be the biggest ancient monument in the Hebrides. It protects the entrance to the island's only sheltered harbour, Castlebay. Southward in Berneray, the lighthouse on Barra Head stands 178 m (583 ft) above the sea, with the greatest arc of visibility in the world.*

Bottom: *On the west coast of the island of Lewis, near the head of Loch Roag, the Standing Stones of Callanish indicate that neolithic man was a resident of the Hebridean islands. One large cairn is encircled by 13 monoliths, and other stones which may have formed concentric circles are dotted about. There is a 'broch' (cylindrical stone tower of Pictish origin) a short distance away.*

Right: *Lobster creels are a familiar sight on the island of Burray, one of the 70 islands which make up the Orkneys, where fishing and cattle-raising are the main occupations of the inhabitants. The island is joined to the Orkney mainland by a causeway. Lobster fishing is very much an independently run business with each two-man crew using a small boat.*

Above: *Ben Nevis is Britain's highest mountain (1343 m/4406 ft) but is easily climbed from Glen Nevis on the south-western slope. Near its summit snow lies in gullies all the year round. There is also an observatory, now in ruins, from which meteorological observations were taken between 1883 and 1904. Below it stands Inverlochy Castle, built for the 1st Lord Abinger in 1863 near the site of the original 13th century fortress and now a luxury hotel.*

Cape Wrath, the north-west extremity of the mainland, is not accessible by car. Durness is the nearest village and it is possible to take a ferry over the Kyle of Durness to Achemore from where, in the summer months, a minibus completes the journey to the cape. The road along the north coast gives spectacular coastal and mountain scenery for the first 64 km (40 miles) to Tongue, but after Tongue the best of the Highlands is southward past Loch Loyal and the four-peaked Ben Loyal to Altnaharra and that other world beyond the Great Glen.

The Great Glen is the natural divide which isolates the northern Highlands, formed some 350 million years ago when a great geological upheaval tore the land across. The divide stretches from Inverness and the Moray Firth to Loch Linnhe and Fort William. Before the 18th century, when General Wade and his successors built military roads into the Highlands during the Jacobite rebellions, the English believed that barbarians and cannibals roamed this inaccessible region. For more than a hundred years after that, the Highlanders remained almost untouched by social progress. Filial obedience to the clan chief and a capacity for enduring hardship were their main characteristics. The MacPhersons once complained of their lord's effeminacy when they saw him brush snow off a stone before using it as a pillow.

Fort William, its single street crowded in summer, nestles in a triangle of lochs and above it towers the massive Ben Nevis, Britain's highest mountain, its 1343 m (4,406 ft) summit often wreathed in cloud. The precipitous north face is for intrepid climbers only, but there is a well-trodden tourist path to the top and the climb, at first over heatherclad slopes, then zig-zagging up rocky hillsides dotted with alpine flowers, is well worth while. From the summit there is a magnificent view of the Great Glen, slicing its way through the mountains. In the distance are the peaks of Ben Lomond and Ben Lawers, to the west are Rhum and Eigg and on a clear day there are even glimpses of the Antrim mountains in Northern Ireland, more than 160 km (100 miles) due south.

From Invergarry, north of Fort William, the famous Road to the Isles skirts Loch Garry, Loch Loyne and Loch Cluanie, their mirror-like surfaces reflecting mountains clad in purple heather or orange bracken.

South of Fort William is the most famous of all Highland glens, the Pass of Glencoe, where Scotland is at its awe-inspiring best, with rugged peaks glowering down on the winding road. Even in midsummer there is chill in the 'Glen of Weeping', the scene of the massacre of 1692, the result of old enmities between the Campbell and MacDonald clans.

Most visitors cherish a secret hope of catching a glimpse of the Loch Ness monster. Overshadowed by steep hills, the loch's dark waters seem a natural hiding place for some giant prehistoric reptile. As long ago as the 6th century St Adamnan recorded a sighting in his biography of St Columba, but it is only since the 1930's that 'Nessie spotting' has become a popular pastime and so far scientific investigators have produced no decisive result. Enthusiasts say that the best chance of a sighting is early on a bright morning from half-way along the loch at Castle Urquhart, which stands in a splendid position on a bluff above the loch. Once one of the largest strongholds in Scotland, it is now only a ruin, but the view is spectacular, even if Nessie does not oblige.

Inverness, known as the 'Capital of the Highlands' has a fine situation astride the River Ness, at the eastern end of the Great Glen, and a fine tradition for attracting the cream of the world's pipers in competition. Here the local people speak pure English, without a trace of Scottish burr, the theory being that they originally learned their English from the garrisons of soldiers from the south, set up along the Glen after the Jacobite rebellion.

Many a country house near Inverness preserves intact the room in which Prince Charles Edward, the Stuart Pretender, slept the night before Culloden in 1746. Bonnie Prince Charlie had sailed from France to the Outer Hebrides the previous year and hoisted his standard at Glenfinnan. The Highland clans rallied to his support and marched southward, proclaiming the Prince's father King James VIII. Within a few months they were retreating north again, pursued by the Hanoverian troops, and the Highlanders began to desert to

Above: *Looking much as it did in the Young Pretender's day, Moil Castle commands the narrows by which travellers pass 'over the sea to Skye'. Its original owner was a Danish noblewoman to whom the Gaels (the Scottish inhabitants of the Island) gave the name Saucy Mary. She stretched a chain to the mainland and demanded toll from the passing ships. The Young Pretender took refuge on Skye after he and his troops were routed at Culloden.*

Right: *Prince Charles Edward Stuart, the Young Pretender, a man of courageous Scottish energy mixed with some Polish blood and spurious Italian charm, faced the Duke of Cumberland, who was British but with strong German connections, on Culloden Moor near Inverness.*

Right: *The old thatched Leanach farmhouse which stood in the middle of the battle-field of Culloden somehow survived the fighting and is now cared for by the National Trust for Scotland.*

Far right *The victory gained by the Duke of Cumberland over the Young Pretender ended the Jacobite cause in Britain. Leader of the government forces, Cumberland went on to pursue the Highland rebels with a savage barbarity. At Culloden the Highlanders' graves, grouped according to their clans, form a rough semi-circle opposite the principal cairn.*

their homes as the spring sowing season arrived. The Prince's pursuers caught up with him on Culloden Moor, 9000 of them against 5000 Jacobites, and the battle was over in 40 minutes, leaving 1000 Jacobites dead and the rest in flight. The Cumberland Stone marks the spot where the leader of the Government Forces took up his position and a rough semicircle of stones marks the graves of the Highlanders.

The Prince escaped and spent five months as a fugitive in the Highlands and the Hebrides. He was aided by Flora MacDonald, a girl from South Uist who, according to legend, took him 'over the sea to Skye' disguised as her maid. Eventually he was rescued by the French.

The crushing of the Jacobite rebellion brought great changes in the Highland way of life. The wearing of kilts and tartans was banned – on the theory that without them, Highlanders would be like other men. It also broke the rule of the clan chiefs. Though the Gaelic word 'clann' simply means children, so that clan members were all supposed to descend from a common ancestor, the chiefs had power of life and death over their retainers and the passing of their feudal rule meant fundamental changes in the whole social system.

However, it would have taken more than English laws to crush the Highlanders. The romantic legend of 'the king over the water' lived on and a hundred years later, old-fashioned lairds were still passing their hands over a decanter of water when they drank the king's health and Georgian wits recited the toast:

'God bless the King – I mean the Faith's Defender.
God bless (no harm in blessing) the Pretender.
But which the former is and which the latter –
God bless us all! That's quite another matter.'

The act forbidding Highland dress was eventually repealed and the proliferation of official tartans dates from George IV's visit to Scotland, wearing the Royal Stuart. Today's tartans are defined by setts (or patterns), the principal ones those of the different clans.

Despite its harsh weather, the Highland region has long been associated with outdoor pursuits. It provides an excellent sporting arena for climbers, skiers, shooting and deer-stalking parties, naturalists, pony-trekkers and devotees of rustic contests and trials of strength.

For those who enjoy peace and quiet in idyllic surroundings there is splendid game-fishing to be found on freshwater lochs and streams all over the region. Shetland alone has 200 lochs and almost every hotel throughout the Highlands and Islands offers local fishing. There is even salmon fishing within a few hundred yards of Inverness town centre. Lovely moors and

Left: *Ambitious climbers train on the ridges which rise above Glenmore and the isolated peaks of the Cairngorm and Monadhliath massifs and Grampian highlands. They can experience climbs of a steepness and complexity unknown elsewhere this side of the Matterhorn. Between Ben Macdhui and Cairn Gorm, using Glenmore and Lairig Ghru, is a magnificent plateau walk between summits.*

Below left: *An athlete at Glenfinnan, archetypal Highland Games setting at the head of a loch in the natural amphitheatre of the hills, exerts himself in the ancient pastime of tossing the caber. The idea is to run with it and, with a combination of brute strength and a twirl, to launch it forward so that it topples on end. This feat is greeted with acclaim at Highland Games, for contestants fail much more often than they succeed.*

Below right: *Glencoe, 'glen of weeping', sombre with memories of the massacre of 1692, has blossomed out as one of the three popular winter playgrounds of Scotland. The other two are Glen Shee and the Cairngorms.*

mountain-sides provide a home for grouse, partridge and pheasant and a good hunting ground for sportsmen.

The Cairngorms is the highest mountain mass in Britain with six peaks over 1219 m (4000 ft) and the winter sports complex is the biggest in Scotland. In the season the railway station platform at Aviemore, when the London-Inverness train pulls in, might easily be Grindelwald in Switzerland. Many Swiss and Austrian instructors are finding rewarding careers in the resorts of the Scottish snow country. The main chairlift goes up 1097 m (3600 ft) almost to the Cairngorm summit. At the top is the highest restaurant in Britain, commanding a magnificent panorama of the Spey valley and beyond. Conditions on the ridges above Glen More and the peaks of the Cairngorm and Monadhliath massifs can resemble those of Nepal and Kashmir, and are often used as training grounds for climbers with Himalayan ambitions.

On the lower slopes of the Cairngorm mountain range, Glen More Forest Park covers the large areas of pine forest surrounding Loch Morlich. Energetic walkers can hike through Scots pine, Douglas fir, larch and alder and perhaps glimpse roe deer and red squirrels or even a wildcat or roam over the hills where cattle thieves once herded stolen animals through the Pass of Ryvoan. Nature watchers can observe birds and wildlife from hides, whilst Britain's only herd of reindeer, introduced from Lapland in 1952, browse high up on the hills of Glen More.

Important features of the Scottish summer season are the Highland Gatherings or Games, once simply meetings of clansfolk, summoned together by the chief, where the old people exchanged gossip and the young men worked off their high spirits with competitions, races and energetic dancing. Feats of strength like hammer throwing, caber tossing and shot putting became regular events. Now the Games, held in many towns between June and September, are commercial events.

Another pastime special to the Highlands is 'shinty', an ancient winter game which, to the stranger, looks like a cross between hockey and football. Enthusiasts eagerly explain its finer points, but uninitiated southerners claim it is a rough and tumble that demands more brawn than skill.

MID-SCOTLAND

Mid-Scotland is far too prosaic a title for the land that lies south of the Highlands and north of the Forth-Clyde basin. The grandeur of its scenery and the rich embroidery stitched into its towns by history calls for some more stirring description. It is a countryside of sudden contrasts. Visitors can explore dark mountains and barren moorlands or gentle, secluded glens with bubbling cascades and travel some of the great scenic roads of Britain to proud old cities, houses and castles famed in legend and literature or bustling fishing harbours.

In Grampian the Spey, the Don and the Dee fan out to carry the melting snows of the Cairngorms through some of Scotland's most lyrical mountain and forest scenery to the shores of the moody North Sea. Off shore, in a long straggling ribbon, lie the oil-rigs, named after birds like Tern, Fulmar and Cormorant or Scottish saints like Ninian and Magnus. In spite of early stories from Aberdeen of scenes reminiscent of the California gold rush, nothing as transient as an oil boom could change the essential character of the sturdy Granite City. The vision of a race of 'tartan sheikhs' has evaporated now and Aberdeen's solid stone and level-headed inhabitants have stood up well to the invasion of the new technology, even if the atmosphere of the city is a little less sober these days.

Ancient treasures are embedded in the canyon-like streets between the 'new' bridge across the Dee (a mere 450 years old) and the 'Auld Brig' over the Don (more than 600). Aberdonians have acquired a reputation for ultra-Scottish parsimony – the sort of penny-pinching which makes a motorist switch off his windscreen wipers when going under a bridge, to avoid wear and tear. Every Aberdonian makes jokes about it, confident that there is no truth in the slur.

Inland, the Dee shimmers over the rocks at Balmoral and Braemar, hiding the salmon from the wading fisherman, just as the heather on the moors above hides the grouse. The Dee in spate becomes a roaring torrent and the bridge at Ballater has a plaque recording the disastrous fate of several previous bridges. Local guides say that the masonry of a dozen grand castles have disappeared into the river bed.

Balmoral is famous for its royal connections and the villages of Deeside have seen the arrival of many crowned heads. When the Tsar and Tsarina of Russia passed through, all the cottages were festooned in black and gold in their honour. The Shah of Persia, visiting Queen Victoria in 1889, was greeted with trappings of pink and apple-green. The Grand Vizier remarked wistfully: 'What a beautiful climate. In our country it never rains like this.'

A few miles west of Balmoral is Braemar, site of the most famous of the Highland Gatherings. This great clan event, on a Saturday in early September, may have its origins 900 years ago when Malcolm Canmore summoned the clans to the Brae of Mar for contests which would enable him to select the strongest men as his soldiers. Aboyne too has a Gathering in September, with a procession led by the 'Cock o' the North', the head of the ducal family of Gordon.

The Grampian valleys have allowed the rivers to widen into long, narrow lochs. Seen from the surrounding hillsides the valleys cradle them like strips of molten silver. From an elevated viewpoint between Pitlochry and Kinloch Rannoch, the 'Queen's View' down Loch Tummel must be the finest in all Scotland – at least Queen Victoria thought so and, understandably, the Scots were very quick to broadcast her enthusiasm.

Anyone who imagines Britain to be overcrowded should walk the glens, the antediluvian forests and cattle tracks of northern Tayside. This is Atholl country, the feudal domains of the Murrays of Atholl, ancestors of the pre-Stuart monarchs. The clan seat is at Blair Atholl and the Duke is the only

Above: *Queen's View is a famous beauty spot with a splendid vista of Loch Tummel. However, the view has changed since Queen Victoria saw it in 1866 – the loch has grown by over 4 miles as the result of the valley being flooded for a new hydro-electric power scheme and the wooded islets were once the tops of hills. Nevertheless, it is still a magnificent sight.*

Right: *Most prestigious of country caravanserais, Gleneagles Hotel, standing on moorland near Auchterader, is a 283-hectare (700 acre) resort comprising luxury hotel, shopping centre, three 18-hole golf courses, railway station and helicopter pad. A new Indoor and Country Club complex, built at a cost of £1,500,000, was recently opened.*

Left: *An air of lingering romance and decayed grandeur is natural to St Andrews. The cathedral and castle are more impressive in their desolation than many large, well-preserved edifices. Legend says that beneath the cathedral lie the bones of St Andrew, buried there by the 8th century monk Regulus, or Rule.*
St Andrews university is the oldest in Scotland and its bicycling, scarlet-gowned students are most academic-looking. The four golf courses of St Andrews (two maintained by the town council and two by the Royal and Ancient Golf Club) extend over the foreshore links north of the town.

Right: *Blair Castle, on the Perth-Inverness road, is the seat of the Duke of Atholl and the headquarters of a private army, the Atholl Highlanders. In ancient times these ducal retainers fought under the fire-and-sword commissions awarded by Scottish monarchs to loyal chiefs. Their duties are now ceremonial and judges, admirals and generals are proud to serve as private soldiers in the 'army'.*

Following page: *If ever the ponds and lochs of Scotland are drained, the bottom will be found to be paved with curling stones. These polished, one-handled lumps of granite are often left out on the ice, only to sink in an overnight thaw. Curling is a uniquely Scottish sport (readily adopted in Canada) which resembles bowls on ice. Here is a popular mass-curling venue, the Lake of Menteith near Aberfoyle.*

British subject allowed to retain a private army. The legacy of mediaeval spellings is confusing: the Duke is 'Atholl' but the whisky distilled at Pitlochry is 'Athol' and the delicious oatmeal, honey and whisky pudding which was once the Highlanders' iron ration and is now one of the delicacies of gourmet cuisine, is 'Athole' brose.

Legends abound in this region. Under a yew tree in the little churchyard of Fortingall at the foot of Glen Lyon, claimed as the oldest tree in the world, the wife of a Roman centurion is said to have given birth to the boy who became Pontius Pilate. In a field at Luncarty near Perth, the Scots king Kenneth escaped catastrophe on a dark night when a yell from an invader who trod on a thistle gave early warning of a surprise Danish attack. Legend says that after this event the thistle was adopted as Scotland's national flower. Stretching credulity even further is the tale that the sculpted stones of Meigle, near Forfar, once lined the tomb of Queen Guinevere, the wife of the early British King Arthur.

31

The river Tummel joins the Tay below Pitlochry and flows on to Perth to form the wide Tay estuary which separates Perth and Dundee from Fife. This estuary is crossed by two famous bridges: the railway bridge which replaced the notorious 'disaster' bridge opened in 1878 and blown down in a gale the following year with the loss of 75 lives, and the modern road bridge which replaced the congested but well-loved ferry.

In the centre of Dundee is the Howff, once a monastery orchard and the city's main graveyard for 300 years until the mid 19th century. It has many interesting old tombstones.

Fat, pink-bellied trout are a speciality of Loch Leven near Kinross. During hard frost, the surface of this shallow exposed lake supports several hundred participants in a grand match for curling enthusiasts known as the North of Scotland versus the South. The market gardens of the Carse of Gowrie, along the Firth of Tay, and Blairgowrie are used for intensive raspberry and strawberry cultivation. This helps explain Dundee's pre-eminence as a jam and fruit cake metropolis.

Before the Forth and Tay road bridges were opened, Fife was a rather aloof region, cut off from the mainstream of north-south tourist traffic. It is now firmly on the tourist route, especially for the growing army of golf followers. The game's capital is the Royal and Ancient Golf Club of St Andrews and the town has four courses which extend over the foreshore links north of the town. The Royal and Ancient was founded in 1754 but golf has been played in Scotland at least since 1457 when it was discussed in parliament because it was interfering with the more essential practice of archery.

Below: *Culross, a small town on the north shore of the Firth of Forth, is one of the best examples of what a 16th century Scottish township must have looked like. The National Trust for Scotland has restored many of its beautiful, interesting and unique 16th and 17th century buildings including Culross Palace. The old snuff-maker's house has the inscription: 'Who would have thocht it, noses would have bocht it'.*

Above: *Pittenweem is one of several interesting small ports along a stretch of the Fife coast known as East Neuk. At one time the boats traded with Holland and Denmark and the fishermen followed the herring as far south as Lowestoft. In Pittenweem fisher-girls used to go down to mend the nets and cure the catch. The East Neuk once waged war on Lothian rivals and fought running battles at sea with lumps of coal. In East Fife's fishing heyday, Pittenweem was the tiniest village with the steepest streets and the biggest fleet and the fish market is still an important place.*

Right: *The Tay Road bridge was built in 1966 at a cost of over £6 million and is one and a half miles long. A pedestrian way crosses the bridge between the four lanes and offers a fine view of Dundee rising up the hillside. At 184 km the Tay is Scotland's longest river and has excellent salmon and trout fishing.*

The streets of the town have the feel of the Middle Ages about them, with quaint little shops and a labyrinth of narrow wynds. The castle ruin, on a grassy headland, dates from 1200 and has a bloody history, being the scene of fierce struggles between Catholics and Protestants during the Reformation, and the murder of Cardinal-bishop Beaton. Its stones have now been put to more peaceful use in the building of houses. The cathedral is also in ruins but the ghost of a 'white lady' remains faithful to the tower, moaning gently from time to time.

A Stuart king described Fife as 'a beggar's mantle fringed with gold, the fringe being the relatively rich fishing harbours and ribbons of sand stretching all the way from Burntisland on the Forth and round Fife Ness to Abernethy in the Firth of Tay.

Alexander Selkirk was born in the fishing village of Largo and after growing up to terrorize the neighbourhood he ran away to sea. In 1704 he was cast ashore on a desert island where he lived for four years and his adventures were fictionalized by Daniel Defoe in *Robinson Crusoe*. He is remembered in a statuette above the door of the 300 year old cottage where he was born.

Inland is Dunfermline, birthplace of many Scottish Kings. In the Abbey Church is the grave of Robert the Bruce, whose body was discovered during 19th century renovations, wrapped in a gold-threaded shroud.

The route westwards from Fife to the ancient kingdom of Argyll, now part of Strathclyde, leads through the wasp waist of Scotland. The Forth-Clyde belt was a cradle of industry, a hot bed of that Scottish mechanical genius which has contributed so much to engineering science. On the canal in 1790 Patrick Miller demonstrated a prototype paddlesteamer and in 1818 Sir John Robinson's *Vulcan*, the first all-iron ship, took the water. Iron foundries on the Carron river at Camelon built heavy guns for Nelson's warships: hence the term 'carronade'.

Central region is not all industry and wild scenery begins on the very doorsteps of manufacturing towns. Here the Highlands meet the Lowlands. At one moment road and railway are gliding parallel across flat meadows; at the next one is toiling past crags and the other is probing cascades of bubbling torrents throwing up their spray.

The rough ravines and heather-covered hillsides of the Braes of Balquidder were Rob Roy's native heath. His tomb, and those of his family, are said to be in Balquidder churchyard and Sir Walter Scott's novel has romanticized

Previous pages: *The gardens of Crarae Lodge are man's answer to the hundred-odd species of wild flowers which nature has planted on the mild, moist banks of Loch Fyne. Crarae, with its exotic assembly of blooms and shrubs and imaginative use of landscaping and colour, is a favourite venue for horticulturists' outings. It helps explain why rich country-house owners through two centuries have sought for Scottish head gardeners. There are 24 km (15 miles) of magnificent scenery on the lochside road between Crarae and the head of Loch Fyne.*

Right: *In a romantic setting beside the Aray where it joins the headwaters of Loch Fyne stands Inveraray Castle, the headquarters of the clan Campbell since the 15th century. The present castle, the home of the Duke of Argyll, the Campbell chief, was completed in 1770. It is an early and outstanding example of the neo-Scottish baronial style and among its treasures it houses a fine collection of armour.*

Above: *Snow on the mountains adds exciting contrasts as this view of Stob Ghabhar (1085 m/ 3565 ft) from across the waters of Loch Tulla proves. Loch Tulla is a small, remote inland loch near the Bridge of Orchy on the road to Glencoe.*

Following pages: *Reflected in the peaceful waters of Loch Awe, between Ben Cruachan and the hills that flank Glen Orchy, Kilchurn Castle belies its warlike past. Kilchurn was a Campbell stronghold and its keep was built by Sir Colin Campbell in 1440, with additions in the 16th and 17th centuries. In 1746, the year of Culloden, it was occupied by Hanoverian troops at the invitation of the Campbells who were anti-Jacobites. The same gale which blew down the Tay rail bridge in 1879 removed one of Kilchurn's towers, but it remains one of the most glorious and splendidly sited ruins in Scotland.*

his exploits though he was, in fact, a freebooter and cattle-stealer. The cave he is supposed to have used is close to Inversnaid on Loch Lomond and Loch Katrine is said to take its name from the old Highland word for a marauder like Rob Roy: 'cateran'. The Trossachs, too, were immortalized by Sir Walter Scott in 'The Lady of the Lake', which seems to mention every bridge and farmhouse. Every season brings its own beauty to the Trossachs, from the variegated greens of spring to the browns and purple of autumn.

The foothill towns of Callander, Doune and Aberfoyle are quiet, stone-built places, a trifle melancholy, but busy enough in the holiday season with their country shops and war memorials, castle ruins and inns; they are a few miles only from the ironworks and refineries, but seemingly a world away.

Though Loch Lomond is probably one of the best known stretches of water in the world, the hills run so closely down to the loch that panoramic views are almost impossible. The place for views is the summit of Rest and be Thankful, on the road to the coast. Below is the gnarled and twisted fist of promontory nicknamed the Duke of Argyll's Bowling Green, turreted country houses immersed in drifts of daffodils at spring-time and clear sheets of water reflecting a profusion of primroses, wild cherry blossom, bluebells and anemones.

The headquarters of the Campbell clan – a name that was for generations associated with the memory of the treachery at Glencoe – is the handsome little town of Inveraray near the head of Loch Fyne, an 18th-century creation, and now tastefully modernized. Dr Johnson, the famous lexicographer, was

Above: *It was the coming of steamers in the 19th century that made Oban a popular tourist town and ferries run to many of the Hebridean islands: Mull, Barra, South Uist, Coll, Tiree, Colonsay and Lismore. On a hill above the busy little town* *stands McCaig's folly, planned in the last century by a banker who wanted to build a magnificent family memorial and provide work for the local unemployed at the same time. Both projects failed when he went bankrupt.*

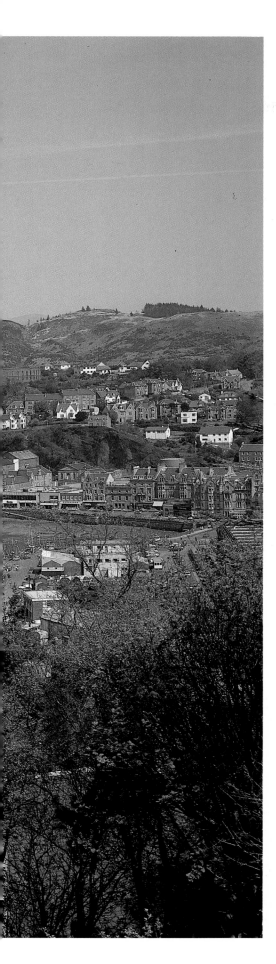

entertained here in 1773 and, as Boswell reports, tasted Scotch whisky for the first time.

It is the centre of a romantic countryside with Oban, to the north, the area's second largest town and a lively holiday centre. Seil, an enchanting little island off the coast of Oban, is joined to the mainland by one of Thomas Telford's bridges, known as the 'bridge over the Atlantic'.

In Strathclyde the sea is always a presence. From far inland can be seen the endless pageant of Clyde shipping – battle cruisers and liners once, now tankers and container ships. Visitors can spend a whole day weaving through the maze of sea lochs and peninsulas where every small village has its pier, with boats ferrying passengers to another pretty little place round the next corner. In many of the villages, the only event of the day seems to be the arrival of the boats.

Strathclyde's offshore territories are those Atlantic barriers generally known as the Western Isles: Mull, Islay, Jura and others. These isles contain the dream homes of pop stars, Westminster politicians and northern industrialists but their presence has little effect on the ways of the locals.

Mull reminds the English of Cornwall and on the waterfront of the capital, Tobermory, sophisticated yachtsmen rub shoulders with weathered fisher-folk. In the bay, treasure seekers search for doubloons from the sunken wreck of the San Juan de Sicilia, an Armada warship which was blown up in 1588, possibly by an English spy. To the south of Mull is the charming little island of Colonsay, a resting place for migrating seafowl, with rabbits hopping on the sand-dunes, grey seals on the off-shore reefs and some rare varieties among the many wild flowers.

Staffa, the 'isle of staves', consists of basalt pillars which were stacked and jointed as they cooled from fountains of lava spouting out of antediluvian eruptions. The grotto on Staffa, known to the locals as the 'musical cave' because of the Aeolian-harp effect of the air currents round the pillars, inspired Mendelssohn's *Hebrides* concert piece, which ends with the overture 'Fingal's Cave'. In his diary he wrote: 'What a wonder is Fingal's Cave! This vast cathedral of the seas with its dark lapping waters within and the brightness of the gleaming waves outside!'

In 563 St Columba left his native Ireland and founded a monastery on Iona, from where his followers carried Christianity throughout Scotland and Northern England. There is nothing left of the monastery but St Oran's Cemetery, 'the Westminster Abbey of Scotland' is Scotland's oldest Christian burial place, where more than 60 kings are said to rest and many carved slabs commemorate clan chiefs.

Tiree is so flat that it was known in Gaelic as 'the kingdom whose summits are lower than the waves' and claims to be the sunniest spot in the west. The local people are crofters and the holidaymakers who come here are seeking peace and solitude. The island of Jura takes its name from the Norse for 'deer' and there are still several thousand red deer roaming the hills. Its twin conical peaks, the Paps of Jura, are a landmark for sailors approaching the west coast.

The islands have remained untouched by the savage events of Scottish history though Duncan, murdered by Macbeth in 1040, was buried on Iona, but the romantic castles of the mid-Scotland mainland could tell many a bloody story.

From the ramparts of Stirling Castle, poised on a precipitous rock above the town, seven battlefields can be seen, including Bannockburn and Stirling Bridge, scenes of the victories of Robert the Bruce and his predecessor William Wallace, folk hero and freedom fighter. Visible, too, are Sheriffmuir and Falkirk, the sites of skirmishes in the 18th century rebellions of the Old and Young Pretenders. Within the castle the 8th Earl of Douglas was stabbed by James II in 1452 and hurled from the window. In the 18th century the skeleton of an armed man, said to be Douglas, was found in the garden.

One of the magnificent military relics of mediaeval Scotland, Dunnottar Castle, stands in ruined splendour on a great crag of the Grampian coast near Stonehaven. It was a toll-gate and frontier post from which the Keith Lords,

Left: *Tobermory ('Well of Mary') is the chief town and fishing port of the island of Mull. It is also the last stepping stone on the route to Staffa and Iona. The harvest of the sea-bottom around the island is principally lobster, and after use, the lobster creels must be scrubbed and perhaps tarred, and piled on the harbour wall to dry in the sun and wind.*

Below: *The island of Staffa is the result of ancient volcanic activity. The great grotto inspired Mendelssohn to write the concert overture 'Fingal's Cave'. Most distinguished travellers in Scotland in the 19th century made Fingal's Cave their farthest point north and sometimes waited for days, as tourists may do today, for a fair passage and a calm sea*

hereditary Earls Marischal of Scotland, commanded the eastern approaches. In 1297 when the English held the castle, William Wallace stormed it and roasted alive the enemy soldiers who fled to the chapel for sanctuary. The armies of Balliol, Bruce, Montrose and Cromwell all besieged it in their turn. When the 17th century witch-hunt was on for the Covenanters, who stood for extreme Protestant Presbyterian belief, Dunnottar's dungeon became a merciless prison where 167 men, women and children were left to die.

Glamis Castle, in the cattle-breeding countryside of Tayside, has been the birthplace of royalty since Macbeth, the 'Thane of Glamis', in the 11th century. Its most recent royal baby was Princess Margaret, born in 1930. The impressive building, with its clusters of rounded turrets, is the epitome of what most people mean by Scottish baronial architecture. Here Malcolm II is supposed to have been murdered and the Malcolm Stone in the village is reputed to be his gravestone. The castle was forfeited to the Crown in the 16th century, after Lady Glamis was burned for witchcraft and conspiracy to murder the king, but later her innocence was established and it was returned to the family. There is a story that every heir to Glamis is entrusted with a dreadful secret when he comes of age, a secret so dire that he never smiles again.

High in the Sidlow Hills is Dunsinane, where the remains of an ancient fort are identified with Macbeth's castle. Shakespeare places Macbeth's final battle and death here, but it is more likely that Macbeth, fleeing after Dunsinane, made his last stand further north at Lumphanan, where a cairn in a ring of trees reputedly marks the spot where he was killed.

It is Scotland's proud boast that she had four universities - Aberdeen, St Andrews, Glasgow and Edinburgh — when England had only Oxford and Cambridge. Young men of modest means were prepared to make enormous sacrifices to ensure a good education. The mid-semester holiday of Scottish universities, used to be known as 'Meal Monday', when students were given a long weekend to hike back to their distant homes and replenish the sack of oatmeal which was their only food supply.

St Andrews, founded by Bishop Henry Wardlaw in 1412, is the oldest and in the 16th century famous Scots like George Buchanan and Andrew Melville studied there. College Chapel contains the pulpit from which John Knox preached his first sermons and a thorn tree planted by Mary Queen of Scots still flourishes in the quadrangle of St Mary's College.

Glasgow, where the first classes took place in the crypt of the cathedral, and Aberdeen were also founded by the church in the 15th century. Marischal College was founded a century later and amalgamated with Aberdeen's existing university. It is now one of the finest granite buildings in the world, with a magnificent pinnacled façade.

Scotland still has a strong academic tradition, though it is a far cry from the 16th century schools of Latinists and theologians to the progressive new university of Stirling, situated on the banks of Allan Water near the town. Its MacRobert Centre is open to non-students for concerts, jazz, recitals, debates, avant-garde films and theatre.

Another just cause for Scottish pride is the distilling, blending and bottling of whisky. The best-known brands of malt whisky are produced within a few miles of one another but each has its own character. Tourists can follow the Whisky Trail which runs through 65 miles of pleasing country, taking in the four famous distilleries of Glenfiddich, Glenfarclas, Tamdhu and Strathisla. The whisky most people drink is not, according to the connoisseurs, the real stuff. This is the unblended or single malt, which costs half as much again as blended Scotch whisky and is produced in small distilleries, most of them dotted over the Grampian foothills. Once it was made illicitly in remote mountain huts.

Above: *Falkland, where rich and poor lived cheek by jowl, was a favourite residence of Stuart monarchs. The well-preserved palace rises among the burgh rooftops, as centrally sited as the town hall or general post office. It has Gothic buttresses and arrow-slits, classical pillars and medallions, and French renaissance towers.*

Right: *Craigievar Castle is a beautiful 17th century tower-house near Alford, supposed to have been the model for Walt Disney's fairy-tale castles. It has changed little since it was built for William Forbes, merchant brother of the Bishop of Aberdeen.*

Right: *Dunnottar Castle, south of Stonehaven, is one of the grand military relics of mediaeval Scotland. When Cromwell ruled England, the Scottish state regalia was brought here for safe keeping. Under siege, the starving defenders smuggled out the regalia to Kinneff church, where it lay buried behind the altar until the monarchy was restored.*

Below: *A statue of Charles I stands in the grounds of Glamis Castle, which was rebuilt in the 17th century in the style of a French château. The 5 m (15 ft) thick walls of the tower date back to the 14th century.*

THE LOWLANDS & BORDER COUNTRY

Travellers who speed through Borders and Lowlands south of Edinburgh and Glasgow, intent on reaching the major cities or the Highlands, are missing much of beauty and interest. Below Edinburgh, over the green Pentland and Moorfoot Hills, lies a little-known region of bare hills and few roads leading to the Cheviots in the east and, in the west, to the lovely land of Galloway, where composer Franz Liszt and poet John Keats both noted the prettiness of the girls and the villages. Where the lands of Scotland and England touch, the ever-changing vistas of Border country shows its historic heritage at every turn in the road with its castles, abbeys and ruined peel towers.

To the east and south of Edinburgh the Great North Road sweeps up from England, crossing the border just north of Berwick-upon-Tweed and skirting the Lammermuir Hills whose heather-glowing slopes give visitors from the south their first sight of authentic Scotland. At Dunbar the road swerves west through lovely East Linton and Haddington on its way into the heart of Edinburgh. In Dunbar castle Mary Queen of Scots stayed with her husband Darnley after he had taken part in the murder of her secretary Rizzio. She later returned with Bothwell after Darnley's murder. Haddington is a distinguished town with an architectural legacy that has been faithfully preserved. Nearby is Lennoxlove, originally the home of Maitland of Lethington, Mary Queen of Scots's secretary of state, and now owned by the Duke of Hamilton. There are many relics of the Queen in the house, including her death mask.

Below: *Rising in the Cheviots, the hills that mark the border country between England and Scotland and the scene of so much bloodshed in the past, Kale Water makes its sparkling way north. Along with many similar streams it flows across Cheviot pastures polka-dotted with sheep to join the salmon-rich Tweed.*

Above: *Traquair House, though enlarged in the reign of Charles I, dates back to the 10th century and is said to be the oldest inhabited house in Scotland. Situated near Peebles, it is open to the public and has several relics of Mary Queen of Scots who stayed there in 1566. A tradition, long since discarded, was that the gates, closed after the Jacobite rising in 1745, would only be re-opened when another Stuart sat on the throne.*

Left: *On rising ground beside the town loch, Linlithgow Palace, the birth-place of Mary Queen of Scots, still wears an air of majesty in spite of its ruined, fire-stained stones. It was the favourite palace of the Stuarts and although accidentally destroyed by fire in 1746, the charm of its interior is still evident while the views from many of its windows must be virtually unchanged. Linlithgow Loch today does double duty as a sailing lake and a bird sanctuary.*

Right: *If the visitor to Edinburgh happens to be staying near the main railway station, he need only look out from his bedroom window to see almost exactly what this photograph shows. Being built, like Rome, on seven hills, Edinburgh abounds in magnificent views.*

Its elevated position and cosmopolitan outlook lead Glaswegians to attack it for being 'West-Endy and east-windy'. In return to such attacks, inhabitants quote the town's long and distinguished history as a capital city and home of Kings, going right back to Edwin in 617 AD, a king of Northumbria from whom the town is thought to have taken its name. However Edinburgh's status as a capital derives from when James II moved his parliament here in the 1450's. The Scottish crown jewels, centuries older than the English crown jewels, are housed in the castle. They were judiciously hidden away during the time of Cromwell and the Act of Union of 1807, then tactfully 'discovered' by a commission including Sir Walter Scott in 1817.

For visitors and for most of the city's inhabitants the highlight of Edinburgh's year is the annual International Festival of Arts from the end of August to mid-September. This is the high-spot of the city's cultural life, with its impressive range of music, drama, dance and exhibitions, when Edinburgh flies its flags, lengthens its licensing hours and fills its streets with marching pipers (as shown far right).

Above: *The clock on the tower of the North British hotel above Edinburgh's Waverley station is kept five minutes fast as encouragement to those rushing for a train. From a viewpoint on Calton Hill, the Gothic spires of central Edinburgh rise above Princes Street. This is said to be the only main street in Europe without a double row of shops, for the south side is all gardens. The nearest spire on the left is the Scott monument.*

Right: *Participants in the Tattoo on the esplanade of Edinburgh Castle parade for the final salute after an evening performance. The Military Tattoo, which runs at the same time as the Edinburgh International Festival, has proved itself very popular. The programme is built around displays by the best of regimental, cavalry and dance troupes from around the world. They make dramatic entrances and exits by way of the drawbridge and portcullis. The most enthusiastic acclaim is usually reserved for the Highland dancers and the massed pipe bands of the Highland regiments. Lighting effects and the batteries and ramparts of the old sturdy citadel provide memorable backcloths for the events. The climax of the spectacle is a solitary piper playing a lament, spotlit on a high tower while all the castle rock is darkened.*

On the coast, the principal holiday town is North Berwick which was 'made' in the latter part of the 19th century by the rich and famous who chose it as their exclusive holiday resort. On North Berwick's celebrated golf course cabinet ministers, bankers and millionaires walked farther in a few hours than they would normally walk in a year. From North Berwick Law, a volcanic viewpoint 186 m (613 ft) above the town, there is a majestic panorama of the Firth of Forth and the Bass Rock. Golf courses elbow each other so closely along the southern shores of the Firth of Forth that the stretch is known as the 'Holy Land of Golf'. The championship course at Muirfield has been the home of the Ancient and Honourable Company of Edinburgh Golfers since 1891, but the game has been played in Edinburgh since 1457.

The visitor to Edinburgh can be left in no doubt that he is in an important place for its centre has all the drama and panache of a capital city. There, serrating the skyline with its towers and battlements, is the castle whose jumbled buildings have been clinging to this volcanic ledge 91.4 m (300 ft) above the city for nearly 1000 years. The castle's oldest building is the beautifully simple little chapel built in 1076 by Margaret, Malcolm III's queen, later canonized as St Margaret. It marks the highest point on the rock. In the royal apartments is the room where Mary Queen of Scots gave birth to the son who was to become James VI of Scotland and James I of England. It was James IV who built the Great Hall which now displays an excellent collection of armour and weapons. The castle also marks the upper end of the Royal Mile, a line of streets passing the High Kirk of St Giles, continuing through Canongate down to the Palace of Holyroodhouse, the official residence of the sovereign in Scotland. This palace, unexpectedly small, is dominated by the green flanks of Arthur's Seat, an extinct 250 m (822 ft) volcano that serves as a magnificent municipal grandstand from which to view the whole of the city and much of the Firth of Forth and the Pentland Hills. Behind the 61 m (200 ft)-high neo-Gothic memorial erected in 1846 to the memory of Scotland's greatest novelist, Sir Walter Scott, is the green heart of the city, Princes Street Gardens, divided into East and West by the Royal Scottish Academy and the National Gallery of Scotland, two impressive buildings which nourish and preserve both Scotland's native art and its rich collection of European masterpieces. The floral clock in the gardens, said to be the oldest in the world, was made in 1903.

Princes Street, the main shopping thoroughfare, runs parallel to the Royal Mile. It has shops on one side only, looking across the Gardens to the Old Town skyline. Behind Princes Street lies the unique 'New Town' instigated in 1770 by Lord Provost Drummond and imaginatively planned by a 23-year-old architect named James Craig. It is a handsome district of wide streets, generous squares and Georgian houses and an outstanding example of intelligent town planning.

In the Grassmarket is the site where 100 Covenanters were martyred in the 17th century. Nearby was the hideout of the notorious body snatchers Burke and Hare in the 19th century.

For visitors and for most of its inhabitants the highlight of Edinburgh's year is the annual International Festival of Music, Drama and the Arts, in the last three weeks of August, when the city throws off any northerly inhibitions it may still possess, flies its flags, lengthens its licensing hours and fills its streets with marching pipers. The Military Tattoo, which runs at the same time as the Festival, began in 1947. The programme is built round displays by the best of regimental, cavalry and dance troupes from around the world, performing on the Castle Esplanade.

It is little more than an hour's journey from Edinburgh to Glasgow but Glaswegians still look on Edinburgh as rather a foreign place. The people of Edinburgh say they are only jealous. Glaswegians, unimpressed, reply that 'Edinburgh may be the capital but Glasgow has the capital!' Daniel Defoe, in the 18th century, described Glasgow as 'the most beautiful little city in Europe'. It is unlikely that today's visitors would agree, though signs of elegance still remain, and the inhabitants say it is 'a great place to get out of'.

Waterways lead out of the city to green and flowery sea lochs. The Clyde is

an astonishingly narrow river, considering the vast ships which have been launched there. Along its south shore the view quickly opens on the widening firth, revealing a pattern of islands and a chain of small holiday resorts separated from each other by prolific woodland and historic houses. On this route are the championship golf courses of Troon and Turnberry, the homeland of Robert Burns around the towns of Ayr and Alloway and Culzean Castle, one of Robert Adam's outstanding achievements. It contains the flat which was given to General Eisenhower in 1947 as a mark of Scotland's gratitude to a great war leader. There are also mementoes of Winston Churchill, Vera Lynn, Glenn Miller and other leading figures of the 1940's.

The islands of Arran and Bute, standing side by side but quite different in character, are easily accessible from Glasgow. Frowning Arran is rugged and mountainous, with steep torrents rushing seawards on all sides and uncultivated moorland rich in prehistoric remains: burial cairns and stone circles. Arran's northern 'highlands', with half a dozen peaks rising to more than 610 m (2000 ft), are divided from the southern 'lowlands' by The String, an historic mountain road that crosses the island. St Columba is said to have used this road on his journey from Ireland to Iona.

Left: *Culzean Castle, designed by Robert Adam, was built in the late 18th century around an ancient tower belonging to the Kennedy family near Ayr. In 1969 the grounds, which include a home farm, became Scotland's first country park.*

Above: *Rothesay, chief town of the island of Bute, is a pleasant resort, popular with trippers from the mainland. Its main historic sights are both interesting ruins: the 13th century castle and St Mary's Chapel, beside the High Kirk.*

Below *Kirkcudbright, a picturesque small port at the mouth of the Dee, is the adopted home of a vigorous colony of potters, painters, sculptors and weavers. The vigour seems to have been traditional in the town for a stone in the graveyard records the death of Billy Marshall, a tinker, at the age of 120. According to Sir Walter Scott, Marshall fathered four children after his 100th birthday. At the harbour stands McLellan's Castle, a turreted mansion built in 1582 by Sir Thomas McLellan, the Provost at the time, with stones from the old friary. Kirkcudbright (the name means 'Church of Cuthbert') is in the centre of Galloway, a region of great beauty and peacefulness and too little visited.*

Smiling Bute has gentle scenery, mostly farming land with patches of moor. In the shelter of the mainland hills, the climate is mild, so that palm trees and fuschias flourish out of doors. Rothesay, the capital, stands on a semi-circular bay dotted with boats and is the traditional destination of 'doon the watter' excursionists from Glasgow.

The northern corner of the island is separated from the mainland by the famous Kyles of Bute. Kyle means narrow water and the Bute ferry leaves the mainland from Colintraive, a name derived from 'the straits of swimming', for at this spot graziers used to swim their cattle across to the island on their way back from market. Visitors can almost touch the rocks on either side of the Kyles as the boat twists among them.

A corniche road embroiders the coast southwards to Stranraer. The seascapes are magnificent and the mountains of Mourne and Antrim Hills in Northern Ireland can often be seen in the distance. Ailsa Craig's solitary pinnacle divides the shipping lanes. Inland, Glen Trool Forest Park has some of the finest scenery in southern Scotland and is the home of wild goats and roe deer and there are many miles of peaceful hiking tracks, far removed from any town or road.

In the west of Galloway, Wigtown stands at the beginning of a pilgrim's route to the Isle of Whithorn, along a promontory called the Machars. A hilltop monument to the Covenanters dominates Wigtown, a reminder of the 17th century religious persecution. On the mudflats of the shore stands the Martyrs' Stake, marking the spot where two women were left to drown in the rising tide in the anti-Covenant witch-hunts.

In the fourth century St Ninian, the first Christian missionary to Scotland, landed on the Isle of Whithorn, which in spite of its name is not an island, and Scottish kings and barons made pilgrimages to the spot with as much reverence as Moslems journeying to Mecca. Whithorn's priory rose on the stones of St Ninian's early chapel and its most precious relics, the bones of the saint himself, were already a thousand years old when they were donated to the Scottish church at Bruges in the 14th century.

From the hills that penetrate into the Galloway peninsula the rivers Nith, Dee, Cree and Stinchar flow through rich farming valleys to the Solway Firth and the Irish Sea. On the coast is the little village of Rockcliffe right on the water's edge with Rough Island, a National Trust bird sanctuary, just off shore and accessible on foot at low tide. A little way up the Urr Water estuary is Kippford, a still unspoilt yachting centre. Between the two is the Mote of Mark, the site of a 6th century hillfort. Important archaeological finds here include iron implements and clay moulds for bronze casting. Across the estuary woodland paths lead to silent, virgin beaches where 18th century smugglers landed wines and tobacco when the moon was low.

Dumfries town, standing solidly in the last bend of the Nith, became a royal burgh 700 years ago. Robert Burns dissipated his final energies, died and was buried here in 1796 and the area has other literary associations. J.M. Barrie, author of *Peter Pan*, went to school at Dumfries Academy. The home of essayist and historian Thomas Carlyle was at nearby Craigenputtock and the Maxwelton Braes of the famous old song 'Annie Laurie' were a little way up the Moniaive valley.

Robert Burns and James Boswell were among those who went to sample the waters at Moffat, six miles from Dumfries, in the hope of relief from digestive troubles. At one time, Moffat was regarded as Scotland's answer to the English spas of Bath and Cheltenham, though the taste of the waters was officially described as 'that of a mixture of rotten eggs beaten up in the scourings from a foul gun'. Baths, hotels and assembly rooms were erected, but somehow Moffat's fame subsided, to be replaced in 1863 by a gold rush. Prospectors, amateur and professional, panned the hill burns and brought in quantities of yellow-veined rock. Miners trekked down from Fife with their picks. Geological analysis put an end to all the dreams: it was only iron pyrites, 'fool's gold'.

There are several national curiosities in the deeply scored moorland neighbourhood of Moffat. A great hollow once used by cattle rustlers to conceal stolen herds is known as the Devil's Bathtub and the Grey Mare's Tail is a streaming cascade 61m (200ft) high near the summit of the lonely road which leads to Selkirk.

Though officially in the 'lowlands', the Lowther Hills are a miniature mountain world. Leadhills, the second highest village in Scotland, has the highest golf course in Britain and the grave of Scotland's longest-lived inhabitant: John Taylor, who died aged 137. In the past, mines here have produced lead, gold and silver, including the gold in the crown of James V and his queen. Local gold also provided a ring for the late Queen Mary and a brooch for the Queen Mother.

The ruins of the four great abbeys of the Scottish Borders - Dryburgh, Jedburgh, Melrose and Kelso – have inspired poets, writers and painters through the centuries and their foundation marked the beginning of Border history as we know it. All four were founded in the reign of David I in the 12th century. He employed his people in building great religious edifices rather than fortresses, though he almost bankrupted his kingdom in the process. David, dubbed by an English chronicler 'that most courtly king of the Scots', had been brought up at the court of William the Conqueror and longed to civilize the country after the Norman-English fashion. He persuaded Norman barons, friends of his youth, to settle north of the Tweed and set the locals a good example. From his reign dates the rise in Scotland of some famous families, Fraser, Lindsay, Lamont, Seton and several others.

The abbeys were designed as colonies for monks from Cistercian and other orders in Normandy and Yorkshire who would develop agriculture, industry and the civilized arts, but fate decreed that for 500 years these magnificent buildings should know no peace. They were sacked and burned, rebuilt, then besieged again. Their history is that of military strongpoints on a bitterly-contested frontier, and their stones proclaim all the turmoil and danger of the border wars.

Below: *Dryburgh, on the banks of the Tweed, grew rich in the Middle Ages but was later mercilessly plundered and burned by Border raiders. The picture shows the vaulted alcoves in which Sir Walter Scott and Earl Haig are buried.*

Above: *Jedburgh Abbey, in a town centre of hilly streets, is undercut by the swift Jed Water racing down to the Teviot and Tweed and is one of the most complete of Border abbeys. After the Reformation, when all the abbeys were dispossessed, part of the building was used as Jedburgh's parish church. The tracery of the north transept windows is still intact and the south-west windows stand symmetrically along the nave.*

Left: *'If thou would'st view fair Melrose aright, Go visit it in the pale moonlight'. So many visitors took Scott's* Last Minstrel *(1805) at his word that a sleepless custodian applied to have the words removed from the poem. Melrose was an imposing pile in its day, if the gaunt shell is any guide. An air of mysticism hangs about the tombs where Michael Scott the magician of medieval renown is buried, and an enigmatic inscription in the north aisle reads: 'Here Lyis the Race of the House of Zair'.*

Right: *Kelso Abbey, much knocked about, was further vandalized by crude restoration work. Now, stripped to its earlier condition, it is the most fragmentary but most atmospheric of the great ecclesiastical ruins.*

Left: *Even in ruin, the 14th century Hermitage Castle, the Border stronghold of the Douglases, looks ready to repel invaders. It has an interesting bakehouse and visitors can see the pit prison where Sir William Douglas, one of the 'Black Douglases', starved one of his prisoners, Sir Alexander Ramsay, to death.*

Below: *Net fishermen at work beside the Union suspension bridge near Berwick-upon-Tweed. Some of Europe's finest salmon are born in the Tweed and return in spring to spawn in their native pools. The heaviest salmon are usually caught in the autumn: September-October.*

Right: *In the heart of Scott's beloved Borderland, a gravel sweep on a hilltop beside the Earlston-Dryburgh road has been designated 'Scott's View'. The panoramic view embraces a score of towers, hills and habitations enshrined in literature and embraced by the Tweed's crescent bends. In the background are the Eildon hills. Under the Eildon tree Thomas the Rhymer, alias Thomas of Ercildoune (Earlston) had his rendezvous with the Queen of Elfland. Before Sir Walter stamped his personality on this district, another Scott inhabited it: Michael Scott, the magician and court astrologer to Frederick II the Holy Roman Emperor, whose death in 1450 he accurately foretold. Back in Scotland Scott was plagued by the devil who set him the never-ending task of spinning ropes of sand at the mouth of the Tweed.*

The decline of the abbeys saw the rise of the Border reivers, or plunderers, and the Mosstroopers, excellent irregular cavalry in battle, turned bandit in quieter times. Families raided one another or joined forces to raid the English. Landowners were required by law to fortify their houses and some of the little country towers which served as strongholds, like Smailholm Tower on a lochside hillock, are still preserved.

Today the Borderers ride out, not to plunder, but to join the great mounted cavalcades of the Common Ridings and the other festivals with which each burgh celebrates the granting of its charter or a local battle. The great Border ballads still tell of the days when courage was admired above all and even the most bloodthirsty reiver was a hero, to be lamented in rhyme if caught and brought to justice.

The principal Border towns are Galashiels, Hawick, Melrose, Jedburgh, Selkirk and Peebles. Parochial rivalries have given way to fierce rugby football traditions and no-one thinks it strange that places no larger than an English village supply players to the Scottish international team. These players carry the support of the whole region for, bitter as local antagonisms may be, all unite in a battle against the 'auld enemy' of England.

A stroll down a grey main street reveals a border town's historical priorities. In Galashiels, a coat of arms on the Town Hall has the motto 'Sour Plums'; back in 1337 men of the town surprised some Englishmen eating plums in an orchard and slaughtered them to a man. Jedburgh's battle-cry was 'Jethart's here!' and Jethart justice (execute the criminal first and try him afterwards) is proverbial in Scotland. Magistrates there, they used to say, would hang you for stealing a sheep but not for murdering your mother-in-law. In a fortified town near the abbey, Mary Queen of Scots lay sick after the harrowing 40 mile ride to see her lover, the Earl of Bothwell, at Hermitage Castle. The towers and walls of the building are still intact.

Selkirk, crowning a ridge above the Ettrick vale, has monuments to Sir Walter Scott (for some years the district sheriff), to Andrew Lang the author and to Mungo Park the African explorer, but its most pathetic memorial is inscribed simply 'O, Flodden Field'. It recalls the dark day of 1513 on the slopes of Cheviot, when Scotland's army was annihilated and her king slain. Of the 100 Selkirk men who joined the fight, only one returned. The battle inspired the well-known lament, 'The Flowers o' the Forest'.

Nowhere in the Border country are visitors far from the sound of water. Navigators along the River Tweed, often called the queen of the salmon rivers, pass dignified mansions, prosperous farms and luxuriously wooded banks. The river flows past haunted and hallowed ground: by ducal Floors Castle and Kelso's fine bridge, past Neidpath's theatrical ruin and on to the Tweedsmuir ascent where it rises.

It was the monks who first established Border wool as an important export which fetched a high price on the Continental market. The quality of the wool, the softness of the water for washing it and the skill of weavers all came together to make the famous 'Tweed' cloth and Hawick is the famous centre for classic sweaters and cashmere twinsets. The Textile Trail gives visitors the chance to trace the history and development of the industry through museum displays, guided tours of working mills and mill shops displaying top quality merchandise.

ENGLAND

England, from the rolling hills and towering forests of its borders with Scotland to the array of tempting south coast resorts, has beauty in abundance, with an ever-varied landscape and ever-changing seascape. It has something to match every mood and serve every taste: the grandeur of the Cornish coastline, the gentler pleasures of Kent orchards or peaceful Devon villages, the lonely wilderness of the East Anglian wildfowl sanctuaries, the sophistication of its city theatres and concert halls, and the dreamy meandering of rivers like the Thames and Avon.

Large areas of unspoiled countryside are preserved from change as National Parks, ranging from the volcanic crags of the Lake District, mirrored in calm sheets of water, to the rocky hillsides and valleys of the Yorkshire Dales, or the granite tors of Dartmoor.

Many of the phases of history had their beginnings in the south-east, which has always been England's front door to both friends and enemies. Through it came the Celts, bringing the Iron Age with them. Uninvited came the Romans, imposing their materialistic civilization on the country and pushing the Celts into its western fringes. The great defensive bastion of Hadrian's Wall, which marches across Northumbria and Cumbria, was built to mark the northernmost frontier of the Roman Empire. The Anglo-Saxons followed the Romans, leaving their churches and literature to mark their passage. In 1066 the Normans landed at Pevensey Bay, winning a decisive battle near Hastings, then marching to London where William built the Tower and tamed the country with sword and fire.

The Midlands saw a different type of invasion in the 19th century, when new inventions and machinery ushered in the Industrial Revolution, which was to change the face of the world. One of the most important sites for industrial archaeologists is Ironbridge in Shropshire, now an impressive museum, where the introduction of a new iron-smelting process brought vast increases in production. Museums throughout the north and Midlands trace the development of the textile and pottery industries, of steam power, the railways and inland waterways.

The English have a reputation for quiet reserve and they avoid grandiose claims for their fine buildings, their art treasures and theatrical traditions, probably because they do not find it necessary to make an effort to impress. They are confident that they can leave it to the visitor to find his own superlatives for the dozens of splendid cathedrals, from Canterbury in the south to Durham in the north, the stately homes which seem to have history built into every stone, the Chichester Festival and the operas of Glyndebourne in Sussex, the performances of the Royal Shakespeare Company and the music of the Aldeburgh Festival in Suffolk.

England preserves its past, not only through its architectural and artistic heritage but in the customs and pageantry, relics from its ancient way of life. The Mumming Plays, acting out the battle between good and evil, still performed in the West Country, Hampshire and West Yorkshire, have their origins in ancient rites belonging to the changing seasons. The Morris Dancers who tour the country areas perform dances once linked with the pagan fertility rites of spring. Modern Druids still gather to honour the summer solstice at Stonehenge as the sun rises on Midsummer Day.

Small festivals abound and visitors often find that the true feeling of England lies not only in the pageantry of the Changing of the Guard outside Buckingham Palace, but also the hundreds of village fêtes on green lawns shaded by great trees, the Harvest Festival in the country churches, the bonfires and fireworks which light the sky on Guy Fawkes Night.

National Parks or Forest Parks

Designated Areas of Outstanding Natural Beauty

0 10 20 30 40 miles
0 10 20 30 40 50 60 Km

Holy Island
Lindisfarne Castle
Bamburgh
Chillingham
Cheviot Hills
Carter Bar
NORTHUMBERLAND NATIONAL PARK
Bellingham
Bewcastle
Hadrian's Wall
Corbridge
Newcastle
Birdoswald
Bywell
Brampton
Hexham
River Tyne
Jarrow
Carlisle
Blanchland
Durham
LAKE DISTRICT NATIONAL PARK
Maryport
Redcar
Loweswater
Derwent Water
Dufton
Whitehaven
Keswick
Ullswater
St. Bees
Helvellyn
Kirkby Stephen
Buttermere
Grasmere
Redcar
Ravenglass
Thirlmere
Ambleside
Richmond
Wast Water
Windermere
Swaledale
Cleveland Hills
Kendal
Wensleydale
NORTH YORK MOORS NATIONAL PARK
Isle of Man
Rievaulx Abbey
Scarborough
YORKSHIRE DALES NATIONAL PARK
Jervaulx Abbey
Filey
Fountains Abbey
Castle Howard
Morecambe
Malham Cove
Brimham Rocks
Knaresborough
Burton Agnes Hall
Lancaster
Gordale Scar
Wharfedale
FOREST OF BOWLAND
Bolton Abbey
York
Clitheroe
Haworth (Bronte parsonage)
Blackpool
Burnley
Leeds
Blackburn
Hebden Bridge
Bradford
Halifax
Huddersfield
Bolton
Edale
MANCHESTER
Blue John Mine
LINCOLNSHIRE WOLDS
Liverpool
Eyam
Speedwell Cavern
Chatsworth
Hardwick Hall
Chester
Haddon Hall
Lincoln
PEAK DISTRICT NATIONAL PARK
Tissington
Stoke-on-Trent
NORFOLK COAST
Wells-next-the-sea
Cromer
Nottingham
Hunstanton
Blakeney
Derby
Sandringham
Ranworth
CANNOCK CHASE
King's Lynn
Norwich
Melbourne Hall
Norfolk Broads
Ironbridge
Hallaton
Gt. Yarmouth
SHROPSHIRE HILLS
Bridgnorth
BIRMINGHAM
Lowestoft
Ludlow
Coventry
Corby
Southwold
Harvington Hall
Kenilworth
Ely
Dunwich
Warwick
River Avon
Haddenham
Newmarket
Bury St. Edmunds
Snape
Worcester
Cambridge
Stowmarket
Aldeburgh
Hereford
Malvern
Evesham
Stratford-upon-Avon
Sulgrave Manor
Long Melford
Lavenham
Woodbridge
MALVERN HILLS
Broadway
Sudbury
Kersey
Ipswich
Goodrich
Cheltenham
Upper and Lower Slaughter
Dedham
Felixstowe
Symonds Yat
Coombe Hill
Bourton-on-the-Water
THE CHILTERNS
Flatford Mill
Chedworth
Blenheim Palace
Colchester
WYE VALLEY
COTSWOLDS
Bibury
Oxford
Chequers
Clacton-on-Sea
Cirencester
Fairford
Dorchester
Chalfont St Giles
Kelmscot Manor
Shillingford
(Milton's Cottage)
Maldon
Abingdon
Wallingford
Cliveden House
Burnham-on-Crouch
Vale of White Horse
Goring Gap
Bristol
Avebury
Pangbourne
Henley
Windsor Castle
Bath
Reading
Sunbury
LONDON
Southend-on-Sea
Savernake Forest
LONDON
Margate
MENDIP HILLS
Lacock Abbey
Windsor Castle
Herne Bay
Broadstairs
Cheddar Caves
NORTH WESSEX DOWNS
Chartwell
Leeds Castle
Ramsgate
Lynton
Lynmouth
Longleat House
Guildford
Gomshall
Hever Castle
Canterbury
Sandwich
Selworthy
Wookey Hole
Wells
SURREY HILLS
Shere
Penshurst Place
KENT DOWNS
Simonsbath
Dunster
Stonehenge
Hindhead
Tunbridge Wells
Dover
Dunkery Beacon
Glastonbury
Abinger Hammer
Biddenden
Clovelly
Chawton (Jane Austen's house)
Petworth House
Cranbrook
Hythe
Westward Ho!
Salisbury
Winchester
Midhurst
ROMNEY MARSH
Romney
EXMOOR NATIONAL PARK
Southampton
Bignor (Roman Villa)
Chanctonbury Ring
Winchelsea
DARTMOOR NATIONAL PARK
Axminster
SUSSEX DOWNS
Arundel
Battle Abbey
Rye
Boscastle
The Cerne Giant
NEW FOREST
Bosham
Brighton
Hastings
Okehampton
Moretonhampstead
Sidmouth
Lyme Regis
Abbotsbury
Bournemouth
Portsmouth
Chichester
Littlehampton
Pevensey
Tintagel
Brown Willy
Chagford
Higher Bockhampton
Selsey
Bognor Regis
Eastbourne
Rough Tor
Dartmoor
Postbridge
Budleigh Salterton
(Thomas Hardy's cottage)
Rottingdean
Padstow
Exeter
Isle of Wight
Newquay
BODMIN MOOR
Princetown
Dawlish
Chesil Beach
Weymouth
Cotehele House
Buckland-in-the-moor
Redruth
Tavistock
Totnes
Plymouth
Saltram House
SOUTH DEVON
Fowey
Dartmouth
Helston
Gerrans Bay
St. Michael's Mount
Kynance Cove

NORTHUMBRIA & YORKSHIRE

Between the two rivers Humber and Tweed and between the crests of the Pennines and the North Sea coast lies one of England's most characterful regions. At the northern end is the ancient Saxon kingdom of Northumbria, ruled over in times when myth and history were inextricably mixed by such colourfully named kings as Edwin, Ecgfried and Oswald. These Anglo-Saxon monarchs took over when the Romans left Britain and, having subdued the resident tribes, spent much of their time warring with their fellow kings in Mercia or Wessex and with the Picts who came marauding from time to time out of what is now known as Scotland.

King Oswald turned out to be rather different from his fellows. Once pacification was well in hand he decided that it was time these rough, unruly northerners should become Christians like himself. So he asked the influential monastery founded by St Columba on Iona to send a missionary to work in Northumbria. They sent a monk called Aidan whose first action was to establish his own island monastery on Lindisfarne – 'the island of the Lincoln people' off the Northumbrian coast.

The seeds of Christianity which Aidan – later St Aidan - sowed in Northumbria germinated and spread, eventually reaching far enough south to merge with the mission begun in Canterbury by St Augustine. From these two points – Lindisfarne, now known as Holy Island, and Canterbury – the conversion of England can be said to have sprung. Today the whole area bristles with reminders that for many centuries Christianity and violence existed side by side. But, in spite of the menacing castles and the defensive solidity of Hadrian's Wall, an air of sanctity pervades the scene: the influence of holy men outweighs the clash of arms. Many people feel this influence most strongly on Holy Island, which can be reached by causeway from the mainland at low tide. Near the ruins of the priory the ancient drink of the monks, mead, is still made.

The conflicts of this age are epitomized in Durham Cathedral where St Cuthbert, who succeeded St Aidan at Lindisfarne, is buried. On its rocky promontory, virtually surrounded by the River Wear, built even more solidly than the castle which shares its eyrie, Durham Cathedral proclaims the strength of the temporal and ecclesiastical powers which its prince-bishops used to wield.

Left: *The rocky crag of Lindisfarne, or Holy Island, was first fortified in 1548 and the castle played its role as defender of the harbour until 1819 when the guns were removed and it fell into disrepair. It was bought in 1902 by Edward Hudson, founder of* Country Life, *who commissioned Sir Edwin Lutyens to restore it. Holy Island has been designated an area of outstanding natural beauty and includes a nature reserve.*

Right: *The bleak winter weather of the high Yorkshire dales is shiveringly captured in this picture of Wensleydale below the Pennine fells with the solitary farmhouse the only sign of life in the frozen landscape. The fells are divided and sub-divided by dry-stone walls. Hundreds of miles of them were built in the 18th century when stone was plentiful and labour was cheap.*

Top right opposite: *Secure on its hill amid shifting sands on the Northumberland coast, Bamburgh Castle defies the North Sea that thunders at its feet in winter storms. Once the palace of the Anglo-Saxon kings of Northumbria, Bamburgh has often been used as a dramatically regal background in historical films.*

Below right opposite: *Durham Cathedral stands on a pinnacle of rock 21.3 m (70 ft) high, rising above the river Wear. In the year 687 St Cuthbert of Lindisfarne made the monks at his death-bed promise that if they had to leave the island they would take his body with them. When Viking raids forced them to leave they settled in Durham and built a church to house the saint's coffin. The present cathedral was built by Normans between 1093 and 1133.*

Below far right opposite: *Staithes, a red-roofed, white-washed jumble of houses clinging to crumbling clay cliffs above the harbour wall, is one of the many once-important but now declining fishing ports along the Yorkshire coast.*

Right: *In some areas Hadrian's Wall, which stretches from Wallsend, east of Newcastle upon Tyne, to Bowness, west of Carlisle, is still surprisingly complete though in other parts many a farmhouse and barn has benefited from its Roman-hewn stone. The wall was 5 m (15 ft) high and up to 3 m (9 ft) thick.*

The air of sanctity is strong in St Paul's Church, Jarrow, where the Venerable Bede, author of England's earliest written history, lived and worked for 50 years up to his death in 753 AD. Here you can see his high-backed chair looking as though he might have been sitting in it only yesterday and would be again tomorrow. It was the Venerable Bede who first described Hadrian's Wall, then more than 600 years old, though it is said that he misinterpreted its age and purpose. The wall was built by the order of the Emperor Hadrian between AD 122 and 130 after he had visited Britain and decided that it would be unwise to attempt to extend the empire any further north. It had 17 forts along its 116 km (72 miles) length and was manned by 5,500 cavalry and 13,000 infantry. Rome withdrew its troops from the wall in AD 383, when they were sent home to defend the city from invading Goths, Vandals and Huns.

One of the best preserved of the wall's forts is Vercovicium, the modern Housesteads. It once garrisoned 1000 Roman troops and contained barracks, a forge, chapel, granary and bakery. A village grew up around the fort with married quarters, shops and temples.

Down the north-west side of Northumberland run the Cheviot Hills. One of the loveliest roads in the region follows the course of the river along Upper Coquet Dale, west from Herinton to the remains of a group of Roman camps at Chew Green, best seen from the hill opposite. Carter Bar, with its famous view over the Scottish Lowlands, was the scene of the last Border raid in 1575. This raid is commemorated by an annual gathering of horse-riders from both sides of the Border. The men of Bellingham hid from northern raiders in the sturdy local church of St Cuthbert's. Cannonballs taken from the wall are on display.

One of the unique sights of Northumbria is the herd of wild white cattle at Chillingham. These horned descendants of the wild ox have roamed the Cheviot foothills at least since the 12th century, when the park was enclosed, and possibly since Roman times. These are genuinely wild creatures and do not allow anyone to come too close. Newly-born calves are hidden in the bracken and if they are touched by human hands their mothers will abandon them. Less exotic are the Blackface and Cheviot sheep whose wool provides the famous Borderland Tweed. There are plenty of shops and mill showrooms displaying locally made cloth and some of the bigger factories make knitting wool, so that shoppers can match up a skirt length with a home-knitted sweater.

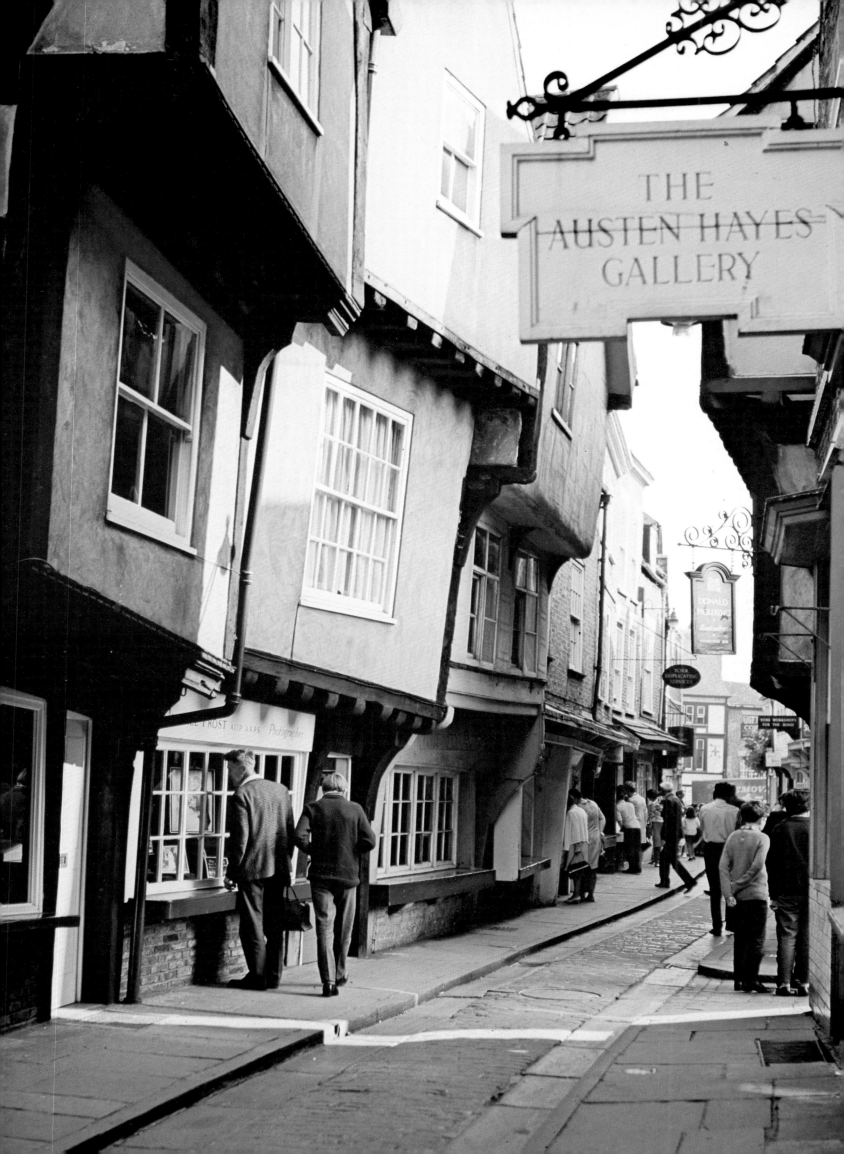

Left: *The Shambles, one of York's many interesting old corners, was mentioned in the Domesday Book and its timber-framed buildings demonstrate what the city must have been like in mediaeval times, long before the days of neatly designed, flat-fronted houses, when each storey overhung the one below until finally neighbours could shake hands across the street. Originally it was a district given over to slaughter-houses.*

Later it was a street of butchers and some of the shops still keep the front slabs where meat was displayed. Today it is a tourist centre of antique shops, boutiques and art galleries, their goods tastefully displayed. The 16th century Roman Catholic martyr Margaret Clitherow, canonized by the Pope in 1969 as St Margaret of York, once lived at No. 35.

Below: *The countryside of the Pennines offers many pleasant contrasts. These rolling upland pastures lie below the bleak barren heights of Haworth moor. There are excellent and varied walks in the area, though most visitors come to see the home of the Brontë sisters at Haworth parsonage, or the nearby Keighley and Worth Valley Railway, a privately owned line run by enthusiasts between Keighley and Oxenhope.*

Right: *Knaresborough, a town of handsome Georgian houses, is picturesquely situated on the river Nidd in North Yorkshire and boating is a popular pastime. High above the river stands the ruined 14th century castle of John of Gaunt, where Richard II was imprisoned in 1399. On the north bank, near Grimbold Bridge, is St Robert's chapel, hewn out of the rock in the 18th century.*

Below: *The sturdy grey houses of Hebden Bridge, a typical mill town in the West Riding of Yorkshire, climb the steep sides of the valley above the river Calder where it joins Hebden Water. The town is connected to the hill-top village of Heptonstall by a pack-horse way. To the north-west is the well-known local beauty spot of Hardcastle Crags.*

Newcastle-upon-Tyne was once a station on the Roman wall and the line of the wall has been traced through the city. Now it is a sprawling commercial centre, but once beyond the commuter belt, along the Tyne valley, there are many fascinating little spots. Bywell was once an important place, peopled by craftsmen servicing the horsemen of the region. Henry VI, fleeing from Hexham field in 1464 after the Lancastrian defeat, took refuge in its castle. All that remains of the flourishing village is a handful of houses, the castle tower – and two churches, within a stone's throw of one another. Legend says that they were built by two rival sisters. St Andrew's has a remarkable Saxon tower and St Peter's stands on the spot where Egbert was consecrated Bishop of Lindisfarne in 802. In the great 18th century flood, when the Tyne burst its banks and submerged Bywell under several feet of water, the horses were taken into St Peter's for safety. Corbridge was a strategically vital spot in Roman times and the Roman station of Corstopitum was first set up as a military headquarters, then as a supply base for the soldiers manning the wall. The storehouse alone covers over 4000 square metres (one acre) of ground and the enormous granaries show the scope and efficiency of Roman public works. Hexham is one of Northumbria's most romantic little market towns, with its 15th century moot hall and curious market place piazza.

The road from Hexham leads over the moors to Blanchland, said to be one of England's most idyllic villages, its little stone houses built amongst the ruins of a once great abbey, with the old cloisters forming the village square and the remains of the refectory part of the local inn. At the head of Allendale is the winter ski centre of Allenheads, once a flourishing lead mining area, and further along is Allendale Town which attracts New Year's Eve crowds to see the celebrated 'Guysers' prancing round a bonfire with lighted tar barrels on their heads, an age old custom which probably dates from winter solstice festivities. The ceremony carried on during the war, when an enclosed fire in a bucket was used so that it could not be seen by German bombers.

The southern half of this region is Yorkshire, England's largest county though now segmented for administrative purposes. It is a land of industrious, down-to-earth, 'brass tack' people made prosperous initially by the nourishing pastures of the Yorkshire moors which fattened and sleekened vast flocks of sheep; then by the purity and power of her great rivers which washed the wool and drove the first mechanical looms, and – later – by the wealth of the coal seams that lie beneath her Pennine borders.

The region has inevitably been scarred by the industrial revolution and its aftermath but the scars are generally very localized and great areas of Northumberland, Durham and Yorkshire have remained unaltered since history began. Much is being done, especially around Durham, to eradicate unsightly slag-heaps and restore the land to fertility.

Yorkshire is famed above all for its dales, the Norse word for valleys, deeply carved by rivers flowing down from the high moorland. Each one has its own special character. Swaledale runs through meadows sprinkled with mountain pansies, then twists and turns between steep fellsides until it emerges from a narrow gorge under the rock where Richmond town and castle stand. The 11th century castle was never attacked because of its strength and impregnable position. Wensleydale, with its green pastureland, is famous for its cheese-making, once a cottage craft but now centred on small factories at Hawes. In the hills just south of Wensleydale lies Semerwater, the lake with a legend. A weary traveller once begged for food and lodging in a nearby town and, when he was turned away, he put a curse on the town, so that it was swallowed up in the waters of the lake.

The course of the river Nidd is unpredictable; it flows underground, into a huge reservoir, then through flat arable fields. Above it stand Brimham Rocks, outcrops of millstone grit weathered into fantastic shapes with names like 'dancing bear' and 'the oyster shell'. At Knaresborough, famous for its witch, Mother Shipton, it cuts through a limestone gorge. Mother Shipton's home was a cave near the Dropping Well, where objects suspended under the dripping water become petrified and there is always an interesting collection of bowler hats, dolls and shoes, all turning slowly into stone.

The river Aire bursts from a subterranean course into Malham Cove, a spectacular limestone amphitheatre of 91 m (300 ft) cliffs. Nearby Gordale Scar produces a magnificent series of waterfalls. Further south, Airedale meets the textile industry in full force, so that mills, chimneys and austere towns border the river. Yorkshire's thriving wool industry grew up in the valleys around Halifax and Huddersfield in the 18th century. The mill owners built houses for their workers and they can still be seen in towns like Hebdon Bridge and Saltaire, the first 'garden village' in Britain. Bradford has a museum with woollen industry exhibits and Halifax Piece Hall, opened in 1779 for the sale of weavers' 'pieces', is now an arts and crafts market and textile museum.

Below: *Rievaulx Abbey, on the edge of the north Yorkshire moors, was founded in 1131 by Cistercian monks who came over from Clairvaux in France. The choir of the abbey church, which many consider to be its finest feature, was added between 1225 and 1230. Both in its architecture and its setting, Rievaulx is one of the most imposing ruins in the north.*

Above: *The octagonal Chapter House is one of the glories of York Minster, dating from the 13th century. The roof is vaulted and the Early Decorated windows have rich tracery. With one exception, their painted glass dates from the reign of Edward I, with scenes from the lives of the saints and the New Testament. Restoration work was necessary after a fire in 1984, which damaged the south transept, including the rose window. Delightful carvings, some beautiful, some comic, decorate the splendid stalls.*

Few visitors would think of touring Yorkshire without seeing the city of York, the capital of the North. Mother Shipton professed: 'Winchester was, London is, York shall be, the finest of the three'. It is the most mediaeval of English towns, with its circle of creamy-coloured stone walls, the fortified 'Bars' or gates, and narrow streets of picturesque old buildings. The Minster grew on the site of four earlier churches, taking two and a half centuries to complete, after beginning in about 1227. The stained glass is world famous and the building shows the handiwork of many craftsmen over the centuries: the heavy squat Norman work in the crypt, the delicate Early English work in the transepts, the central tower in the fine lines of the Perpendicular period. Every four years York stages a major festival, with the Minster as the setting for orchestral and choral concerts, and the York Cycle of Mystery Plays, religious drama dating from 1340, is performed by local people.

Besides York Minster, the region has a wealth of mediaeval buildings. Fountains Abbey, standing on broad, sweeping lawns, is magnificent even in ruin. It displays an impressive system of mediaeval drains and waterworks. The remains of Rievaulx Abbey make a breathtaking picture when viewed from the ornamental terrace above and Bolton Abbey, a priory founded in the 18th century for Augustinian Canons, is situated on a graceful curve of the river Wharfe, where it can be crossed by a footbridge or stepping stones. There are records of the vast quantities of cheese consumed by the monks of Bolton and Jervaulx Abbeys, and Wensleydale cheese probably has a French origin, for the monks had introduced the method they brought with them at the time of the Norman Conquest. At first the cheese was made from ewe's milk but after the dissolution, and the scattering of the Abbey flocks, cow's milk was substituted.

Above: *At the north-east corner of York Minster is the Treasurer's House, parts of which date from the reign of Edward I, although the present house is mainly 17th and 18th century. The office of treasurer, first created by Thomas, Archbishop of York in 1070, was abolished by Henry VIII and the house passed into private ownership until 1930 when the then owner, Frank Green, gave it to the National Trust.*

Above: *Whitby has been a fishing port for several hundred years and still has its fishing fleet. Terraces of red-roofed cottages rise from the harbour and on the cliff stand the remains of the 13th century castle. Behind the town lies the beautiful landscape of the North York Moors national park.*

Left: *The magnificent fountain designed for the Great Exhibition of 1851 is the centrepiece of the gardens at Castle Howard, outside York. The house was designed by Vanbrugh for Charles Howard, 3rd Earl of Carlisle in the early 18th century and is still the seat of the Howard family. The interior is impressive, containing many art treasures, china and statuary and the chapel has pre-Raphaelite stained glass.*

Two further architectural treasures of Yorkshire are Castle Howard and Burton Agnes Hall. Castle Howard, outside York, is a vast house begun by Vanbrugh in 1702 and continued while he was working on Blenheim Palace. It took 37 years to build and by the time it was finished both Vanbrugh and the 3rd Earl of Carlisle, who commissioned it, were dead. Room after room is packed with art treasures and the grounds, with ornamental waters, statuary and a temple, complete the splendour. The English television series 'Brideshead Revisited' was filmed here. Burton Agnes, near Bridlington, is a dignified Elizabethan manor house with plaster-work ceilings, an oak-panelled drawing room and elaborately furnished state bedrooms. It also has a ghost: Anne Griffith, daughter of the original owner. She loved the house so much she made her family promise, when she was dying, that her skull should always remain in the house. Twice it was removed, so the story goes, and twice so much uproar swept through the house that it had to be returned.

North along the coast from Flamborough Head is the dramatic cliff scenery of what is sometimes called the 'forgotten coast', though many visitors have discovered the attractions of Filey, Scarborough, Whitby and Redcar. It was at Scarborough, its two sandy bays divided by a headland, that the craze for sea-bathing began in the mid-nineteenth century. On a sunny day it has a Mediterranean aspect, its sweeps of crescents and Regency terraces rising above the long marine drive. Storms batter the coast in winter and each town has its own stories of heroic sea rescues and ships lost.

The river Esk cuts a ravine through the moors where it flows into the sea, making a natural harbour where the ancient port of Whitby nestles. The synod of Whitby, held in 664, consolidated Christianity in the land and in the monastery cowsheds a cowherd called Caedmon wrote what is said to be the first poem in the English language, telling the story of creation. Captain Cook served his apprenticeship in a house in Grape Lane in the days when Whitby was an important whaling station.

Robin Hood and two of his henchmen are supposed to have sought shelter in Whitby, firing three arrows into the air from the top of the tower and vowing to stay wherever they landed. This turned out to be a short way away, in a cleft in the cliffs. A cluster of red-roofed cottages cling precariously to the cliffside at Robin Hood's Bay. The streets are often only wide enough for one fisherman with a basket on his back and land has always been so scarce that parents often built a house in their own small garden for a son when he married. Because of its situation, this was once the centre of a vast smuggling trade organised quite openly on the coast and later it was a busy fishing port, with fishermen salting down the catch and carrying it to Pickering and York – even smuggling salt to avoid the salt tax.

Right: *The Chinese Room at Burton Agnes Hall on Humberside. The lacquer panels that line the walls were specially made in China to the design of the fifth Baronet, Sir Griffith Boynton (1712-61), whose portrait hangs over the fireplace. The handsome house dating from 1600 with an Inigo Jones addition from 1628, has fine carved ceilings, beautifully furnished rooms and an excellent collection of Impressionist paintings with works by Manet and Gauguin.*

CUMBRIA, THE LAKES & LANCASHIRE

When the Pennines were squeezed up to form the backbone of northern England the counties to the east (though they did not exist at the time) got a bigger share of moorland and fell than the counties to the west. As if to compensate for this lop-sided territorial division a featureless area near the Irish Sea coast emerged to create England's only mountainous region – a miniature Switzerland of incomparable beauty – the Lake District.

It is not a large area – Switzerland itself is 25 times larger – and from the 950m (3118 ft) peak of Helvellyn, it is possible on a clear day to see it all, and beyond to the hills of Scotland and the Irish Sea. But within the Lake District there are some 100 peaks over 600 m (2000 ft), 15 lakes (Windermere is over 16 km (10 miles) long) and ten spectacular waterfalls.

For much of the year the Lake District is thronged with tourists and the M6 motorway, which slices through the north-west region from the West Midlands to the Scottish border, brings an ever-growing stream from the south to enjoy its beauty but 200 years ago its virtues were unsung and its peaks and valleys unvisited. Then, at the beginning of the 19th century, a young man who was born and brought up near Grasmere appointed himself what today would be known as the area's Public Relations Officer. He wrote a masterly *Guide to the Lakes* which was published in 1810 under his own name: William Wordsworth. In it he wrote that the whole area was 'capable of satisfying the most intense cravings for the tranquil and the lovely and the perfect to which man, the noblest of her creatures, is subject'. Lofty idealism of this calibre was exactly what the early Victorians needed to inspire their romantic enthusiasm for nature. The rush to Lakeland was begun. Ruskin was pessimistic about the region's future. In a letter to Canon Rawnsley he said: 'It's all of no use. You will soon have a tourist railway up Scafell, and another up Helvellyn, and another up Skiddaw, and then a connecting line all round'. Happily Ruskin's worst fears have not been fulfilled.

One of the finest scenic main highways in the country runs from Ambleside north to Keswick, running through Grasmere and Rydal, both homes of William Wordsworth, and alongside the wood-fringed reservoir-lake of Thirlmere, overshadowed to the east by the heights of Helvellyn.

Grasmere is the site of one of the most famous of the traditional Lakeland sports meetings in August. Competitions include fell-racing, the local form of wrestling and hound trails. The meeting celebrated its centenary in 1952. Grasmere and Ambleside are among the few places which still celebrate 'rush-bearing', which used to be a common custom in the 15th and 16th

Left: *Wordsworth's line 'one bare dwelling, one abode, no more' might easily have been written about this isolated Langdale farmhouse which is just across the fells from the poet's cottage at Grasmere. The road up Langdale from Ambleside leads to an impressive view of Langdale Pikes.*

Right: *This view of Derwent Water emphasizes one of the great charms of the Lake District: the juxtaposition of a gentle landscape with the wild background of the fells. At the edge of the lake, near Friar's Crag (Ruskin's favourite view-point), is a memorial plaque to Canon Rawnsley, a former vicar of Keswick and co-founder of the National Trust in 1895.*

Above: *Honister Crag is one of Lakeland's most dramatic crags, its sides scarred with slate quarries, its sheer rocks bleak and formidable. The summit can be reached on foot from the top of Honister Pass and then, as the picture shows, a great panorama of lakes and fells unfolds. The road leading down to Buttermere was once dreaded by motorists but it has been much improved.*

centuries, when rushes were strewn on earthen church floors once a year to keep them dry. Now, on a summer Saturday, a procession moves to the church carrying designs made from rushes and flowers.

Splendid rock-climbing is possible on mountains like Great Gable, the Pillar and the majestic Scafell, and there are magnificent prospects from the summits but it is perhaps the walker, rather than the climber or the motorist, who discovers the true charm of Lakeland. There are so many beauty spots to explore that choice becomes the only problem. In the Ullswater area are Aira Force, a silver stream of water tumbling down 21 m (70 ft) between steep rock walls, where a love-sick maiden once drowned, leaving her grieving suitor to live out his life as a hermit in a spot nearby, and the trout-filled waters of the isolated Angle Tarn, with its pretty little islands. On Moor Divock, a wind-swept plateau off the lake's north-east shore, are wild ponies, lapwings and curlews, and a strange assortment of standing stones, a stone circle, cairns, mounds and pits dating back 3000 to 4000 years. No-one knows who raised Cap Stone or why, but it still stands as a reminder of prehistoric man.

Lakeland possesses a variety of flowers, ferns and mosses which is probably unequalled anywhere else in the country. In spring the woods are dotted with anemone, primrose and violet. In June the old packhorse trails are bright with honeysuckle, wild roses, geraniums and yellow poppies. In distant spots rarities like the bee-orchis, bog asphodel and birds'-eye primrose may still be found. Parnassus grass grows on marshy ground at the head of the dales. The bracken is one of the glories of the district. It gives colour to the scene throughout the year, except in July and August, when it is a dense, green, waist-high jungle.

The beauty of the area has attracted visitors for centuries. Wordsworth was born at Cockermouth and is buried in Grasmere churchyard. Southey lived for 40 years at Greta Hall, near Keswick, and Thomas de Quincey lived at Nab Cottage on Rydal Water. Another famous local character was John Peel, born at Caldbeck in 1776, who 'view-halloed' over the surrounding fells in search of foxes for 55 years.

Several traditional Cumbrian crafts survive – Kendal's Museum of Lakeland Life preserves those which have now disappeared from the villages, as well as selling, in the attached shop, pottery, glass, jewellery, toys and rugs made by local craftsmen. Visitors can still watch weaving, leatherworking and woodcarving at some of the tourist centres in the area.

Market days are important for the farmers of the region, especially markets like the autumn sheep auction at Kirkby Stephen, when buyers from all over the north bid for rams reared on the nearby fells, and the September horse and pony sales of the Cowper Day fair. Sheep-farming is the dominant industry of the Dales, the native sheep being the Herdwick. These small sheep look very much at home with their grizzled faces; they are able to climb like goats and leap over virtually any wall.

Some Lake District views are so much photographed that they seen familiar, even when seen for the first time: Derwent Water from Friars Crag, with peak after peak jostling away into the distance, or eerie Wast Water, with the towering Screes on the right and the peak of Great Gable ahead. Roads are scarce and over-busy in summer, but views are always spectacular. The 'Buttermere Round' runs along the shore of Derwent Water, through Grange and the woods of Borrowdale over the steep Honister Pass and down into Buttermere, as peaceful and pastoral as its name. On the remarkable Roman road over Hardknott Pass, 396 m (1300 ft) high and crowned by the remains of a Roman camp, motorists wrestle with hairpin bends on a gradient of one in four. Much lonelier is the unfenced road over Birker Moor from Dunnerdale to Eskdale, a panorama of some of the highest land in England unfolding all round and the Bootle Fell road over Black Combe, with bracken and heather stretching for miles on one side, and the expanse of the Irish Sea into the horizon on the other. Beside the road to Troutbeck, near Ullswater, you come within a mile or so of the magnificent falls known as Aira Force with a sheer drop of some 21 m (70 ft). With Glencoyne Park on one side and Gowbarrow Park on the other it is a breathtaking spot. Ullswater, the second

Left: *The pleasant little village of Grange, in Borrowdale, stands beside two separate channels of the Derwent, crossed by a stone bridge with two arches. This picture shows the view from Grange Fell which, together with Borrowdale Birches, was bought by the National Trust in 1910 as a memorial to King Edward VII and named King's How. Near Grange is the Bowder Stone, an amazingly balanced rock weighing about 2000 tonnes.*

Below: *On the western edge of the Pennines in the river Eden valley north of Appleby, the village of Dufton is a welcoming oasis in a world of moorland and high fells. Here, around a generous village green, most of the houses are built from the local red sandstone which gives the surrounding fields their rich, bronze colouring. In the mid-18th century Dufton was an important lead-mining centre and there is a well-worn path to Great Rundale, a steep hillside beyond Dufton Pike, where the old workings may still be seen. Dufton is on the route of the Pennine Way, the 400 km (250 mile) track, mapped and signposted, which may be walked from Edale in Derbyshire to Kirk Yetholm on the Scottish side of the Cheviots. A clapper bridge of stone slabs carries the Pennine Way over Dufton's Great Rundale Beck.*

Right: *The fells surrounding Crummock Water are less stark than many of Lakeland's mountains and their grassy slopes contribute to the graceful, serene look of one of the most delightful lakes of the area. Walkers can enjoy the varied scenery on a 14 km (9 mile) circuit of Crummock Water.*

Above: *Lake District connoisseurs are quick to desert some of the more popular lakes during holiday seasons in order to find the peace and solitude that is Lakeland's great virtue. Loweswater is one of the smaller, less accessible but no less lovely lakes on the western fringe of the district. This view across the lake from the road through Crabtree shows Holme Wood dominated by the 542 m (1781 ft) peak of Carling Knott on Loweswater Fell. The circuit of Loweswater, using the road on the north side and lanes and footpaths through Holme Wood on the south, makes a very pleasant hour's walk.*

Above: *The Forest of Bowland in Lancashire is one of the loneliest parts of the county. Not surprisingly considering the idiosyncrasy of the English language hardly any of it is forest, mostly consisting of wild moorland fell. The area contains Pendle Hill and Pendle village, famous as the home of the Lancashire witches, two old hags and their families who were hanged for witchcraft in 1612.*

Left: *Pine trees soften the rather severe outlines of Buttermere, where the forbidding mountains descend abruptly to the water's edge. In the north-west corner Sour Milk Gill comes down the fells from Bleaberry Tarn in a series of thin cataracts and a stream joins the lakes of Buttermere and Crummock Water.*

largest of the lakes, was particularly admired by Wordsworth. His *Ode to the Daffodils* was written after a visit in spring to Gowbarrow Park, which is now National Trust property.

Lake Windermere, the largest of the lakes, contains several small islands, and pleasure steamers traverse the Lake. The road round Lake Windermere drops down into Ambleside, with its ideal setting near the head of the Lake.

The intense magnetism of the Lakes has diverted attention from the rest of the region which is surprisingly interesting and attractive, though not without industrial scars around Liverpool and Manchester, its two principal cities.

To the north of the region there is another and very different city – Carlisle, the sentinel city near the Scottish border and a one-time fort on Hadrian's Wall which ended some 19 km (12 miles) to the west. It is the centre of a wild and solitary though fertile region flanked by Pennine moorlands to the east and the racing tidal waters of the Solway Firth to the west. The fortress was taken by the Scots on several occasions, but they never held it permanently. In 1745 the Young Pretender rode in on a white horse with the famous 'hundred pipers' and established his headquarters. The castle has a Norman keep with a windowless cell named after MacIvor, Sir Walter Scott's hero in 'Waverley'. Mary, Queen of Scots, was a prisoner in the tower for two months in 1568, though her apartment was destroyed early in the 19th century, along with the banqueting hall. There is a fine view from the ramparts.

At the western end of Hadrian's Wall is Bowness-on-Solway, where stones from the old Roman camp are built into the walls of the village. Reminders of the Roman occupation are dotted all around the area. Stone for Hadrian's Wall was quarried near Brampton and there is a moving inscription on a rock, high above the river belt, carved by a Roman standard-bearer.

All down the Cumbrian coast, except for the industrialized strip between Maryport and Whitehaven, there are deserted sandy beaches where the only sounds are of retreating waves and the plaintive cry of seabirds. Bird-watchers can see dunlins, godwits, oystercatchers, sandpipers and wild geese. Across the estuary from Ravenglass is the largest breeding-colony of black-headed gulls in Europe. Sea-urchins and starfish cling to the shore and visitors sometimes see dolphins, porpoises and grey seals.

For the gregarious there is always Blackpool and Morecambe and the other Lancashire coastal resorts (not forgetting the Isle of Man) where the northerners show the rest of the world how they like to enjoy themselves even if 'Kiss-me-quick' hats are not everyone's idea of a good time. It is easy to be toffee-nosed about Blackpool, but northerners are very demanding people and for the food they like and the entertainment they enjoy the standards they demand are high.

Inland from Blackpool and north towards Lancaster lies one of those stretches of countryside that, to the southerner at any rate, is unexpected in Lancashire: the Forest of Bowland, a green and brown wilderness of high pasture and fell stretching from close to Clitheroe almost to Lancaster. The only road across the Forest climbs through the Trough of Bowland, a stream-bordered, tree-lined valley sheltering under the steep flank of Blaze Moss, a 518 m (1700 ft) high hill.

For those blessed with the 'seeing eye' there is much beauty to be found in the harbour bustle of Liverpool, first settled nearly 2000 years ago, firmly established on the West Indian trade and now the largest port in Britain. It is the only city in the country which can claim to have two cathedrals both built in the present century, though it is probably more widely known as the birth-place of the Beatles.

The construction of the Manchester Ship Canal in 1894 enabled Manchester to become the third largest port in England. Its many cultural and architectural treasures, include the Cathedral, a 15th century Gothic building with superbly carved pew ends, five art galleries and the oldest public library in Europe. The renowned Royal Exchange Theatre is built in the old cotton exchange, once packed with thousands of dealers, fixing world prices.

Yes, there is plenty to see and do in the north-west outside the Lake District where, as an old Yorkshire man once remarked, 'there's nowt but scenery'.

THE MIDLANDS

S earch as you will, it is difficult to find a common denominator in the Midlands. How can there be in a region whose industries vary from coal mining and heavy engineering to lace making and whose scenery changes from the muscular gritstone 'edges' of Derbyshire to the fruit orchards of Worcester, blanketed with fleecy pink and white blossom in spring-time. It is difficult, too, to define the exact boundaries of the Midlands. Roughly speaking, they cover a 96km (60mile) radius from the mediaeval cross on the village green at Meriden in Warwickshire, said to be the exact centre of England. But it is best not to try to define the Midlands too exactly in terms of area and accept the fact that they are diverse, diverting and definitely underrated.

Touristically the Midlands suffer from the widely-held belief that the only good thing they possess is Stratford-upon-Avon and the Shakespeare cult on which it thrives. Stratford is a lovely town, historically, literarily and theatrically important, but to visit it without much more than a glance at the surrounding regions is to neglect much of England's most delectable scenery and ignore some of her richest treasures.

A random dip into some of the individual Midland counties shows how much they have to offer besides Shakespeare. Warwickshire, the bard's own county, has the stately ruins of Kenilworth Castle where Robert Dudley, Earl of Leicester, entertained Elizabeth I so lavishly that he all but bankrupted himself, the menacing defences of Warwick Castle and several imposing country houses, among them Compton Wynyates, begun by Edmund Compton in 1480 and finished by his son William. The mellow brick house with its formal topiary gardens was originally moated but the Comptons had to fill in the moat after the Civil War as a penalty for supporting the Royalist cause. The river Avon flows through water meadows, under ancient bridges and past picturesque mills and half-timbered houses. Birmingham itself has more miles of canals than Venice, cruised by narrow canal boats. The city's symphony orchestra is renowned throughout Britain and the Town Hall has been the centre of the region's musical life since Mendelssohn conducted

Above: *Haddon Hall in Derbyshire is a fine example of mediaeval architecture. Though originally a fortified house, it was never besieged and it has belonged to the Manners family since 1567. The chapel has 15th century wall-paintings and a Norman font.*

Right: *Compton Wynyates, near Banbury, was begun by Edmund Compton in 1480. The mellow brick house is surrounded by rising parkland which places it in a hollow. It was originally moated but the Comptons had to fill in the moat as a penalty for supporting the Royalist cause.*

Left: *Warwick Castle is everyone's idea of what a mediaeval fortress should look like. Below its walls the Avon flows placidly on its way to Stratford. The interior was transformed into a stately home in the 17th century but badly damaged by fire in 1770. In the state apartments there is a magnificent collection of furniture and armour.*

Above: *The Early English nave of Lincoln is built of limestone from the hill on which the cathedral stands, but the handsome piers are ornamental with multiple shafts of Purbeck marble.*

Below: *To get away from the busy tourist traffic of Stratford-upon-Avon, it is only necessary to walk along the banks of the Avon to get this pastoral view of St Mary's church where the poet is buried.*

the first performance of *Elijah* there in 1847. The work of Birmingham Repertory Theatre is justly famous, and the City Art Gallery and Museum has an important collection of Pre-Raphaelite paintings.

Neighbouring Northamptonshire, except near the Warwickshire borders, is a flatter, more open landscape, mainly agricultural but industrially important for its deposits of iron ore at Corby. Being a limestone area the county has beautiful churches, many with elegant spires, and castles both inhabited and ruined. One evocative spot is a mere grassy mound beside the river Nene. Here stood Fotheringhay Castle where Mary Queen of Scots was beheaded in 1587 after 19 years of frustrating detention during which she had been shuttled around the Midlands from one custodian's house to another's. Of special interest particularly to American visitors is Sulgrave Manor which is the home of George Washington's ancestors.

Derbyshire is a complete contrast, at least in the north where the so-called Peak District is to be found. To the question which many people ask: 'Which is *the* Peak?' the answer is simple: there is not one. The district gets its name from the Peacs, an ancient British tribe which lived in the area before the Romans came. In the Peak District National Park, the Pennine Way – a 400km (250miles) track for walkers leading to the Scottish border – begins at Edale beneath the massive 600m (200ft) hump of Kinder Scout. Derbyshire's stately homes are world-famous: Chatsworth, home of the Duke of Devonshire; Haddon Hall, traditionally the scene of a romantic 16th century elopement by Dorothy Vernon, daughter of the owner; Hardwick Hall, built by the Countess of Shrewsbury (Bess of Hardwick) with the money accumulated from four advantageous marriages; Kedleston Hall, for 800 years the home of the Curzons; and Melbourne Hall which gave its name to Melbourne, Australia, and where Thomas Cook, of travel fame, began his working life as a gardener's boy. The Romans first discovered Blue John, a translucent stone which could be worked into striking ornaments, 2000 years ago. Both Nero and Petronius paid enormous amounts of money for Blue John vases. Mining has left the show caverns at Blue John in Castleton. Speedwell cavern was once a lead mine and visitors travel through by boat, while the Nestus Mine recreates the sights and sounds of a working mine.

In Hereford and Worcester the Malvern Hills rise like a shark's fin above the distant Vale of Evesham, the market garden of the Midlands. It was while wandering on these hills one summer evening that Sir Edward Elgar heard a

Below: *Lincoln Cathedral on Steephill, 76 m (230 ft) above the lower streets, dominates the city and the surrounding countryside. Built by the Normans, it must surely be the only cathedral in England to have been damaged by earthquake, an event which happened in 1185. According to a contemporary account the building was 'cleft from top to bottom'. At once Bishop Hugh of Avalon began restoring and extending it and the cathedral as it stands today was virtually completed by 1280. Since that time the only major alteration has been the heightening of the three towers which are such an impressive feature. The splendid west front is richly decorated with carvings and 11 statues of kings, from William I to Edward III, stand over the central doorway.*

Following pages: *The Lord Leycester Hospital in Warwick was founded in 1571 by Robert Dudley, Earl of Leicester, as a hospital (in the early sense of the word) for the 'poor and impotent'. The buildings were originally the headquarters of Warwick's Town Guilds and their chapel, St James, is on the left of the picture. Today the Hospital is a home for retired or disabled ex-servicemen.*

voice singing the lovely folk-tune which became the theme of his 'Introduction and Allegro for Strings'. Elgar's music captures the essence of Worcestershire as well as, if not better than, words can ever hope to do.

The river Wye rises in the Cambrian mountains, a clean, dancing river, plays its slow movement as it passes the pink stone pile of Hereford Cathedral, swings into an 8km (5mile) loop at Symonds Yat and finally separates England and Wales before merging with the Severn below Chepstow. Its banks are 'a succession of nameless beauties' said the poet Gray. There is an unbroken series of beautiful landscapes – lofty woodland, rocky gorges and rich agricultural country – as well as castles, churches and pleasant towns. The touring centre is Ross-on-Wye, a quiet town centred on its arcaded market hall. Nearby is Goodrich and its romantic ruined castle which was defended for Charles I during the Civil War. It eventually fell after a siege of four and a half months.

Mediaeval monks used the water from Holy Well and St Anne's Well as curatives and Malvern is still famous for its pure spring water, which it probably owes its pureness to its hard rocks, for rainwater can dissolve few deposits. In 1842 two doctors converted a hotel into England's first hydropathic establishment and the town gained the title of 'metropolis of the water cure'. Though water cures are no longer fashionable, Great Malvern is still a cheerful little town, full of imposing Victorian houses and a wealth of rhododendron gardens clinging to the dizzy slopes of the hillside.

Dovecotes and hiding holes are specialities of the district. The 'hides' go back to the time of the religious persecutions. Harvington Hall has hides behind trapdoors, as well as a stair that lifts out and a beam that pivots. Dovecotes were kept, from the Middle Ages onwards, so that the lord of the manor could always have a fresh treat for the table. In the 17th century there were about 26,000 of them, much to the desperation of the farmers, whose crops were pillaged by flocks of birds. Only a handful remain. At Sarnesfield the dovecote was the tower of the 13th century church, which contains over 100 resting places, and the circular dovecote at Garway, which once belonged to the Knights Templar, has walls nearly four feet thick and more than 660 holes.

Shropshire has become inextricably associated with A.E. Housman, the poet, who died in 1936. He wrote nostalgically of Wenlock Edge, the Wrekin and the country bordering the upper reaches of the Severn. Housman was, in fact, a Worcestershire man, but that is one of the quirks of topography common in the well-mixed Midlands.

The Wrekin has taken on a new tourist significance over the past few years, because of the popularity of Ironbridge and its huge industrial museum complex. Here Abraham Darby first used coke to smelt iron in 1709 and the great iron bridge itself was erected in 1779. A series of museums illustrates the pioneering developments of the Industrial Revolution.

Bridgnorth and Ludlow both began life as fortified riverside towns. Bridgnorth, which is divided into High Town and Low Town, separated by a steeply winding road, retains only the keep of its Norman castle. It leans at an angle of 17 degrees – three times greater than the leaning tower of Pisa – but it has stood there safely for 800 years. Ludlow is a planned mediaeval castle-town and amid the extensive ruins of its pink sandstone castle visitors can see summer performances of classic dramas. Milton's 'Comus' was first performed here in 1634.

The 'five towns' of the Staffordshire Potteries were famous long before Arnold Bennett wrote about them, for many of the most famous names in china – Wedgwood, Spode, Copeland and Royal Doulton among them – come from this area.

Cheshire has one of the most beautiful mediaeval towns in Britain. Chester is enclosed by ancient red sandstone walls, its four main gates arching across the roads. One of its most famous sites is the Rows, consisting of arcades running along the first floor of the half-timbered houses, forming unique shopping galleries.

The Midlands can lay claim to several of the most magnificent cathedrals in the country. Hereford, once the Saxon capital of West Mercia, has been the

Right opposite: *Mam Tor, a 518 m (1700 ft) mountain in north Derbyshire, is the southern outpost of the region known as the High Peak. This is the really rugged northern half of Derbyshire's Peak District, an area of rocky outcrops on high moorlands, crossed by the Pennine Way. Mam Tor has been known since Elizabethan times as the shivering mountain because of the way its almost continuous landslides of shale and grit reflect the sunlight. People living in the Midlands and North of England have long regarded the Peak District as their natural playground. Indeed it was largely the pressure of public opinion generated by the thousands of walkers from Manchester and Sheffield that led, in the early 1930s, to the public being granted access to the privately owned mountains and moors in the area and to the establishment, in 1951, of the Peak District National Park.*

Below: *Dr Johnson considered that 'he who has seen Dovedale has no need to visit the Highlands' and, even if he was guilty of exaggeration, most visitors agree on the beauty of Dovedale, a wooded ravine in the Peak District, which twists through limestone cliffs full of caves and rocks which have weathered into strange shapes, with names like Lion Rock, Jacob's Ladder and Lover's Leap.*

seat of a bishop since 672 AD. The cathedral is mainly Norman, but shows the alterations of several centuries. It has a rare mediaeval library where all the books are chained to the wall and one of the oldest maps in the world, the Mappa Mundi, made in the early 14th century when the world was supposed to be flat, with Jerusalem in the centre. The cathedral takes turns with Worcester and Gloucester in hosting the yearly 'Three Choirs Festival'.

The Norman bishop Remigius built his church on rising ground to be 'as strong as the place was strong and as fair as the place was fair', so Lincoln Cathedral dominates the city and surrounding country. It dates from the 11th to 15th centuries and has a fine west front and stately triple towers. Inside, on the north side of the Choir, the famous 'Lincoln Imp' leers down from among intricately carved foliage. This work of some jocular mediaeval mason went almost unnoticed until the middle of the 19th century when James Usher, a local jeweller, designed him into a tie-pin which was presented to the Prince of Wales, later Edward VII.

Worcester Cathedral is originally Norman and Bishop Wulfstan's splendid crypt remains, but the major part of the building dates from the 14th century. The choir-stalls, preserved from 1379, are carved with various quaint scenes and among the many monuments is an effigy of King John clad in royal robes, considered to be the oldest royal effigy in England. His tomb was opened in 1797 and the skeleton was found intact. In the vaulted cloisters, the piers have square openings, probably so that a watchful eye could be kept on the monks while they worked. The monastic refectory now serves as the hall of King's School.

Coventry has a cathedral of a very different kind. In 1940 one of the worst bombing raids of the war laid waste the major part of the city, including the Cathedral Church of St Michael. Only part of the walls and the 91m (300ft) spire remain, but visitors can now walk through the ruins to the most controversial of modern cathedrals, designed by Sir Basil Spence and completed in 1962. It displays a vast tapestry by Graham Sutherland, a baptistry window by John Piper and a bronze of St Michael by Epstein.

Above: *The Horn Dance of Abbot's Bromley in Staffordshire is a strange survival from prehistoric times. It takes place early in September, when a procession makes a circuit of the town and local farms. Among the characters are the Deer Men, who carry reindeer antlers thought to be 1000 years old and perform their dance at various venues from dawn onwards.*

In the 19th century Tennyson and Lander re-told the legend of Lady Godiva, wife of Leofric, Earl of Chester, who rode naked through the streets to persuade her husband to reduce taxes. Her statue stands at the entrance to the city's new shopping centre and animated figures on the clock tower depict both Lady Godiva and Peeping Tom, the only person to break the townspeople's pledge to remain behind shuttered windows during her ride. He is supposed to have been struck blind for his sins.

Many old local customs have survived in the region, like the Shrovetide football at Atherstone in Warwickshire, said to have started in the 13th century, when Warwickshire and Leicestershire men fought over a bag of gold, and another is the Easter Bottle-Kicking at Hallaton in Leicestershire, when youths from Hallaton and the neighbouring village of Medbourne fight for the 'bottles', or small casks of beer, each team trying to carry them over a brook into their own parish.

Derbyshire's famous well-dressing may go back to the pagan ceremonies of propitiating the gods of water, though many say it originated at the time of the Black Death when the villagers of Tissington escaped the sickness and gave credit to the pure waters of their well. Several villages celebrate on Ascension Day and various other dates, decorating the village wells with tapestry-like pictures made in trays of soft clay, with flowers, fir cones, pebbles and leaves arranged in Biblical scenes. Clergy and choir go from well to well, giving a blessing.

Eyam, another Derbyshire village, also dresses its wells, but Eyam was not spared from the Plague. Plaques on the houses tell the story of the brave villagers who, under the leadership of the vicar, voluntarily cut themselves off from the outside world once the sickness struck. When the Plague abated, 260 of the inhabitants were dead. Tombs dot the village in unexpected places and many skeletons lie buried beneath the flagstones of the old cottages. Once the church had been closed to prevent infection, the parishioners gathered for worship around a cavern in the valley, known as Cucklet Church. On the last Sunday in August, Plague Sunday, a service in memory of the local martyrs is held here.

Above: *This fine half-timbered 16th century building is the oldest house in Bridgnorth. It was the birthplace, in 1729, of Thomas Percy, who became Bishop of Dromore. This ancient Shropshire market town is split by the river Severn into High Town and Low Town, linked by steps and by the steep Castle Hill Cliff Railway.*

Right: *Ironbridge took its name from the first cold-blast iron bridge built in the World in 1779, cast at Coalbrookdale, 'the cradle of the iron trade', and still spanning the Severn Gorge. The gorge is now the site of an extensive series of museums charting the history of the iron, coal and clay industries. Several visits are needed to absorb all that is on show.*

Below: *The highest point of the lovely Malvern Hills in Hereford and Worcester is the 398 m (1307 ft) Worcester Beacon, Macaulay's 'lonely height'. From the top there is a magnificent view of fifteen counties, three cathedrals and five abbeys. St Anne's Well, one of the famous springs, gushes from its slopes.*

EAST ANGLIA

In East Anglia the sky comes into its own: clear, luminous blue arching up from limitless horizons to proclaim that East Anglia has no end and no beginning. And, indeed, in some respects it has not. On its east side the hungry sea gnaws away at its cliffs and dunes while to the west, where huge shallow meres and marshes once cut it off from the rest of England, today's fenland fields – hedgeless acres of rich dark soil - spread endlessly outward towards the sky.

But to set some limits, however arbitrary, East Anglia may be said to cover certainly the counties of Norfolk and Suffolk, possibly parts of Lincolnshire where it borders the Wash and the estuaries of Essex, and finally Cambridgeshire where its ill-defined inland boundaries lie. Physically the area has much in common with the Netherlands, but what all East Anglians share is a sturdy – some call it stubborn – independence bred into them through centuries of isolation from their neighbours.

Until the 17th century the Fens were a watery waste stretching from south of the Isle of Ely (which was literally an island then) as far as the Wash, the great shallow indentation of the North Sea separating western Norfolk from eastern Lincolnshire. To strangers to the area the Fens presented an almost impassable barrier and anyone who did manage to find his way across was regarded with suspicion and dubbed a 'foreigner'. Even today in the villages of East Anglia you will often hear people born in other parts of England referred to as foreigners.

As early as the reigns of Elizabeth I and James I plans were made to drain the Fens, but it was not until Charles I was insecurely on the throne that any practical steps were taken. A Dutch engineer named Vermuyden was engaged to mastermind the operation but Charles ran out of money. Then came the Civil War and operations were again delayed. Finally in 1653, the original plan was completed and hundreds of square kilometres of land were gradually brought under the plough.

Norwich is perhaps the queen of East Anglian cities though its position today cannot compare with its status in the Middle Ages when, after London and Bristol, it was the third city in the kingdom, its prosperity based on wool. In Norwich everything continues to convey this former prominence and a continuing prosperity, coupled with obvious civic pride.

George Borrow wrote of Norwich: 'A fine city – whichever way you view it'. The most famous view is from Mousehold Heath, where Kett banded together his desperate peasant followers before marching on the city in the Peasants' Revolt of 1549. The old walled city, with no less than 33 ancient churches, is

Right: *Sailing for pleasure on the Norfolk Broads became popular only towards the end of the last century. As the work of the trading wherries and reed cutters declined, the holiday-maker took over and turned these waterways into a playground for amateur sailors. In recent years a sail has become a comparatively rare sight as more and more visitors demand power-driven craft. As a result these waters are becoming a growing menace to the rich wild life of the area.*

Right, inset: *Willy Lott's cottage, adjoining Flatford Mill, was the subject of one of John Constable's most famous paintings. So little has the scene changed that Constable would have no difficulty recognizing the cottage from this photograph.*

Left: *Salt flats and sand dunes like these abound along the coasts of Norfolk and Suffolk and are poor protection against the North Sea. In the floods of January, 1952, when many people were drowned, dozens of coastal villages were inundated. The East Anglian coast is gradually retreating and, over the centuries, as here at Dunwich, whole towns and villages have been swallowed by the waves.*

Below: *The East Anglian wool trade which, in the 14th and 15th centuries, made this region one of the wealthiest in England, has bequeathed some architectural gems. One of the richest jewel boxes is the Suffolk village of Lavenham, which was famous for its blue cloth. In the village centre, whichever way you turn, there are well-* *preserved (though internally modernized) mediaeval houses. The Guildhall in the Market Square is in the care of the National Trust and there are several notable old inns, including The Angel and The Swan, which incorporates the old Wool Hall.*

like an illustration from a mediaeval manuscript. The mainly Norman cathedral is surrounded by a secluded close of delightful old buildings, among them the school where Nelson was a pupil. Elm Hill remains a sensitively preserved corner of mediaeval Norwich, a cobbled, traffic-free street which broadens out at one point into a square courtyard where stands the elm tree which gives the street its name. The old Guildhall looks out onto the open-air market with its colourful awnings, called 'tilts', and stalls selling all types of local produce.

In the 14th and 15th centuries, the East Anglian wool trade made this region one of the wealthiest in the country. After that, the development of water power meant that the weaving industry moved to the north of England, where there were sufficient hill streams to provide energy, so East Anglia remained unspoiled by the Industrial Revolution. In its heyday, Lavenham was so prosperous that the weavers were able to build substantial houses and the town is full of beautiful half timbered buildings, decorated plaster walls and top storeys which bulge out into the street. The Old Wool Hall, once threatened with demolition, has been incorporated into 'The Swan' and the impressive Guildhall, dating from the 1530s, is a museum with exhibitions of local industries. Rivalries between the wool villages ran high and the people of Lavenham were determined that their church should have the grandest tower in the area. It is 43m (141ft) high and was mainly financed by a rich clothier, Thomas Spring, whose son was so proud of his brand new coat-of-arms that he had it depicted 32 times on the top of the tower. Stoke-by-Nayland also has a mighty tower, standing on a hill so that it is a landmark for miles, which Constable used in many of his landscapes.

Eastward from the Fens the land rises markedly, though the naming by some atlases of the low hills of Suffolk as the 'East Anglian Heights' rather overstates the case. All the same, East Anglia is not as flat as it is often said to be. Both Norfolk and Suffolk are endowed with gentle hills and valleys which give much of the landscape a pleasant, undulating intimacy beneath the generous skies. 'You can, in no direction, go a quarter of a mile,' wrote

William Cobbett in his *Rural Rides*, 'without finding views that a painter might crave.' And, indeed, anyone familiar with the works of John Crome, John Sell Cotman, John Constable and Thomas Gainsborough – East Anglians to a man – will know exactly what he meant, for these artists captured the simple charm of East Anglia in what are now considered to be the finest English landscape paintings of the early 19th century.

Many of the scenes and villages painted by Constable still survive unspoiled, in spite of the throngs of tourists, all trying to pinpoint the exact spot where the painter sat to execute each picture. He wrote of his birthplace, East Bergholt, near the Essex-Suffolk border, 'I love every stile and stump and lane in the village; as long as I am able to hold a brush I shall never cease to paint them', and the pretty village, built on a ridge above the river, has many attractive old houses and a church with an external bell-house, where the bells hang upside down and are rung by hand, without the aid of ropes. Along the River Stour is the 18th century Flatford Mill, with the mill, mill house and Willy Lott's cottage standing unchanged from the days when Constable worked there.

Nearby is Colchester, the oldest recorded town in England, with a history stretching back to the Iron Age. The Romans called the town Camulodunum and enjoyed the famous local oysters so much, they shipped large quantities back home. The Roman walls circling the town still stand and the Normans took stone from Roman buildings for the castle, which has the largest keep in England. The castle was under siege for 12 months in 1648 by Cromwell's army and when it surrendered, the two Royalist commanders were shot as rebels. The late 15th century Siege House, headquarters of the parliamentary leader, still has bullet holes in its timbers. In the 16th century, links with the Continent led to an influx of Protestant weavers, refugees from the Low Countries, whose style of building can still be seen in the Dutch quarter.

South of Colchester lies a different, wild world of salty marshes, low meadows and oyster beds, ports and yachting centres like Maldon and Burnham-on-Crouch, where fishermen recount their catches in pubs.

The folk of Long Melford were determined to give their town a church which would be the wonder of the century. It has an amazing range of windows, ninety-seven of them, an important collection of stained glass and, in the Clopton Chantry, a mighty monument to Sir William Cordell, Solicitor General and Master of the Rolls. His beautiful Elizabethan House, Melford Hall, now belongs to the National Trust. In 1578, during Elizabeth I's royal progress, he was the first Suffolk man to entertain her and is said to have set such a lavish example of hospitality that many of the other land-owners of the county, forced to follow suit, were almost ruined.

Sudbury, the largest of the wool towns, does not have the antique charm of some of the others, but it has several interesting buildings: the house where Thomas Gainsborough was born, the 15th century Salter's Hall with its Pickwickian associations, and St Peter's Church, with a painted 17th century nave roof and a famous piece of 15th century embroidery, the Sudbury Pall, still used at the funerals of aldermen.

East Anglia has a long and fascinating sea coast, with all types of resorts, from busy seaside centres with the full complement of illuminations, donkey rides and day and night entertainment to quiet hide-away villages. Towns like Clacton, Great Yarmouth and Southend are all lively holiday centres, but the stretch of coastline between Felixstowe and Lowestoft has quite a different character. The pace is slower here, shingle beaches shelve steeply from sand-dunes, rivers meander to the sea.

The 16th century Moot Hall at Aldeburgh was once the centre of the town, but the sea has encroached until it now stands at the water's edge. It is a dignified, peaceful spot – except in June when the annual Aldeburgh Festival, founded by Benjamin Britten in 1948, attracts many thousands of visitors to hear some of the best musicians in the world. The sea has treated Dunwich even more harshly than Aldeburgh. In the Middle Ages it was a great port, now it is a tiny hamlet, most of its streets and important buildings, including nine churches, swallowed up by the sea. There is occasional underwater

Below: *The red brick windmill of Cley next the Sea, its white cap and sails catching the sunlight, is much photographed and painted. The village, with houses of brick and cobble dressings, was once a busy sea-port but is now inland, standing at the edge of salt-marshes which echo with the cries of numerous and varied wild birds.*

Above: *In Kersey, one of Suffolk's pretty weaving villages, interesting old colour-washed houses line the main street which dips down to a shallow ford. The village gave its name to hard-wearing Kersey cloth. The splendid Perpendicular church was built from the profits of the wool trade and has a flint tower and a porch with fine 15th century carved panels.*

exploration of the submerged town and fishermen say they can hear the church bells from beneath the waves, out in their boats at night. Southwold was renowned for its fishing industry as far back as Domesday records and has always owed its prosperity to the sea, but now it is a constant battle to keep the harbour mouth open. The Battle of Sole Bay in 1672 between the Dutch and English fleets took place just off the coast here and is commemorated in the local brewery's Broadside Ale.

Norfolk also has a stretch of wild beauty along its coast, between Cromer and Hunstanton. Blakeney's steep street of flint cottages slopes down to a natural, sheltered harbour full of boats. At Wells-next-the-Sea pinewoods border the sandy beach and a fleet of whelk and shrimp boats operate from the harbour. Holkham has an enormous Palladian mansion, once the home of the 'Coke of Norfolk', famous for his agricultural developments in the late 18th century.

Today on the Isle of Ely stands – and has stood for nearly 1000 years – one of England's architectural treasures: Ely Cathedral, begun in 1083 on the site of an earlier Benedictine abbey. In 1322 the Norman central tower collapsed, to be replaced by something quite unique in ecclesiastical architecture: the 'Octagon', a gigantic eight-sided lantern tower 22.5m (74ft) across. In the flat lands of the fens it stands on its low island like a lighthouse on a hill. South of Ely lie the city and university of Cambridge with some half-dozen of its world famous colleges backing on to the river. The 'backs' as they are called, particularly in a daffodil-rich spring, are one of the great visual experiences of East Anglia – a perfect blend of young growth and ancient architecture bordering the placid waters of the Cam.

Historians have never managed to explain exactly how and why a university started at Cambridge. Alfred the Great established a college of priests at Ely and monks from Ely set up schools at Cambridge, which had been a centre for local trade from the earliest times. Scholars certainly began gathering in

Left: *Abbot Simon of Ely started the building of his cathedral at the age of 87 while his brother, Bishop Walkelin, was building Winchester Cathedral. By 1106 the choir was completed and the bodies of four saints, Etheldreda, Sexburga, Withburga and Ermenhilda, were moved from the old Saxon church and reinterred behind the high altar. By 1189 the main work was completed with the building of the massive West Tower. The Lady Chapel was begun in 1321 and was originally ablaze with stained glass and richly decorated with scenes from the legendary life of the Virgin, all stolen or destroyed in the Reformation.*

Below: *A year after the Lady Chapel was begun, Ely's Norman central tower collapsed. But out of disaster came triumph, when Ely's lantern was built – a masterpiece of mediaeval engineering and architecture with its unique stone octagon and wooden lantern, sheathed in lead and framed with eight enormous 18 m (60 ft) oak posts.*

Above: *King's College Chapel, seen beyond the punters on the Cam, is not only the architectural gem of Cambridge but also England's finest example of the Perpendicular style. It was begun by Henry VI in 1446 but, because of delays caused by the Wars of the Roses, not completed until 1515, six years after Henry VIII's accession. The next 26 years were occupied by the Flemish glaziers putting in the superb windows. In 1962 the chapel received a splendid gift: 'The Adoration of the Magi' by Peter Paul Rubens. It is now the chapel's altarpiece. In this picture, King's College is to the right of the chapel and the beautifully proportioned Clare College, built in 1638, to the left.*

Above: *This butcher's shop in Newmarket, heart of the 'sport of kings' since the 17th century, exudes an almost Regency swagger with the Royal Arms proudly displayed. Their presence indicates the proprietor has been granted the Royal Warrant by a member of the Royal Family to supply goods to the household concerned. The proprietor or director is personally responsible for seeing that over 40 rules governing holders of the Royal warrant are properly observed.*

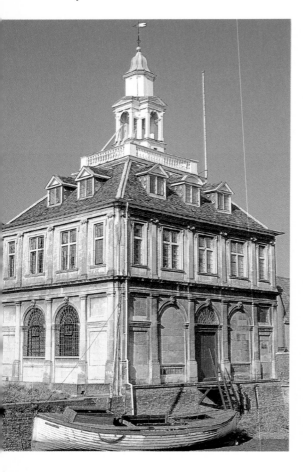

Cambridge in the early 12th century and by 1226 they had organised sufficiently to elect a Chancellor. The first college, Peterhouse, was founded in 1284 by Hugh de Balsham, Bishop of Ely.

One of the most picturesque of Cambridge colleges is Queens', so called because it enjoyed first the patronage of Queen Mary of Anjou, then of Elizabeth Woodville, wife of Edward IV. In one corner of the main court, which is a symphony of mellow Tudor brick, is the Erasmus Tower, where the famous philosopher lived while teaching at the college in the 16th century. The president's lodge is a spectacular Tudor building with a brick cloister below and two storeys of typically East Anglian half timbering. Crossing the Cam between Cloister Court and the college gardens is the 'mathematical bridge', made of wood and designed according to mathematical principles so that no nails or other fastenings were needed. Unfortunately, curious Victorian scientists took it apart to see how it worked and were unable to put it together, so the present bridge is a copy. Corpus Christi, founded by two town guilds, has the earliest English example of a mediaeval quadrangle, and a library with a priceless collection of ancient manuscripts. Trinity College, founded by Henry VIII, is as big as some universities and its output includes such famous men as Byron, Tennyson, Newton and Macaulay. Outside the Great Gate stands an apple tree, supposed to descend from the one under which Isaac Newton formulated the theory of gravity.

A few miles inland from the Norfolk coast are the Broads, the shallow reed-fringed lakes which lie along the sides of the rivers. They are freshwater lakes, made by mediaeval men digging for peat, and they give wide-ranging opportunities for boating. It is hard to say where water begins and the land ends, for what passes for 'land' often turns out to be flooded reed beds or alder swamps. In summer, the Broads can be overcrowded and noisy but in spring and autumn they become still and mysterious again with wild duck quacking contentedly in the reeds.

The wild stretches of countryside in East Anglia are dotted with nature reserves and bird sanctuaries, a paradise for naturalists. The Nature Conservancy Centre at Ranworth is one of the few places where visitors can safely walk through the reeds and fens fringing a broad and learn something about the problems of the area. Holme Dunes Nature Reserve, near Hunstanton, is a place of salt-marshes and sand dunes, where all kinds of migrating birds pass through in the autumn, on their way south from the Arctic. Minsmere, on the Suffolk coast, has hides in the marsh and heathlands, where watchers may see herons and terns, spoonbills, Bewick's swans and an occasional osprey. In winter, the area between the old and new Bedford rivers, in Cambridgeshire, is allowed to flood naturally, providing a home for pintails, gadwalls, Bewick's and Whooper swans and other wintering wildfowl.

More than any other part of Britain, the under-populated counties of Norfolk and Suffolk have attracted modern cottage craftsmen and in many towns and villages there are opportunities to see pottery, ironwork, woodwork, basketry and jewellery-making in progress, and to purchase the finished goods. In Norfolk there are craft centres at Snape and Erpingham with interesting studio workshops. Bury St Edmunds has a 75-year-old factory using the wood from a nearby coppice to make a range of traditional wooden tools. Several museums illustrate the past life and work of the area: for instance the Museum of East Anglian Life at Stowmarket, Suffolk, the Bridewell Museum of Local Industries in Norwich and the Farmland Museum at Haddenham, Cambridgeshire.

The decline of the wool trade coincided with the rise of agriculture in East Anglia and to two of Norfolk's large landowners – Townshend of Raynham and Coke of Holkham – must go the credit for laying the foundations of much agricultural practice in the 18th century, enabling the region's widespread sandy soils to produce heavy crops of grain and sugar beet.

One of the charms of East Anglia lies in the fact that it is only lightly industrialized and it is evident that where the pressures which come with urban living are less intense, the rewards of living seem, by contrast, incomparably richer.

Below: *The red brick Shire Hall at Woodbridge, a market town situated on the river Deben in Suffolk, dates back to Elizabethan times. The town has many interesting buildings, including the Abbey, begun in 1564, a half-timbered house with an old weighing-machine attached and the famous 18th century tidal mill on the estuary. Little Grange was once the home of Edward Fitzgerald, translator of* The Rubaiyat of Omar Khayyam.

THE THAMES VALLEY & THE COTSWOLDS

The Thames is a wealthy river deriving its substantial income from a long list of benefactors: the Rodings of Essex and the Downs of Dunstable; the Chilterns and the Vale of Aylesbury, the Uplands of Northamptonshire and the Vale of White Horse; the Downs of Marlborough and Lambourn and the Cotswold Hills; the Heights of Hindhead and Haslemere and the suburban slopes of the North Downs. From all these surrounding hills and valleys tributaries trickle, gurgle, flow and surge towards the Thames to make it the longest, largest and most picturesque river in England. And what a fascinating collection of names these tributaries have: Cherwell, Windrush, Stort, Ock, Roding, Evenlode, Loddon, Kennet, Mole, Wey and a dozen others. Each has a character of its own; each adds its individuality to the complex character of 'sweet Thames'.

The Thames in London is a tidal river, rising and falling some 6m (20 ft) with each tide, but above Teddington (tide-ending-town) it changes its life style, throws off its sober workaday suit and becomes a cheerful, beflagged pleasure-boat river, meandering nearly twice the distance roads and railways need to reach its source on the lower slopes of the Cotswolds near Cirencester. Here, in a meadow beside the Tetbury road, a bearded, recumbent figure of Father Thames, sculptured in stone, marks the official beginning of the river's 334 km (210 miles) journey to the sea.

The Cotswold towns and villages with their honey-coloured stone houses have a timeless beauty. Building with Cotswold stone went on even in prehistoric times. The burial mound of Belas Knap near Cheltenham was built 5000 years ago in just the same way that local masons still build dry-stone walls. It has four chambers and when it was opened up, nearly 40 skeletons were found. There are at least 30 of these long barrows in the Cotswolds; another good example is Hetty Pegler's Tump, near Stroud, on a quiet hill-top with tremendous views. No-one knows why the barrow was named after Hester Pegler, the wife of a 17th century landowner.

Above: *Cliveden's weekend gatherings have seen much history made especially after the house was bought by the Astors. Queen Victoria and her Ministers were frequent visitors. The appeasement conferences took place here in a bid to avert World War II and so (on a different political level) did the events leading to the 1960's Profumo scandal.*

Right: *Chipping Campden, in the Cotswolds, is one of Britain's most picturesque towns. Built of the distinctive honey coloured stone, nearly every building in the town is pre-1800 and, the wealthy wool merchant, William Grevel's house in the High Street is over 600 years old. The Jacobean Market Hall must be one of the most photographed buildings in England.*

Right: *Chipping Campden's Market Hall, built in 1627 by Sir Baptist Hicks (his arms appear at one end), was used for the sale of poultry and dairy produce. It is a gabled building with a cobbled floor, arches and stone balustrades, and is just one of the many fine buildings in the care of the National Trust.*

Below: *Every building contributes to the charm of the pretty Cotswold village of Upper Slaughter. No new houses have been built there since 1904. The name Slaughter is not as bloodthirsty as it sounds: it comes from the old English word 'sloghtre' which means muddy place.*

Today's villages, their stone mellowed to a soft yellowish-grey, still have many of the 400-500 year old houses and churches financed by the wealth brought to the wool merchants by the huge flocks of long-woolled sheep, known as the 'Cotswold Lions', who grazed on the hillsides. They seem to have grown naturally out of the countryside and new buildings blend in with the old to make a harmonious picture. If Broadway and Bourton-on-the-Water have more than their fair share of visitors, which can spoil the atmosphere on a summer weekend, it is only because they are such pleasing places. Broadway's splendid main street is lined with lovely buildings, including Tudor House and the Lygon Arms, a 17th century coaching inn. At Bourton-on-the-Water the river Windrush flows sparkling down the main street, bordered by lawns and crossed by miniature bridges.

Unlike most Cotswold towns, Stow-on-the-Wold does not nestle in the shelter of the hill-side, hence the local saying 'Stow-on-the-Wold, where the windes blow cold'. It has a large important looking market place and it was once well-known all over Europe for its sheep fairs, where as many as 20,000 animals might be sold. There is an old market cross and well-preserved stocks, sheltered by trees. Nearby are some of the prettiest of English villages, including Upper and Lower Swell and Upper and Lower Slaughter. Lower Slaughter, with its terraced rose-covered cottages, rippling stream and watermill and quietly bobbing ducks, is almost too idyllic to be true.

In the southern Cotswolds, the Coln valley, where the river makes its unhurried way to join the Thames at Lechlade, has three places of outstanding interest. At Chedworth stands an extensive Roman villa with a complete bath suite exposed to view. Fairford church has 28 windows of 500 year old stained glass, which were carefully hidden from risk of attack such as in Puritan times. The stained glass illustrates amazing pictures of the lost souls in hell, tortured by horned devils and rather less interesting representations of the cherubim and seraphim of heaven (though these two representations are worth studying for their quiet pastoral scenes, said to be taken from the surrounding countryside). In the village street at Bibury a picture postcard row of stone cottages, first built in the 14th century and once used as a wool store, border a stream known for its trout.

Cliveden means 'valley among cliffs' and the thick woodlands rise up on either side, with the stately mansion looking down from the cliff-top. Once famous for its weekend gatherings of politicians, it was given to the National Trust by the Astor family. Two previous houses burned down and the present building was designed by Sir Charles Barry, architect of the Houses of Parliament, so its grand air is understandable. To the east lies Burnham Beeches, a breath-taking sight in the russet and gold of autumn. The woodlands are the remains of the prehistoric forest which once covered the Chilterns and some of the hollow pollard beeches are believed to be between 600 and 800 years old.

At Cricklade, a handsome, stone-built town on the Roman road to Cirencester, the adolescent Thames can support only canoes and shallow-draught dinghies but at Lechlade, 16 km (10 miles) below, sizeable launches can come up the bridge. When St Paul's Cathedral was built in London, the stone used was loaded into barges here for the journey down the Thames.

The river from here to Dorchester is ambiguously known as 'Thames or Isis': the result of an age-old misunderstanding about the Roman name for the river, Thameisis, thought to be a combination of Thames and Isis. As a tributary, the Thame, joins the Thames at Dorchester, it was widely assumed that the river above Dorchester must be the Isis. The confusion need not worry anyone: the Thames by any other name flows just as sweet.

Threading its way through placid meadows, past Bablock Hythe, where the ferry claims to have been carrying men and their goods across the Thames for a thousand years, the river goes up to Oxford and finds a rival: the upstart Cherwell flowing in from Northamptonshire. Most of the University buildings lie between the two rivers but one of Oxford's most famous landmarks - Magdalen tower - is reflected in the waters of the Cherwell, not the Thames. The two join forces only south of the city, below Folly Bridge on

Below: *The sixteenth century gatehouse and quadrangle of Corpus Christi College, Oxford, are shown here. The college was founded in 1516 by Bishop Richard Fox, a close friend of Bishop Oldham, the founder of Manchester Grammar School. The unusual obelisk in the middle of the quadrangle is a sundial given to the college in 1581 by Charles Turnbull. The actual dial, which is near the top of the pillar, is surmounted by a pelican (the badge of Corpus Christi) and below there is a perpetual calendar.*

Above: *The attractive Radcliffe Camera was completed in 1749 and, with its great dome, it is as impressive as any building in Oxford. It was built with money bequeathed to the University by Dr John Radcliffe, a court physician and fellow of Lincoln College, for the provision of a new library. It is now used as a reading room for the Bodleian.*

the way to Abingdon, where the now dormant Thames glides through the town's triple bridge and past its Wren-style colonnaded Town Hall.

There was a community at Oxford, or 'ford for oxen', in Saxon times; later it was a busy centre for the wool trade and by the 12th century it was a centre of learning. One theory is that it was founded by English students expelled from the University of Paris in 1167. University College was the first to be established in 1249, with Balliol and Merton following within the next fifteen years. Matthew Arnold called Oxford 'that sweet city with her dreaming spires' and though it is now an industrial, as well as a university city, the beauty of its buildings remains unaltered and, when viewed from one of the surrounding hillsides, its spires and turrets still dream in the sunlight.

It is well worth while taking time to explore Oxford, for almost every college has noteworthy features, as well as its own charm and grace. In the magnificent sweep of mellowed buildings along 'the High', or High Street, Oriel and University Colleges on the south side face Queen's, Brasenose and the University church of St Mary the Virgin. Magdalen is one of the richest colleges, its splendid tower famous for the May morning hymn, traditionally sung from the summit at sunrise on May 1. Christ Church College, founded by Cardinal Wolsey in 1525, has the largest quad in Oxford and in Tom Tower is the great bell which tolls 101 strokes at 21.05 each night because there were originally 101 students who had to be in college by curfew. The Bodleian Library, which contains more than three million books, and the Sheldonian Theatre, designed by Wren and presented to the University in 1669, are among the many sights which should not be missed.

Between Oxford and Reading the upper Thames winds first northwards, then southwards, before it reaches the dramatic stretch through the Goring Gap, where it cuts deep through the chalk hills to separate the Berkshire Downs from the Chiltern Hills and steep hills rise on either side, topped by beech and chestnut trees. The first town on this stretch of the river is Abingdon, one of the oldest in the whole valley. There was a Saxon abbey here as early as the 6th century, though little survived the Dissolution. Almshouses built in 1446 are still in use and there are two mediaeval churches, one of them with five aisles. At Clifton Hampden, a pretty village with 400 year old thatched cottages, the *Three Men in a Boat*, the characters created by Jerome K. Jerome, visited the Barley Mow Inn.

Dorchester was a Roman station, a Saxon missionary centre and an important cathedral city from 634 – 707. It is now a pleasant village with a huge abbey church containing a fine 'Jesse' window, showing the family tree of Jesus Christ, mediaeval glass, wallpaintings – and even an amusing epitaph to a lady who died in 1799, 'a martyr to excessive sensibility'. Although Shillingford has a beautifully proportioned three-arch bridge Wallingford bridge has a magnificent 17 arches, built at the beginning of the last century because floods so often made the way impassable. An earlier bridge had its four centre arches replaced by a wooden drawbridge which could be raised to improve the town's defences.

After the Goring Gap, the river flows past pretty villages and the large houses of the rich commuter belt, their well-tended gardens sweeping down to the water's edge, before the scenery becomes more industrialized around Reading. Near Pangbourne, visitors try to guess which of the stately homes of the area was turned into Toad Hall in *The Wind in the Willows*, for it was this stretch of the river which inspired the author, Kenneth Grahame. Mapledurham, too, has literary associations, for part of the English television series *The Forsyte Saga* was set in the quiet, leafy little village. Mapledurham House is a pink-brick Tudor manor which was fortified for the king during the Civil War. The owners, the Blount family, were Roman Catholics and there is an 18th century chapel as well as a secret passage and priest hole, as reminders of the days of religious persecution.

At Henley the Thames stops winding for long enough to make a good regatta course. The Henley Royal Regatta, held in early July, is one of the high spots in the social calendar, as well as being probably the most important river regatta in the world, attracting the top oarsmen. It began in 1833 when

Above: *Blenheim Palace was given to the 1st Duke of Marlborough by Queen Anne and Parliament in gratitude for his victory over the French in 1704 at Blenheim. Built, at immense cost, by Vanbrugh and Hawksmoor, it stands on a superb site, 'The most monumental mansion in England'. In 1764-74 the formal gardens were swept away as Capability Brown landscaped the park, laid out, it is said, according to the battle plan at Blenheim.*

local townspeople initiated the best known cup, the Grand Challenge Cup. Later in July comes the Swan Upping ceremony, the aim of which is to identify all the new cygnets on the river between London and Henley and mark them according to their ownership. Supposed to have been brought to Britain by Richard I during the crusades, swans on the Thames have always been royal birds but Queen Elizabeth I permitted the Vintners' and Dyers' guilds to own some of the swans. Every year a little fleet of skiffs set out, under the command of the Queen's Swan Keeper, to catch and mark the young birds. The Queen's Swan Keeper is resplendent in scarlet livery, a single feather in his peaked cap, while the Dyers' and Vintners' keepers wear blue, and green and white respectively.

Soon after Henley, on one of the prettiest stretches of the Thames, comes Medmenham Abbey, with its sinister associations. Though it stands on the site of an old Cistercian monastery, what remains today is mainly a pseudo-ruin of 300 years ago, the scene of the orgies and blasphemous rituals of the Hellfire Club founded by Sir Francis Dashwood in 1745 with the motto 'do as you please'. Nearby Bisham Abbey has a more respectable history for here were buried four Earls of Salisbury and Richard Neville, Earl of Warwick, 'The Kingmaker'. After the Dissolution, the Hoby family built their house with materials from the old abbey and one of the Hobys was custodian to Princess Elizabeth, who was kept here for three years during the reign of her sister Mary. Another member of the family, Lady Elizabeth Hoby, is said to haunt the house, wringing her hands, because she shut her little son up in a windowless room until he died, simply because his lesson books were untidy.

Right: *The Fourth of June at Eton College is an annual holiday instituted by George III to celebrate his birthday. The procession of boats on the Thames is a traditional feature of the day and the 'wet-bobs', as the oarsmen at Eton are known, dress as sailors of George III's time and wear flowers round their hats. During the procession stroke and bow remain seated and row while the rest of the eight stand with their oars raised. Cox's job – he is in full naval uniform with sword – must indeed be quite a tricky one.*

Above: *Enjoying the riverside view from the terrace of an inn is a popular pastime at Henley-on-Thames, though other visitors prefer the many ways of messing about in boats. The town makes an attractive picture from the river, with its square-turreted church.*

Right: *Hambleden Mill stands in good repair, a reminder of the days when every village had one, whether worked by wind or water, to grind its corn. Indeed, the jolly miller was frequently a popular figure in contemporary literature. A mill was recorded at Hambleden in the Domesday Book and there has been one on the site ever since. In the quiet village of Hambleden itself Lord Cardigan, leader and survivor of the charge of the Light Brigade, was born.*

Below: *The Thames locks are convivial meeting places as well as a means of getting up and down the river without 'shooting' the weir. Most of them are immaculately kept with brightly painted lock-keeper's houses and gardens full of summer flowers. The lock at Goring is on a particularly busy stretch of the river with Goring on the Oxfordshire bank and the popular Swan Inn at Streatley on the Berkshire side and connecting them the Goring bridge.*

Left: *The fertile pastureland of the Chilterns grows a wide variety of crops. A particularly welcome one for the colour it brings to the landscape is rape oil seed, shown here. The Chilterns are a rich reservoir of natural history, both flora and fauna. The rare ghost orchid and the edible dormouse (it was the Romans who tried eating it) are both indigenous to the area; 1,500 miles of footpaths help the walker in his search for them.*

Right: *As old as Christianity, the White Horse of Uffington gallops perpetually across the Berkshire Downs in the vale that bears its name. It is the most ancient and best known of Britain's 17 white horses and lies near to the early Iron Age hill fort, Uffington Castle. The writer Thomas Hughes was born in the village and the opening chapter of* Tom Brown's Schooldays *is a loving description of the features and surrounding countryside.*

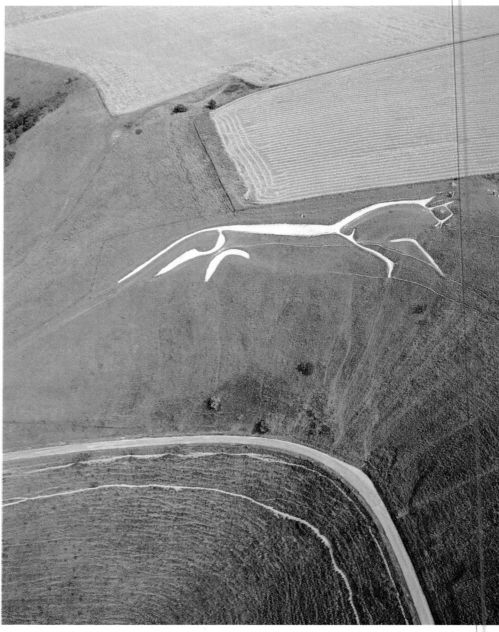

The weir and lock at Marlow combine to make a well-known beauty spot and the town itself is handsome with dignified Georgian houses. The house where Shelley lived in 1817 still stands; his second wife Mary wrote *Frankenstein* here. Beyond the lock are several pretty little islands, the water swirling round them on its way from the weir, and Quarry Woods rise on the Berkshire bank, with Winter Hill giving a panoramic view of the Thames valley from Henley to Maidenhead. On the high ground is Cookham Dene, with dense woodland on one side, furze-clad commons on the other.

Round the next bend of the river lies Cookham. At the lock, the towpath is carpeted with wild flowers and willows droop gracefully towards the water while in the town red-brick cottages surround a large green. Stanley Spencer the artist lived here and his painting of the *Resurrection,* which hangs in the Tate Gallery, shows Jesus at the door of Cookham Church.

Beyond Maidenhead, which has long been a popular resort and boating centre, is Bray, dreamy and peaceful in spite of busy roads nearby. It is hardly surprising that the notorious vicar, thought to be Simon Aleyn, was willing to alter his religion four times to suit the monarch of the day, to be sure of holding on to a good living.

The goal of most Thames valley visitors is Windsor Castle on its hill, dominating the skyline and keeping a parental eye on Eton College on the Buckinghamshire bank. Built on a chalk hill to give all-round visibility, the Thames formed a natural moat; the Tower of London was only a day's march away, and it was adjacent to the royal hunting grounds of Windsor Forest. Part of that forest, now Windsor Great Park, stretches southwards from the castle, with the famous Long Walk, a 5 km (3 mile) avenue created by Charles II. Queen Anne extended it as far as Ascot and the royal family drive down it in open carriages to the races during Ascot week.

A spot with less happy associations in the history of the monarchy is Runnymede, the meadows where, on 15 June 1215, King John signed the Magna Carta, the forerunner of the American Bill of Rights and the United Nations Charter. Tradition says that the barons camped on one bank of the Thames, the King's party on the other, and the two then met on the neutral ground of Magna Carta island.

The Chilterns are part of a chalk belt which stretches from Yorkshire to Dorset. Its valleys were carved by rivers which, apart from the Thames, have long since disappeared. It is beech-wood country and, early last century, local craftsmen known as 'chair-bodgers' set up their simple pole-lathes in almost every glade, making sections for chairs, which were then assembled in the town factories. When it was overtaken by modern mass-production methods the craft almost died out but local craftsmen are now attempting to revive it, making traditional wooden furniture. High Wycombe has a local history museum with a collection of the locally-made 'Windsor' chairs.

Though the Chilterns are often neglected by tourists in search of 'sights' they are excellent walking and wandering country, their woodlands carpeted with bluebells in spring, cool and shaded in summer and a blaze of colour in autumn. One of the highest points is Coombe Hill which offers panoramic views across the Vale of Aylesbury. On its summit, the granite monument to the Buckinghamshire men who died in the Boer War is a landmark for miles. To the south-west lies Chequers, the official country residence of the Prime Minister. It was built in 1565 and for the first two years Lady Mary Grey, sister of the luckless Lady Jane Grey, was confined here because she had married without the consent of Queen Elizabeth. To the west is Cymbeline's Mount, supposedly the place where the sons of the Celtic king Cunobelinus were killed in a battle against the Romans.

South of the Thames between Lechlade and Abingdon lies the Vale of the White Horse. The figure, which is 111 m (365 ft) long and 40 m (130 ft) tall, is thought to have been cut in the first century AD, perhaps as a tribal emblem. It was once credited with magical powers. Nearby is the flat-topped Dragon Hill, where St George is supposed to have slain the dragon. According to legend, the patch of bare chalk on top was left when the dragon's poisonous blood killed off the vegetation.

Below: *Chequers, the Prime Minister's official country residence, has seen many top-level conferences and crisis meetings over the years. Originally built in 1565, the house has undergone many alterations over the years. Though it contains the country's best collection of Civil War treasures, the public is never allowed inside to see them.*

THE SOUTH EASTERN COUNTIES

The white cliffs which are many people's first sight of England – at Dover or Newhaven – are the sliced-off ends of two ranges of chalk hills that outline the limits of the region: the North and South Downs. Between them lies so much beautiful country and so many interesting places that visitors to Britain often travel no further.

At either end of this region stand the two great cathedrals of Canterbury and Winchester – Canterbury where Thomas à Becket was murdered and Winchester where King Alfred was buried. Between the two and running along the ridge of the North Downs are the remains of a Bronze Age track which was almost certainly the main east-west trade route in ancient times. But after the murder of Becket in 1170 and his subsequent canonization, so many pilgrims going to Canterbury used the route that parts of it have become traditionally known as the Pilgrims' Way. One of the best places to locate it is just south-east of Guildford where St Martha's church stands independent of any village on a spur of the Downs. The old track runs past the church which is thought to have been the site of a chantry chapel and from it there is a view that epitomizes southern England: tree upon tree, field after field, hill and hollow for 40km (25miles) to the south where, on a clear day, the mushroom shape of Chanctonbury Ring may be seen. This grove of trees planted in the 18th century on the site of an Iron Age earthwork is as much a landmark on the South Downs as St Martha's is on the North.

Pilgrims and less devout visitors still flock to Canterbury in their thousands. The majestic cathedral was only part of the city's monastic settlement. The cloisters and chapter house lie to the north, though in most monastic communities they were on the sunny side. A row of crumbling pillars marks the site of the infirmary and the Kent war memorial stands on what was once the Canons' bowling green. Around the pretty Green Court, the monks carried on important activities like brewing and baking. Almost half the city walls and several bastion gateways still stand and the massive west gateway has hardly altered in 600 years. St Thomas's Hospital was founded in 1180 to give shelter to poor pilgrims flocking to the Cathedral Shrine. They slept on rushes in the long vaulted hall downstairs and ate upstairs in the refectory. Later pilgrims, with the price of a night's lodging, might have stayed at the old Falstaff inn.

Canterbury has other literary associations besides Chaucer's *Canterbury Tales*. Elizabethan poet and playwright Christopher Marlowe was born here and novelist Joseph Conrad is buried in Canterbury Cemetery. In St Dunstan's Street is the 16th century House of Agnes, described by Charles Dickens in *David Copperfield*.

Once, when King Alfred reigned from 871 to 900, Winchester was the capital of England and the cathedral coffers contain the remains of Saxon and Danish kings, among them Canute. More modern tombs include those of Jane Austen and Izaak Walton. The close contains the Pilgrims' School, with its 13th century hall, and the half-timbered Tudor Cheyne Court. Of the ancient castle, only the great hall where Parliament sat for 300 years remains, its main feature the so-called Round Table of King Arthur. Though it is only about 700 years old, it is tempting to imagine that it was a copy of the original.

Chichester's Cathedral dates from Norman times. It was built on the site of an old Saxon church and there was an old Sussex prophecy which said:

'If Chichester church steeple fall
In England there's no king at all.'

In 1861, when a Queen sat on the throne, the spire collapsed, to be rebuilt five years later. Today, Chichester is best known for the summer-season at its Festival Theatre, when major classical and modern productions are staged.

Above: *There is nothing in England quite like the Sussex Downs, a long range of chalk hills, almost devoid of features but full of charm and personality. Every crest presents a view of the sea or the Weald, every valley shelters some delightful village. Along their length the South Downs Way runs for some 130 km (80 ml), providing a traffic-free bridleway for walkers, riders and cyclists. The photograph shows the Downs near Berwick, between Eastbourne and Lewes.*

Left: *Kent, the 'garden of England', is known for its hop fields and the countryside is dotted with little round, fat oast houses with pointed ventilating cowls. They were built for use in drying hops but many have been converted into characterful houses.*

Right: *Romantic Leeds Castle in Kent stands on rocky knolls in a lake which is home to rare swans and ducks. Henry VIII's first wife, Catherine of Aragon, lived at the castle, so did Edward I's two wives, Eleanor and Margaret, and it was a prison for Elizabeth I before she came to the throne and for French and Dutch soldiers in 1665.*

Below: *Vintage steam trains run between Sheffield Park and Horsted Keynes during the summer and at weekends. British Rail closed the line in 1960 but a group of enthusiasts re-opened it as the Bluebell Railway. There is a railway museum at Sheffield Park station in East Sussex, which was built in 1882.*

Above: *The Lanes are the remains of the old town of Brighton, from the days when it was known as Brighthelmstone, before it became a fashionable resort. They take their name from 'laine', the old Sussex word for a measure of land, and make a delightful enclave full of antique shops, boutiques and restaurants, bounded by East, West and North Streets.*

As a complete contrast to the ancient cathedrals, the modern cathedral of Guildford stands in the simplicity of rose-pink brick on Stag Hill, north-west of the town. The architect, Sir Edward Maufe, relied more on the grace of simplified Gothic lines than on ornate decoration.

The south-east has the most popular and populous sea coast in the whole of Britain. Londoners flock to the north Kent resorts such as Herne Bay, Margate and Broadstairs where sand, sea and sunshine still form the firm basis for a day at the seaside. The other south coast resorts, stretching round the Kent coast from Ramsgate, along the shores of Sussex to Chichester harbour, offer ever changing scenery and cater for every taste, from the slightly formal elegance of Eastbourne, with its broad terraced drives, its lawns and carpets of flowers, to unassuming Littlehampton, which offers a wide range of family amusements and some of the best and safest bathing on the coast. The Isle of Wight is the 'garden island' full of sunshine.

The south-east resorts have always enjoyed the patronage of royalty. Bognor Regis got its name when George V convalesced there in 1929 and Queen Victoria called it her 'dear little Bognor'. Nineteenth century storms washed much of old Bognor into the sea, including a barracks used in the Napoleonic Wars. Brighton blossomed from the moment the Prince Regent paid his first visit in 1783 and apart from the amazing Pavilion it has retained a large number of imposing Regency houses, as well as a jumble of little streets lined with antique shops and known as 'The Lanes', the legacy of the 17th century fishing village.

There are many quieter, picturesque spots, too. At Rottingdean, once a smugglers' village, Georgian houses cluster round a village green, complete with pond. The artist Burne-Jones lived by the green for the last 20 years of his life and Kipling lived across the road for four years. Climping, near Little-hampton, has a great expanse of deserted sand and the lovely Pagham Harbour is now a bird sanctuary. Geologists come from far and wide to discover marine fossils in Bracklesham Beds on the Selsey peninsula.

One notable exception to the chain of seaside resorts is the stretch of coast between Winchelsea and Hythe known as Romney Marsh, its inland boundary marked by the line of the Royal Military Canal – a leftover from the Napoleonic Wars, as are the Martello Towers that dot this coast. At the head of the canal stood a battery and a drawbridge, which could cut off communication between Folkestone and Hythe. The marsh is a deserted area of meadows and dykes, only preserved from the sea by a great sloping embankment, the Dymchurch Wall.

Sheep graze where the sea once gave access to the Cinque Ports of Romney, Hythe, Winchelsea and Rye, which have seen their harbours change to dry land. The original five fortified ports, part of a defence system to ward off invasion from the Continent in the Middle Ages, were Hastings, Sandwich, Dover, Romney and Hythe. Winchelsea and Rye were added later. The ports provided ships to serve the king for a certain number of days each year and in return enjoyed special privileges; they were self-governing and could trade toll-free with any corporation in the land. In the 13th century the fleet from the Cinque Ports was strong enough to take on the whole French navy. Hythe is built on terraces rising from the canal to the mediaeval parish church, which has a vaulted crypt lined with thousands of skulls and bones. It is the starting point for the world's only miniature main line steam railway, the Romney, Hythe and Dymchurch. Rye, with its steep cobbled streets and

Below: *Brockham's village green with its old water pump and impressive backdrop of the North Downs has provided a magnificent venue for village cricket for centuries. W. G. Grace played here, endangering the church windows with his mighty hits. In recent years because of the damage inflicted on parked cars around the green by batsmen hitting boundaries a more secluded pitch has been used.*

Above: *Rye's cobbled Mermaid Street is typical of this little town built on Romney Marsh. Now nearly two miles from the sea, it was one of the two 'ancient towns' linked with the Cinque Ports. Though its hill protects it from flooding by the sea it did not save it in 1377 when the French attacked the town and left it a smouldering ruin.*

half-timbered houses, has attracted artists since Van Dyck sketched it in the 17th century. Henry James spent several years here, living in the Georgian Lamb House and writing *The Ambassadors* and *The Golden Bowl*. Rye used to be a great centre for smuggling, made easier by the vaulted cellars which made excellent hiding places for contraband, and the connecting attics between the houses, convenient for a quick get-away.

Apart from the industrial sprawl that spreads out from Southampton to Portsmouth, the region has retained a surprisingly rural profile. Even Surrey, so firmly in the commuter belt that it is nicknamed the 'Cockney's back yard', has wooded hills, hedgerows dotted with wild flowers and pretty little villages. The green meadows of the Wey valley still reach right into the heart of Guildford. Near Shere, on the banks of the Tillingbourne under the North Downs, is the tree-shrouded Silent Pool where King John is supposed to have spied on a local girl bathing, causing her such shame that she drowned herself. Abinger Hammer is known for its water-cress beds, fed by underground springs, and the old mill at Gomshall, now converted into a restaurant, is mentioned in the Domesday Book. Hindhead stands high on the hillside amid woods and heathlands and nearby is the Devil's Punchbowl, a deep hollow with a stone to mark the spot where the murderers of an unknown sailor were hanged in 1786. Haslemere, with its lovely wooded setting, is known for its annual Dolmetsch Festival of old English music and a thorn tree on the green at Chiddingfold is said to be over 500 years old.

Kent is the 'garden of England' with its orchards, market gardens and fat, red-roofed oast-houses and its little towns and villages are unspoiled. Hammer ponds, whose waters were once used to supply power for local ironworks, are now undisturbed, reedy pools. From Cranbrook, an old cloth-weaving town with weather-board houses, there are peaceful woodland walks. Biddenden has its mediaeval cloth hall and its legend of the 'Maids of

Right: *'Jack the Smith' still wields his hammer to strike the hours on the famous clock beside the Guildford-Dorking road at Abinger Hammer. The village took its name, not from the clock, but from the iron-working which depended on water-power from the river Tillingbourne and flourished until the industry moved to the north in the 17th century.*

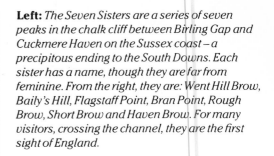

Left: *The Seven Sisters are a series of seven peaks in the chalk cliff between Birling Gap and Cuckmere Haven on the Sussex coast – a precipitous ending to the South Downs. Each sister has a name, though they are far from feminine. From the right, they are: Went Hill Brow, Baily's Hill, Flagstaff Point, Bran Point, Rough Brow, Short Brow and Haven Brow. For many visitors, crossing the channel, they are the first sight of England.*

Biddenden', twins who were born here in the 12th century, joined at the hip and shoulder, and bequeathed a piece of land to provide a dole for the poor. On Easter Monday visitors can eat biscuits embossed with pictures of the maids. Even the busy town of Tunbridge Wells retains its rocky, wooded centre where Queen Henrietta Maria camped for six weeks in 1630 while taking the waters discovered earlier by Lord North.

In West Sussex, the South Downs stand sentinel over peaceful villages like Bramber, with its ruined Norman castle, and Amberley, set on a ridge over the river and backed by the Downs. Its winding streets, with thatched cottages and colourful gardens, seem to have no plan and the village ends to the west in a 14th century castle overlooking frequently flooded meadows known as the 'Wild Brooks'. Arundel still looks like the mediaeval stronghold it once was, with the castle towering on the skyline, the houses rising one above the other up the hillside. The extensive Castle Park has fine beech

Below: *Bosham is an attractive waterside village with a spired church that is 'the oldest site of christianity in Sussex'. King Harold is shown in the Bayeux Tapestry taking the sacrament here before the Battle of Hastings. The waterfront road is regularly flooded at high tide which supports the belief that it was at Bosham that King Canute attempted to command the waves.*

Above: *The New Forest goes back to the Domesday Book and two of William the Conqueror's sons met their deaths in the forest. As well as the oak and beech forests after which it is named, it contains flowery pasture, moor and heathland and several old villages, some, like Minstead and Lyndhurst, with interesting churches or halls. The sure-footed ponies are a familiar sight to visitors. About 3000 roam freely, though they are all owned by those with 'commoners' grazing rights. They are regularly rounded up for branding or for selling at the twice-yearly Beaulieu road sales.*

trees and a lake which has inspired many painters. Near Chichester, at Singleton, the Weald and Downland Open Air Museum displays re-erected historic buildings including a Tudor market hall and a working watermill.

The marks of Roman occupation still remain in the south-east. The Roman Palace at Fishbourne, in West Sussex, dates from the first century and is the largest Roman mansion ever found in the country. The garden has been reconstructed and laid out with the shrubs and trees it would have grown originally. The Roman villa at Bignor, north-east of Chichester, has mosaic floors with designs showing Medusa, Venus and the Four Seasons.

East Sussex calls itself the '1066 Country'. It was at Pevensey that the invasion forces of William, Duke of Normandy, landed and the landing is depicted in the Bayeux Tapestry, showing sailors unloading the ships and leading the horses onto dry land. There was already a Roman fortress here and the Normans built their own fortress in the south-east corner of the walls. It was defended by five towers and a moat.

The town of Battle grew up in the shadow of the abbey built by the Conqueror in celebration of his great victory over the Saxon army led by King Harold. The battle began at nine o'clock on an October morning and it was not until late in the afternoon that King Harold was felled by an arrow and the Norman forces slaughtered every Saxon they could catch. There is disagreement over what happened to Harold's body: one account says that William buried it on the cliff at Hastings, another that Harold's mother took it to Waltham Abbey, in Essex. William founded the Abbey of St Martin, with the high altar marking the spot where the Saxon king fell. It flourished until the Dissolution when it was given to a royal favourite, Sir Antony Browne, who demolished most of it and converted the rest into a mansion for himself. One of the dispossessed monks, it is said, prophesied that Sir Antony's line would end 'by fire and by water'. The prophecy was at last fulfilled in the 18th century when the home of his descendants, Cowdray House, burned down and, in the same year, the last heir was drowned in the Rhine.

In 1079 William turned the New Forest, in the south-west corner of Hampshire, into a royal hunting preserve. Now the public is as free as the deer and ponies to wander through the forest.

In the centuries following the Norman Conquest, the nobility built many castles and stately homes in the south-eastern counties. One of the most beautiful, at least from the outside, is the restored Leeds Castle, near Maidstone, its walls and turrets rising sheer from the lake which forms a natural moat. Hever Castle near Edenbridge, which started life as a fortified manor house in the 13th century, was the girlhood home of the ill-fated Anne Boleyn. Henry VIII courted her here then later after Anne had been executed and he was divorcing his fourth wife, Anne of Cleves, he gave Hever to her. Penshurst Place, Tunbridge Wells, originally dating from the 14th century, was the home of the poet Sir Philip Sidney. His *Arcadia*, written with his sister Mary, was inspired by the countryside around Penshurst.

Petworth House, an imposing mansion rebuilt by the 6th Duke of Somerset in the 17th century, is a treasure gallery of pictures and sculpture. Turner stayed here and loved to paint the stately building and its deer park. In the marble hall, overlooking the park, the owner received the Prince Regent, the Tsar of Russia and other sovereigns of the anti-Napoleonic alliance in 1814. Goodwood House, near Chichester, built by James Wyatt nearly 200 years ago, also has a remarkable collection of paintings and sculpture, including works by Van Dyck, Lely, Reynolds, Romney and Canaletto. Nearby is the Goodwood Race-course, its traditional July meeting established in 1802.

Moving to more modern history, there is Chartwell, in Kent, Winston Churchill's country home. There has been a house on the site, built beside the 'well on the Chart', a natural spring which feeds the lake, since the Middle Ages. In the study, with its old wood beams, Churchill wrote his *History of the English Speaking Peoples* and his chronicles of the Second World War and a studio in the garden contains several of his paintings. As well as a wide collection of memorabilia, visitors can enjoy the trees he planted in the orchard and the rose garden planted to mark the Churchills' golden wedding.

Right: *Chartwell, Winston Churchill's home, is full of his character. In his study, above the picture of Blenheim, his birthplace, hangs the flag flown above the first European city to be liberated. On his desk are photos of his family and busts of Nelson and Napoleon. His ever-present box of cigars sits on the table by his armchair and the carpet was a gift from the Shah of Persia. A replica of his banner as a Knight of the Garter hangs from the rafters.*

Above: *Beaulieu Abbey was a rich and powerful Cistercian house at the mouth of the Beaulieu river in the New Forest; now only parts of it remain, including the Palace House, once the gate-house, now the home of Lord Montagu. His National Motor Museum has a famous collection of vintage cars, motorcycles and bicycles. The abbey ruins and the Parish church are also well worth visiting.*

Right: *Arundel Castle, overlooking the river Arun in West Sussex, has been the ancestral home of the Dukes of Norfolk for over 700 years. Built by Roger de Montmorency in the late 11th century, it houses a fine collection of furniture as well as pictures by Van Dyck, Reynolds, Gainsborough and Lawrence.*

THE WEST COUNTRY

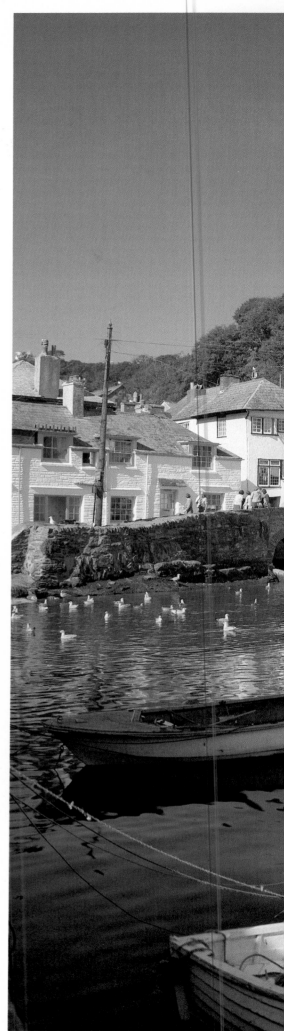

Writing in brief about the West Country is like attempting to summarize the contents of the *Encyclopaedia Britannica* ; the problem is not what to include, but what to leave out. The counties of the west-pointing peninsula offer so much variety in scenery, sights and atmosphere that at first sight it can be difficult to pinpoint exactly what they have in common.

Scenically the chalk uplands of Salisbury Plain could not be more different from the granite crops of Cornwall's Penrith Peninsula, yet both share man's prehistoric puzzles. While Stonehenge is probably the most celebrated stone circle in Europe, few visitors find the little circle of the 'Merry Maidens' of St Buryan. Yet both stand equally silent and mysterious, challenging us to unravel their meaning. Legend says that at St Buryan 19 girls dancing on the Sabbath were turned into stone by the Devil, but it is possible that the circle was actually a sepulchre, for the surroundings are dotted with burial mounds. Naturally, historians have paid far more attention to Stonehenge and the other major circle at nearby Avebury, for in prehistoric times this was the busiest part of the country. No one knows for certain the purpose of the two giant circles, but they may have been open temples for sun worship. The building of Stonehenge began 5000 years ago and it has been reckoned that it would have taken 1000 men as long as two weeks to drag the enormous sandstone blocks from the Marlborough Downs. The stones at Avebury are unhewn and their shapes, tall and straight or short and dumpy, may represent male and female figures.

Though such a large part of the region is predominantly rural, with large tracts designated as 'areas of outstanding natural beauty', there are a number of notable historic towns. In Avon there is Bath, famous as a spa in Roman

Above: *Originally Stonehenge seems to have consisted of two circles and two horseshoes of stones, surrounded by a 91 m (300 ft) earthwork. The larger circle was made up of 30 huge monoliths with great lintel stones and some of these are still in position. Its purpose is a prehistoric mystery.*

Right: *The slate-roofed houses of Polperro are steeply stacked above the double harbour where vermilion, violet and turquoise boats nod at anchor. It has become such a tourist magnet in high summer that it is difficult to realize that it was once a quiet, self-sufficient Cornish fishing harbour.*

Above: *Bath's Pulteney Bridge, built in 1771 to the design of Robert Adam, serves the dual purpose of a covered arcade of shops and a bridge across the river Avon. Bath's mineral springs were first recognized by the Romans who established their settlement of Aquae Sulis here in AD 44 but the city's great period of growth was in Georgian times.*

Far right: *Wells Cathedral is the cathedral of the diocese of Bath and Wells. The unique feature of the cathedral's interior is the crossing arch, in the form of a truncated figure of eight, placed beneath the central tower in 1338 to prevent its threatened collapse. The cathedral's greatest glory is the west front, with some 400 stone statues.*

times when it was called Aquae Sulis, the 'waters of Sul', who was a Celtic goddess. In the 18th century it became the most fashionable resort in the country, under the patronage of Beau Nash, and the look of today's city, its Pump and Assembly Rooms, terraces and crescents, is largely Georgian. Visitors may still take the waters, as did Gainsborough, Queen Victoria, Jane Austen and Lord Nelson. Dickens, in *Pickwick Papers* , described the taste as being like 'warm flat-irons'. One of the more modern attractions is the summer festival of music and the arts.

Old Sarum, the site of the original city in Roman times, now provides excellent views of New Sarum and Salisbury in Wiltshire. The Cathedral, begun with the new city in the 15th century, offers one of the finest examples of Early English architecture, an octagonal chapter house, a dial-less 14th century clock and vaulted cloisters. The serene Close, with its well-kept lawns, has some of Salisbury's most interesting buildings.

Exeter's Cathedral stands at the point of the Roman city centre and its twin Norman towers flank the nave with its impressively long stretch of Gothic vaulting. During the last war the carved wooden Bishop's throne was dismantled and stored for safety – a fortunate decision, as it would have sustained a direct hit in the bombing. Exeter still shows evidence of its past as a flourishing port in the 17th century Customs House, the Ship Inn frequented by Drake and Raleigh, and the imaginative Maritime Museum.

Wells, situated at the foot of the Mendip Hills, has city status but no city feel about it; this is a place which seems untouched by time. The Cathedral looks out over the peaceful green, entered through the Penniless Porch, where beggars used to congregate. At the moated Bishop's Palace, generations of swans have learned to ring a bell to ask for food. Cathedral priests once lived in the mediaeval Vicars' Close.

Anyone with a feel for the religious history of the region will want to explore not only the cathedrals, but Sherborne Abbey and the ruins of Glastonbury and Malmesbury, prosperous and influential abbeys before

they fell victim to the Dissolution in the 16th century. At Glastonbury the last abbot was executed on the top of Glastonbury Tor and his head stuck on the abbey gate. After that the abbey was used as a useful source of stone for local building. Malmesbury grew up around the Benedictine abbey above the River Avon. It was founded in the 7th century by St Aldhelm and the Norman remains still house the tomb of King Athelstan. In the tower of the abbey church at Sherborne, on the northern border of Dorset, is 'Great Tom', the tenor bell given by Cardinal Wolsey.

The list of interesting West Country houses and castles is long, too. Cotehele, an early 16th century Cornish manor house, built of granite around two courts, is almost unchanged from the time it was built. Saltram House, near Plymouth, has a superb Robert Adam saloon and dining room, so grand in fact was the former that when George III and his family stayed there they never used the saloon. Wiltshire's Lacock Abbey was originally a nunnery, converted to a private house in the 16th century, and it is still possible to see the sacristy, the chapter house, the cloisters, refectory and dormitory. Wiltshire also has one of England's most famous stately homes, Longleat House, standing in grounds landscaped by Capability Brown. The state-rooms are lavishly decorated, with 16th century tapestries, paintings by Titian and Reynolds, and Sèvres porcelain laid out for a banquet in the hall where Queen Elizabeth I once dined. The Marquess of Bath was the first entrepreneur of the peerage to open his home regularly to visitors and has since added the Safari Park, where motorists drive past a succession of lions, giraffes, elephants and rhino and so on. Safari boats on the lake sail past monkey islands, hippos and sea lions.

Each of the West Country counties has its wilderness, though some are wilder than others. Wildest of all is Devon's Dartmoor, officially designated as one of Britain's national parks and covering 90,000 hectares (350 square miles). Its granite uplands were extensively inhabited in the Bronze and Iron Ages, as the remains of many stone hut circles prove, but today, apart from the villages close to the crossing roads and Her Majesty's Prison at Princetown, it is deserted except for wild deer and ponies. Near Huccaby stands a house which was built in the 19th century, 'between dawn and dusk of a single day'. This feat gave the owner perpetual rights of tenure and grazing, under an ancient Dartmoor law.

The Dunsford Nature Reserve runs through the woods on the north bank of the River Teign, ablaze with wild daffodils in spring and twenty different species of butterflies. Further west along the Teign is the granite-arched Fingle Bridge, part of a packhorse trail from the 16th century. The hilltops above are crowned by Prestonbury and Cranbook Castles, two Iron Age hill-forts originally built to hold the native inhabitants of Dartmoor in check.

Right: There is hardly a discordant note in the wide main street of Dunster, in Somerset, with its quaint eight-sided Yarn Market and tactfully modernized houses. The castle, on a wooded hillside, was built by Mohun, Earl of Somerset in the 11th century. It was held for the Crown during the Civil War and only fell after a siege of 160 days.

Above: *The narrow Cheddar Gorge winds along between steep limestone cliffs which rise to 137 m (450 ft) in places. The hills are riddled with caves, notably Gough's and Cox's, rich in strangely-shaped stalactites and stalagmites. At the end of the gorge stands the Somerset village of Cheddar, which gave its name to the famous cheese, now mainly made elsewhere. The village has paid the price of the tourist boom and is overwhelmed with visitors in summer.*

Right: *Whether illuminated at night or in the bright light of day, Bristol's city centre makes a handsome sight. The city, situated on the river Avon, 11 km (7 miles) from the Bristol Channel, was one of the chief centres of the African slave trade in the 18th century but its trade today is in basic cargoes like grain, timber and tobacco.*

133

On the road from Two Bridges to Moretonhampstead the Warren House Inn was built for the miners of the last century who walked past every day on their way to work in the valley below. Close by is the eerie Wistman's Wood with its twisted oaks and lichened boulders, said to be a sacred grave of the Druids. Conan Doyle took his inspiration for *The Hound of the Baskervilles* from Hound Tor on Dartmoor. He based the legend of Sir Hugo Baskerville, killed by a ghastly hound from hell which haunted the Tor, on the story of Sir Richard Cabell, a wrong-doer buried at Buckfastleigh Church in 1677. Local people maintained they saw black hell-hounds bounding across the moor to leap upon his tomb.

A ring of pleasant little towns surround the moor – flower filled Chagford, nestling in a valley, Okehampton and its ruined castle and Tavistock, where Sir Francis Drake was born. At Buckfastleigh is the modern Benedictine Buckfast Abbey built in local limestone on old foundations, known for its tonic wine and honey. The Dart Valley Steam Railway runs from Buckfastleigh to Totnes. On the moor itself are endlessly photographed villages like Postbridge, a little oasis with a clapper bridge, Buckland in the Moor with its moorstone cottages and thatched roofs set amid beech trees and Widecombe in the Moor, made famous by the song about Uncle Tom Cobley.

Exmoor, which lies two-thirds in Somerset and one-third in Devon, was one of the five ancient royal forests of Britain and it remained a royal demesne until it was sold to John Knight, a member of a well-known Shrewsbury family, in 1818. At the time it was a waste land with only a single farmhouse, but he initiated farming, planted hedges and enclosed fields so that the severity of the lower slopes is softened and the village gardens bring splashes of colour in summer. The Knight family lived in a mansion in Simonsbath, right at the heart of Exmoor. To the south-east are two local beauty spots, Tarr Steps and the Punchbowl. The 'steps', great stone slabs forming a bridge across the River Barle, link prehistoric tracks on either side of the water. The Punchbowl is a natural amphitheatre on the northern side of Winsford Hill, carpeted with bracken, rowan and thorn trees.

R.D. Blackmore based his novel *Lorna Doone* on tales of a band of outlaws who terrorized Exmoor in the 17th century. It is possible to trace many of the scenes from the story, from the hidden Doone Valley, in Hoccombe Combe, along Badgworthy Water, where the remains of buildings supposedly occupied by the fearsome Doones crumble into ruins, to the 520m (1707ft) Dunkery Beacon where the hero first sees the robbers in the glare of the beacon fire 'like clouds upon a red sunset'.

The two highest points in Cornwall, Brown Willy (417m/1375ft) and Rough Tor (400m/1311ft) are found close to one another on Bodmin Moor, a high granite-strewn area lying between the upper reaches of the rivers Inny and Camel. There is only one road across the moor and it was the appalling state of this road in the 17th century that prevented Bodmin from becoming the county town of Cornwall: the assize judges could not be persuaded to venture further west than Launceston. The same road still gives an idea of what Cornwall was like a century ago, though the forbidding Jamaica Inn, made famous by Daphne du Maurier's novel, is now a haunt of tourists rather than smugglers. Near Jamaica Inn is Dozmary Pool, mysterious because no stream runs into it and said to be bottomless. Local legend says that the spirit of a wicked lord named Tregeagle is condemned for ever to empty the pool with a limpet shell with a hole in the bottom.

Many West Country legends are as fascinating as the landscape. Gerrans Bay takes its name from King Geraint, possibly Geraint of King Arthur's Round Table, who built his castle on the west side of the bay. After his death his tribesmen rowed him across the water in a gold boat with silver oars to be interred in the burial mound on Carne Beacon. Two thorn trees growing at Glastonbury are, it is said, direct descendants of an original thorn which sprang from the ground where Joseph of Arimathea, newly arrived to preach, leaned on his staff to pray. Glastonbury is also linked with the haunting stories of King Arthur, as the Isle of Avalon on which he was buried. Tintagel, where the remains of an ancient castle cling to the cliffside, thrives on claims

Above: *Once a busy pilchard fishing port of the north Cornish coast, St Ives is now the haunt of artists. Its charming harbour, old houses and quaint alleyways make it a popular resort. The 15th century church is dedicated to the 5th century St Ia who was martyred here and it contains a madonna sculpted by Dame Barbara Hepworth.*

Above: *The ruins of the so-called King Arthur's Castle cling to a cliff-side at Tintagel. It was a stronghold of the Earls of Cornwall from the 12th century onwards and traces of a Celtic monastery have been excavated on the site. In the village is the 14th century manor house which was used as a post office in Victorian times and is now in the care of the National Trust.*

that King Arthur was born here, even though no archaeological evidence has been found to support them. At the foot of the cliff is Merlin's cave. According to tradition the Round Table is buried under Castle Hill and on midsummer eve it rises, shining, from the earth.

The true glory of the West Country is, of course, the long and magnificent coast that borders this pointing finger of land. One of the best ways to see it is on the South West Peninsula Coast Path which extends, with only a couple of short breaks, from Studland in Dorset right round to Minehead in Somerset, its full length 829km (515miles).

Dorset has a delightful unspoiled coastline with inviting sandy beaches at resorts like Weymouth, which found prosperity when George II took up residence there, Bournemouth, beloved of the Victorians, and Lyme Regis, granted its first borough charter in 1284. Between Weymouth and Lyme Regis is the long pebble ridge of Chesil Beach, where the sharp-eyed can find coloured jaspers and quartz, and visit the 500 year old St Catherine's Chapel on a hill-top at Abbotsbury and the nearby swannery.

Devon has two quite different coasts. The north has towering cliffs, dramatic valleys and roads which plunge suddenly seawards. Lynton and Lynmouth are the twin towns of the Exmoor coast. Rich English holidaymakers discovered Lynmouth in the Napoleonic Wars when they were unable to travel to Europe. Shelley, in 1821, found the cliffs and valleys indescribably grand and roses blowing in open air in winter. Lynmouth nestles 152m (500ft) below Lynton, linked by a steep cliff railway, at the spot where two valleys meet. None of the inhabitants will ever forget the disastrous floods of 1952 when more than 30 people drowned and many houses were swept away. The little Victorian resort of Westward Ho was developed to capitalize on the success of Charles Kingsley's novel in 1855 and Clovelly, rising from the harbour which is the only inlet for boats in many kilometres of rugged cliffs, is still one of the most photographed villages in England. Only pedestrians and donkeys can negotiate the precipitous cobbled street past flower-decked cottages which seem to climb on one another's shoulders.

Right: *The little Cornish seaport of Fowey is still a busy commercial centre exporting china clay. The narrow, winding streets contain many interesting old houses and the church of St Finbarrus is 14th century in origin. It contains monuments to the Rashleigh family of Menabilly, the 17th-19th century house nearby. Daphne du Maurier lived at Menabilly for many years and wrote some of her best known novels there.*

The south coast is Devon's 'riviera' with red sandstone cliffs, sandy coves and a wide range of pleasant resorts: the elegant Regency buildings of Sidmouth, the uncommercialized Edwardian villas of Budleigh Salterton or the peace of chestnut-shaded lawns and gardens in Dawlish. Dartmouth has been an important harbour since Roman times and ships gathered there for the Crusades. Two castles guard the mouth of the river, and a thick chain could be stretched between them as an added defence. On the borders of Devon and Cornwall is Plymouth, a city redolent with maritime history, for the Pilgrim Fathers sailed from there for the New World in 1620, 'having been kindly entertained and courteously used by divers friends there dwelling' and on the Hoe, Sir Francis Drake played bowls as the Armada approached.

For lovers of marine drama the many headlands on the north Cornish coast provide seas crashing down on unyielding rocks. For yachtsmen the more sheltered south coasts with their wide bays and deep estuaries offer not only safe sailing but also friendly harbours and magnificent scenery. Newquay has ten beaches all to itself and plenty of opportunities for surf-riding, cliff-caves and headlands of springy turf dotted with wild flowers. Penzance, its subtropical gardens ablaze with blooms, has quite a different atmosphere. It looks out towards St Michael's Mount, a spot supposed to have been hallowed by the appearance of St Michael the Archangel to a hermit, and is the departure point for the Scilly Isles, where spring flowers bloom in December. At Kynance Cove, near Lizard Point, the special sights are the caves. The 'devil's letter box and bellows' are strange fissures which suck in water, then spew it out in a sheet of spray, with an angry, puffing roar.

Cornwall, isolated from the rest of the country by difficult travelling conditions until the middle of the last century, so that it became known as 'the land beyond England', has preserved many of its ancient customs. The Padstow hobby-horse is probably pagan in origin, when the 'hobby-horse' and the 'teaser' prancing in mock battle at the beginning of May symbolize the conflict between winter and summer, or good and evil. Every now and then, as the procession dances through the town to the traditional song 'let us unite, for summer is a cummin in', a girl is whipped beneath the horse's skirt to have her face blackened; a survival of a fertility rite. Helston's 'furry dance' when couples in formal morning dress dance in and out of the houses to bring good luck, is also a welcome for spring. 'Furry' probably comes from the Celtic word 'feur', a holiday, but the Victorians preferred to call it the 'floral dance', to remove unpleasant pagan associations. Minehead, in Somerset, also has a hobby horse ceremony and Hinton St George celebrates Punky Night in October, when children process through the streets carrying home-made lanterns. Kingsteignton, in Devon, has a Ram Roasting Fair, dating back to a time when the sacrifice of a ram made the village stream flow again and Ashburton still holds its mediaeval ceremony of Ale Tasting and Bread Weighing where local taverns and bakeries have their wares tested.

West Country villages, especially in Cornwall and Devon, still light bonfires on the hilltops on Midsummer Eve when girls throw flowers and herbs into the flames, young couples leap hand in hand over the fire to ensure happiness and fertility, and flaming tar barrels become mobile bonfires.

Tin mining in Cornwall goes back to prehistoric and Roman times but its great boom was in the last century when 300 mines were active. By 1890 the bottom had dropped out of the market but visitors can learn the history of the industry in the tunnels of Poldark Mining at Helston and at Redruth is Tolgus Tin, a tin-streaming mill still able to work much as it did two centuries ago. Not all the long-established industries have died out in the region – lace is still made at Honiton, where it was probably introduced by the Huguenots in the 16th century, and Axminster still makes its famous carpets. An Axminster made by Thomas Whitby, founder of the firm, is in the saloon at Saltram.

The clays of Devon and Cornwall are specially good and since the potter Bernard Leach established his pottery at St Ives in 1920, many craftsmen have established studios there. At Torrington, visitors can watch handblown glass being made at the Dartington Glass Factory. The West Country still has many products like cream, cider and meat pasties, which are justly famous.

WALES

Visitors crossing the Welsh borders cannot remain long under the impression that Wales is simply another part of England. There may be no passport checks, no currency change, but the Welsh have always been a fiercely independent people, with their own language and customs and with deep national aspirations to run their own affairs in their own way. An Englishman in a North Wales public house, surrounded by Welshmen chatting in their own tongue, or listening to the singing in chapel on Sunday, can feel that he is truly 'abroad'.

This separateness began in the 8th century AD when King Offa of Mercia built the dyke that bears his name. It ran from Prestatyn on the Dee in the north to the Severn estuary near Chepstow and long stretches of it are visible today. It was built not so much as a defence but as a boundary – a boundary to separate the Celts of Wales from the Anglo-Saxons of England. But it was such a formidable division that not only did it keep the Celts out of England but it also kept the English out of Wales. Gradually the strangers in the other world beyond Offa's Dyke became known as the Welsh, a word derived from the Anglo-Saxon for 'foreigners'.

Norman lords encroached on Welsh land not by invasion but by a series of skirmishes, building castles to guard their pieces of conquered territory. With the rise of a new breed of Welsh princes, determined to make themselves supreme in the whole country, a major clash was inevitable. Once Edward I had defeated the second of the Llywelyns, who had styled himself Prince of Wales, he built a chain of vast fortresses, including Conwy, Caernarfon and Harlech, which remained impregnable for a hundred years. One last attempt to snatch back independence came with the revolt of Owain Glyndwr (Owen Glendower), the great hero of Welsh nationalism. It was doomed to failure and the English exacted heavy penalties but it is often said that modern Wales began in 1410 for since then the Welsh have never lost the feeling that, whatever the legal and political ties with England, they will always remain a separate nation. The face of the land changed in the 19th century, when the iron industry boomed, coaltips encroached on the hill-sides of the south, slate mines burrowed into the hills of the north. Yet industrialization has left a remarkable amount of the countryside unscathed and large areas have become national parks: the grandeur of Snowdonia, the lakes, hills and waterfalls of the Brecon Beacons, the varied beauties of the Pembrokeshire Coast. In the heartland of Wales, the farming country where markets and sheep-dog trials are the important events and on peninsulas like Lleyn and Gower, the small villages seem to belong to a more leisurely age.

The Welsh are justly proud of their cultural traditions, for they have produced probably more great actors and singers per head of population than any other nation in the world. Their male voice choirs are renowned, often at their best singing traditional hymns. All that is best in Welsh culture has its expression in the National Eisteddfod, held alternately in north and south Wales every August and embracing solo and choral singing, recitation and the playing of musical instruments. The Bardic chair and crown are awarded for Welsh poetry and the ceremony makes a lasting impression on any visitor to it.

At least one in four Welsh people speaks Welsh as naturally as they speak English and several thousand, particularly in country areas, speak only Welsh. However, no stranger to Wales need be daunted by this. Perhaps because of their isolation, the Welsh have always preserved the innate Celtic hospitality and visitors, once they have established their own authenticity, receive a warm and genuine welcome.

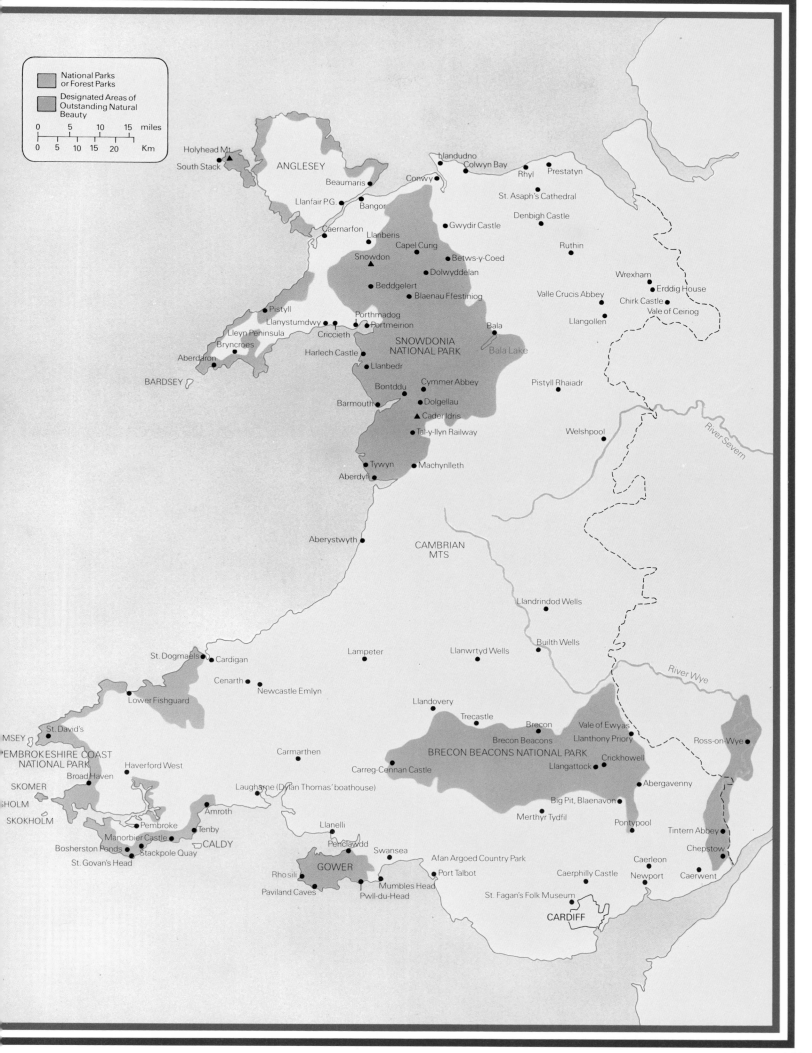

Legend

- National Parks or Forest Parks
- Designated Areas of Outstanding Natural Beauty

Scale:
0 5 10 15 miles
0 5 10 15 20 Km

Holyhead Mt
South Stack
ANGLESEY
Beaumaris
Conwy
llandudno
Colwyn Bay
Rhyl
Prestatyn
Llanfair P.G.
Bangor
St. Asaph's Cathedral
Caernarfon
Denbigh Castle
Llanberis
Gwydir Castle
Capel Curig
Ruthin
Snowdon
Betws-y-Coed
Dolwyddelan
Wrexham
Erddig House
Beddgelert
Valle Crucis Abbey
Chirk Castle
Blaenau Ffestiniog
Vale of Ceiriog
Pistyll
Porthmadog
Llangollen
Llanystumdwy
Portmeirion
Bala
Lleyn Peninsula
Criccieth
SNOWDONIA
NATIONAL PARK
Bryncroes
Harlech Castle
Bala Lake
Aberdaron
Llanbedr
BARDSEY
Bontddu
Cymmer Abbey
Pistyll Rhaiadr
Barmouth
Dolgellau
Cader Idris
Welshpool
Tal-y-llyn Railway
Tywyn
Machynlleth
Aberdyfi
River Severn
Aberystwyth
CAMBRIAN
MTS
Llandrindod Wells
Builth Wells
St. Dogmaels
Cardigan
Lampeter
Llanwrtyd Wells
Cenarth
River Wye
Newcastle Emlyn
Lower Fishguard
Llandovery
Trecastle
St. David's
Brecon
Vale of Ewyas
MSEY
Brecon Beacons
Llanthony Priory
Ross-on-Wye
PEMBROKESHIRE COAST
NATIONAL PARK
Carmarthen
BRECON BEACONS NATIONAL PARK
Crickhowell
SKOMER
Haverford West
Carreg-Cennan Castle
Llangattock
HOLM
Broad Haven
Abergavenny
SKOKHOLM
Laugharne (Dylan Thomas' boathouse)
Big Pit, Blaenavon
Amroth
Llanelli
Merthyr Tydfil
Pontypool
Pembroke
Tenby
Tintern Abbey
Manorbier Castle
CALDY
Penclawdd
Chepstow
Bosherston Ponds
Stackpole Quay
Swansea
Afan Argoed Country Park
Caerleon
St. Govan's Head
GOWER
Caerphilly Castle
Newport
Caerwent
Rhosili
Mumbles Head
Port Talbot
Paviland Caves
Pwll-du-Head
St. Fagan's Folk Museum
CARDIFF

NORTH WALES

Anticipating the Welshness of Wales, the visitor entering the country on the northern coast road from Chester may be disappointed to note how 'English' Colwyn Bay, Rhyl and Prestatyn have become under the influence of holidaymakers from the north of England. The mood changes noticeably at Llandudno, a rather elegant resort nestling between two headlands – the Great and Little Ormes. 'Llan' is the commonest prefix in Welsh place names and is the Welsh word for 'church', so it was appropriate that it should have been at Llandudno – 'the church of Tudno' - that the Rev. Charles Dodgson, better known as Lewis Carroll, first met Alice Liddell whom he immortalized in Alice in Wonderland. From Great Orme Head, whose 207m (679ft) summit may be reached by railway or cablecar, there is a spectacular panoramic view which takes in Snowdonia, Anglesey, the Isle of Man and the Lakeland peaks. The train trip along the Vale of Conwy is one of the most rewarding British Rail can offer. Conwy itself claims the smallest house in Britain, the spot where the first sweet peas in Britain were grown by Queen Eleanor of Castile, and some of the best mussels to be had. The great fortress dominates the town which shelters within its 805m (half mile) of walls, complete with 21 semi-circular defence towers. Further up the lovely valley are the restored Tudor mansion of Gwydir Castle, where white peacocks roam the grounds, and the Trefriw Woollen Mills, where visitors can see all that is involved in producing Welsh weaves. From Bangor the main road crosses Thomas Telford's 304m (1000ft) long suspension bridge built in 1826 and arrives in Anglesey close to a village that is famous only for the 58 letters of its name: Llanfairpwllgwyngyllgogerychwyrndrobwllllantysyliogogogoch, generally abbreviated to Llanfair PG. Anglesey lacks only mountains. It is a beautiful, rugged and productive island with numberless sandy beaches and bays, and a wealth of archaeological remains. On the south-east slope of Holyhead Mountain are remains from the earliest history

Right: *The massive bulk of Conway Castle makes Thomas Telford's bridge in the foreground an insignificant piece of engineering in comparison. The castle was built by Edward I in 1283 in just five years as a means of subjugating Llywelyn, the last – and most independent – of the independent Welsh princes. It crowns the town of Conway, one of the few examples left of a completely walled medieval town.*

Left: *Lake Bala is the largest natural lake in Wales (some of the man-made reservoir lakes are larger). It is 6.4 km (4 ml) long and 46 m (150 ft) deep at its deepest point, a busy sailing and fishing centre. At the north end of the lake is the little town of Bala, an excellent tourist centre with a treelined main street and some good hotels. The valley of the river Dee, which flows into Lake Bala, is surrounded by three mountain groups which provide spectacular scenery. From the lakeside in Bala, the peaks of Aran Benllyn and Cader Idris, both nudging 900 m (3000 ft), can be seen.*

Above: *Wales is rich in railways – particularly the narrow-gauge steam railways which travel scenic routes, like the Ffestiniog Railway which travels between Porthmadog and Blaenau Ffestiniog. The railway's ancestor was the horse-drawn tramway, of exactly the same gauge (596.9 mm/1 ft 11½ in), completed in 1836 and constructed to carry slates from the quarries to Blaenau Ffestiniog. Originally the power for the journey back from the quarries was provided by gravity but, in 1863, steam engines were introduced and passengers were carried soon afterwards.*

Right: *In the heart of Snowdonia and in the shadows of Moel Hebog is Beddgelert. The name means 'grave of Gelert' and there is some confusion over who Gelert was. He was probably a 6th century British saint but legend says that Gelert was the faithful hound slain by Prince Llywelyn who believed, wrongly, that it had attacked his baby son, when in fact it had killed a wolf to protect him. The legend seems to have originated with an enterprising local landlord.*

Right: *The Isle of Anglesey has over 160 km (100 miles) of coastline and this serene view illustrates one facet of its ever-changing scenery, which ranges from tiny, shell-scattered coves to wide stretches of beach or dramatic cliffs.*

Below: *This picture shows a peaceful hillside scene near Bala. One of the best books on Wales, George Borrow's* Wild Wales, *published in 1862, describes his approach to Bala: 'Shortly after leaving the village of the toll-gate I came to a beautiful valley. On my right hand was a river, the farther bank of which was fringed with trees; on my left was a gentle ascent, the lower part of which was covered with yellow luxuriant corn; a little farther on was a green grove, behind which rose up a moel (bare, rounded hill). A more bewitching scene I have never beheld.'*

of Anglesey, a circle of stone huts where metal-workers lived in pre-Christian days. The ramparts of an Iron Age fort, probably once a refuge for villagers from the coast from raiders across the Irish sea, circle the summit and the panorama takes in the Wicklow mountains in Ireland, the Isle of Man, the Snowdon peaks and the mountains of Cumbria. The cliffs sweep down to the lonely islet of South Stack, noisy with the cries of seabirds. Grey seals breed in the caves, cormorants perch on rocks, their wings outspread to dry, razorbills, guillemots and puffins crowd the ledges.

The river Dyfrdwy flows down from the moors through Bala Lake, emerging at the northern end as the Dee without, so tradition says, the waters of the river ever mingling with those of the lake. The little town of Bala was one of the centres of the Methodist revival in North Wales and there is a statue of the Rev. Thomas Charles who founded the British and Foreign Bible Society, after a 16 year-old girl, walking barefoot across the mountains to buy a bible from him, made him realise the need to distribute the scriptures. A worthwhile excursion in the area is the Pistyll Rhaeadr, or 'spout waterfall', which drops about 76m (250ft) in stages, through a natural rock arch. George Borrow described its 'thin, beautiful threads' as being like 'an immense skein of silk agitated and disturbed by tempestuous blasts'.

Capel Curig, Beddgelert and Betws-y-Coed are favourite centres for exploring Snowdonia. Capel Curig is well known to anglers and rock-climbers and the church is dedicated to a 6th century saint called Curig who chose this remote spot in which to preach. Beddgelert stands at the meeting point of two rivers and three valleys. The road to the north-east follows the valley of Nantgwynant with its twin lakes, the road to the south leads through the Pass of Aberglaslyn, where the turbulent river cuts its way between pine-clad

Below: *Abersoch is an attractive village at the mouth of the river Soch within the sheltering arm of Cardigan Bay. Sailing is a great attraction here and in the summer months the estuary and the waters of the bay are alive with coloured sails. The two offshore islands of St Trudwal are the home of guillemots and puffins and a favourite haunt of bird-watchers. The islands were bought in 1934 by the Welsh architect Clough Williams-Ellis to save them from any type of development.*

Above: *Caernarfon was another of the fortresses built by Edward I to dominate the newly-subdued Welsh. Prince Charles's investiture in Caernarfon Castle in 1969 was a re-enactment of a ceremony which first took place almost 700 years ago when the future Edward II was presented to the Welsh people as the first Prince of Wales. Edward I had promised them a prince 'unable to speak English' and his son was only a few months old at the time.*

Right: *The transference of an architectural idiom from one country to another is rarely successful and to do so from the sunlight of Italy to the greyer skies of Wales would seem to be courting disaster. Yet Portmeirion, on a wooded peninsula between Porthmadog and Harlech, has succeeded. It began in 1926 when Clough Williams-Ellis set out to create a living exhibition of the baroque architecture and landscaping of an Italian village. In the 1960's it provided the suitably bizarre and other worldly set for the popular television series 'The Prisoner'.*

crags. At Betws-y-Coed a straggle of grey houses look over a pretty glen where a stream twinkles over rocks, round boulders and beneath the 15th century bridge. Most visitors make for the Swallow and Conwy Falls but another interesting excursion is the walk through forest and farmland to Ty Mawr, the birthplace of Bishop Morgan, the first translator of the Bible into Welsh in the 16th century, laying the foundations of Welsh Protestantism.

The splendid scenic road from Betws-y-Coed to Blaenau Ffestiniog winds first through the Lledr valley, then into more open, wilder country with mountain views. On the way is Dolwyddelan with a castle which seems moulded to its mightly crag. Llywelyn the Great is said to have been born here in the 12th century and the castle saw many battles in the struggle against Edward I before it eventually fell in 1283.

Blaenau Ffestiniog is a town of slate, the blue-grey slate which provides its roofing, paving and fencing. The quarries have gouged into the surrounding mountains for in the last century slate was a booming industry in North Wales, supplying roofing for half England. After the turn of the century, with the arrival of clay roofing tiles, demand declined sharply. At Llechwedd Slate Caverns visitors tour tunnels and caverns by miners' tram and walk 122m (400ft) through deep chambers absorbing the recreated atmosphere of a working mine of Victorian times. The enormous Gloddfa Ganol mine has authentic quarrymen's cottages and a kilometre of workings. The narrow gauge trains of the Ffestiniog Railway follow the route which took the slate to Porthmadog harbour, ready for shipping all over the world.

Near Porthmadog is the extraordinary Italianate village of Portmeirion, between two river estuaries. It was the dream town of Welsh architect Clough Williams-Ellis who set out to prove that developing an old estate need not mean spoiling it. It began in 1926 and over the years has grown into one of the show-places of Wales, as well as the location for several films and the British television series *The Prisoner*. Many architectural treasures have been rescued from the demolition hammers and incorporated in the buildings: a Renaissance fireplace, a 17th century plastered ceiling, an old colonnade from Bristol, and so on.

To the west the Lleyn Peninsula, the picturesque upper arm of Cardigan Bay, pushes out into the Irish Sea, an unhurried and peaceful area. Off the tip of the peninsula is Bardsey Island, where monks from north-east Wales settled when they were forced to flee to escape massacre by the Saxons. Early poets claimed that the bones of 20,000 holy men were buried there and the island became an important place of pilgrimage. It has the remains of a 6th century abbey and bird observatory which monitors winter migration. All along the promontory are signs of the old pilgrims' trail. They worshipped at St Beuno's chapel at Pistyll, which still has its 'leper's window' on the north side of the chancel, and refreshed themselves at St Mary's Well at Bryncroes and near Aberdaron at Ffynnon Fair, which always yields fresh water, even though it is often covered by the sea. Their rest-house is a small white-washed cottage in the village.

Lleyn is proud of its distinguished politician Lloyd George who is buried at Llanystumdwy ('the church at the bend of the river') where he spent much of his childhood. The grave is encased in local stone and covered by a boulder where the 'Welsh wizard' used to sit watching his beloved stream.

On the mainland over the Menai Strait, Snowdon, its 1085m (3560ft) summit higher than any other mountain in England or Wales, is the great natural feature. The climb to the top is little more than a challenging walk, though weather conditions can change for the worse with alarming speed. The summit itself, called Yr Wyddfa Fawr (the tomb) is the legendary burial mound of an unpleasant giant who wore a cloak made from the beards of men he had slain and was finally routed by King Arthur. Beneath it lies the tarn of Glaslyn, the 'green lake', taking its deep colour from the copper mined on its shores in the last century. According to Welsh folklore it is the home of the monster Afanc, who terrorized the Vale of Conwy until the inhabitants finally managed to bind him in chains and drag him up the mountain to hurl him into Glaslyn. For those who do not wish to climb Snowdon or travel up

Below: *On a lonely, bird-haunted cliff-edge at the tip of Anglesey stands South Stack Lighthouse. The way down the stack gives naturalists excellent views of the colonies of sea-birds. Daniel Alexander, who built the lighthouse in 1808, was also responsible for the building of Dartmoor prison and the colonnades of Queen's House, Greenwich.*

Right: *Situated on the island of Anglesey, looking out over the Menai Strait to the mountains of the mainland, Beaumaris is a popular yachting centre. The castle, which stands near the shore, was the last of the Welsh castles built by Edward I. It had a turbulent history and is now a ruin.*

Below: *The Lleyn peninsula provides shelter for the pleasing family resort of Criccieth on the shore of Tremadog Bay and the town commands dramatic views of Snowdonia to the north and across the bay to Harlech in the south. There was a Welsh castle here before the English, led by Edward I, took it by force in 1285 and strengthened its defences. Now only the ruins remain on the hill.*

149

Above: *This scene of rocky isolation, near the village of Nant Peris, gives a taste of the wild beauty which draws walkers and climbers to Snowdonia. The Pass of Llanberis, running south-east from the village, is the most scenic route between Caernarfon and Betws-y-Coed, through great walls of rock and hillsides strewn with boulders and debris.*

on the steam-operated mountain railway from Llanberis, the classic road tour is from Caernarfon to Llanberis over the Llanberis Pass, turn right to Beddgelert and right again to Caernarfon, a delightful round trip of about 48km (30ml).

Snowdon is the centre of the Snowdonia National Park, 220,000 hectares (845 sq.ml.) of countryside preserved against unsuitable development and stretching from Llanberis in the north to the Dovey estuary on Cardigan Bay to the south. The Welsh call the whole wild region 'the land of eagles'. In the south west of the park the great mass of volcanic rock which is Cader Idris rolls through 16km (10ml) of countryside. The name means 'Chair of Idris' and whoever Idris may be, probably a Celtic chieftain, he chose an impressive spot. Charles Darwin said 'old Cader is a grand fellow and shows himself superbly with everchanging light. Do come and see him'. Like Snowdon, Cader Idris has its legends: Llyn Cau, dark in the shadow of rocks, is supposed to harbour a monster like that of Loch Ness in its waters and anyone who falls asleep on the bank is supposed to wake up to find himself mad, or blind – or a poet!

Hundreds of years of Welsh history are embodied in the ruined Harlech Castle, standing on a rocky spur which once overlooked the water. The sea has receded since, but there are still outstandingly beautiful views of Lleyn, Snowdon and Cardigan Bay. Owain Glyndwr captured the castle in 1404, but his movement for Welsh independence came to an end when it fell to the English a few years later. In 1468 it was the last castle to hold out for the Lancastrians against the Yorkists, when the defenders were eventually

starved out, their sufferings giving rise to the well-known march 'Men of Harlech'. It was also the last Welsh castle to hold out for Charles I against the Parliamentarians, finally surrendering in 1647.

There is a strong local tradition of an underground passage leading from Harlech Castle to the so-called Roman steps at Llanbedr, but this is only one of the mysteries of the steps. The 2000 flat stones climbing the mountainside to a paved way at the top of the pass are commonly believed to be the work of Romans, making a lookout post, but are more likely to be a mediaeval pack-way from one valley to the next.

The charming little town of Barmouth stands at the mouth of the Mawddach estuary, which stretches to the sea from the valley sheltered by the range of Cader Idris.

According to John Ruskin, the Victorian art critic, there was only one walk that excelled the walk from Dolgellau to Barmouth and that was the one from Barmouth to Dolgellau. Now the main road runs through the beauty of his favourite path. On the way it passes near St David's gold-mine, near Bontddu, which produced the nugget of gold used for several royal wedding rings including those of Queen Elizabeth II, Princess Margaret and Princess Anne, leaving just enough for a ring for the Princess of Wales.

Visitors can follow the history of the Welsh 'gold rush' of the 19th century along a footpath through the Mawddach valley. Overgrown ruins mark the site of mines where the strike was seldom rich enough to warrant the cost of getting the gold out of the ground. The Gwyn-fynydd mine was one of the more successful, staying in operation until 1938. The remains of the tunnel,

Right: *Most of the signs of Porthmadog's heyday, when the harbour was packed with ships engaged in the slate trade, have gone and today the town is primarily a holiday and sailing centre which offers safe bathing from excellent sandy beaches and makes a useful touring centre for north and west Wales.*

the strong room and the tramway can still be seen. Other splendid walks from Dolgellau are the torrent walk and the precipice walk, cut like a ledge, high on the hillside. North of the town are the ruins of Cymmer Abbey, a 12th century Cistercian foundation.

The road from Dolgellau to Tywyn has views across the wooded estuary on one side and on the other the towering mountainside and Tywyn is the starting point for another of the 'great little railways' of Wales, running for 11km (7ml) through a pretty valley and originally constructed for the slate traffic. A valley road also bends from Tywyn to the lake of Tal-y-Llyn, a shallow, shining sheet of water reflecting the surrounding mountains.

Machynlleth, standing inland on the south side of the Dovey, has its place in history for it was here that Owain Glyndwr was proclaimed Prince of Wales and set up his parliament in 1404, in the building which still stands in Maen Gwyn Street. Inside are slate slabs taken from the town streets, listing the tolls payable for the passage of sheep and cattle into the town. The road along the Dovey estuary was only finished in 1827 so Aberdovey, or Aberdyfi, was sheltered from the major events of Welsh history as the gorse-covered hills shelter it from the north wind but the plaintive song 'The Bells of Aberdovey' have ensured its fame. The legend goes that an ancient city lies submerged by the waves off the coast of Aberdovey and on a quiet evening the bells can be heard singing softly.

The countryside between Machynlleth and Welshpool, near the English border, is high moorland, little visited and only thinly inhabited, though with its own wild beauty; further north, however, the Vale of Llangollen is green and tree-filled. Llangollen itself is famous for its International Musical Eisteddfod, held in July every year since 1947 and attracting competitors from all over the world. The town takes its name from a 7th century hermit, St Collen, and its mediaeval bridge is one of the traditional 'seven wonders of Wales'. Famous, too, is Plas Newydd, the mansion home for 50 years of two eccentric women, Lady Eleanor Butler and Miss Sarah Ponsonby, known as the 'Ladies of Llangollen'. They entertained many celebrated men, including Scott and the Duke of Wellington, who were expected to make a gift of a curio or carving. Wordsworth, however, offered a sonnet.

One of the most striking landmarks of the Vale of Llangollen is the ruined castle of Dinas Bran, on a conical hill facing the town, the 13th century refuge of a Welsh prince who supported the English king against his own people. A tree-shaded walk along the canal leads to the remains of Valle Crucis Abbey, the 'abbey of the vale of the cross', founded in 1201 for Cistercian monks and sharing the fate of the monasteries under Henry VIII. In a neighbouring field stands Eliseg's Pillar, a remarkable survival from the early Christian era. Eliseg was a ruler of Powys in the 9th century.

North of Llangollen lies the Vale of Clwyd where Ruthin's red stone castle is well known for its mediaeval banquets. On the limestone block in the square, King Arthur is supposed to have ordered one of his rivals beheaded. The castle held out against an attack by Owain Glyndwr but fell after a siege by Parliamentarians in 1646. Denbigh Castle too, after being captured and recaptured in the Wars of the Roses, finally fell to the Parliamentarians. To the north is the smallest cathedral in the country, St Asaph's.

The Vale of Ceiriog rivals the Vale of Llangollen for natural loveliness and on the edge stands Chirk Castle, its splendidly ornate iron gates leading to an impressively long drive, vast lawns and neat topiary. The strong fortress was built in 1310 – the battlements wide enough for at least two soldiers to march abreast while manning the defences. The house has been continuously inhabited for 650 years and among many interesting paintings is one by a foreign artist which shows a local scene with ships sailing over dry land. The story goes that his Welsh patron told him to include sheep on the hills and he misunderstood. A complete contrast is Erddig, near Wrexham, a typical squire's home of the 17th century, with much of its original furniture and outbuildings including bakery, laundry, sawmill and smithy. The gardens, with their fine avenue of yew trees, Victorian flower garden and orchard, have been lovingly restored by the National Trust.

Left: *On the coast road between Penmaenpool and Barmouth, motorists can enjoy views over the Mawddach estuary though, as always, the walker will have more time to enjoy the peaceful countryside. There is plenty to explore in the area, from the workings of old gold mines to the remains of the Cistercian Cymmer Abbey.*

SOUTH WALES

Any visiting spectator at a Llanelli v. Swansea rugby match would find it hard to believe that he was in what was once the most 'English' part of Wales. Yet many of the southern towns – Chepstow, Cardiff, Caerphilly, Swansea, Newport, Llanelli, Carmarthen, Pembroke and Haverfordwest – grew out of mainly English settlements around the castles built by the marauding Norman barons. The indigenous Welsh retreated into the hills and valleys, rebelling from time to time but not returning to claim their own until the Industrial Revolution and its demand for labour in the coal mines and ironworks attracted them back to a new form of serfdom.

Today the Welshmen of South Wales may not be quite as vociferously Welsh-speaking as their brothers and sisters in the north, but they share all the other good qualities of Welshmen everywhere including their aptitude for singing and their ready hospitality. In one thing they excel: their devotion to the sport of rugby football.

The southern half of Wales is a very beautiful land of mountains (though not as high as those in the north), lakes, waterfalls and rivers; of superb coastal scenery, especially on the Pembroke coast; with the two National Parks covering hundreds of unspoilt square miles; with some fine Roman remains at Caerleon and Caerwent; with castles and monasteries both ruined and working; and the valleys, mainly sadly scarred because of the wealth of coal that lay beneath them, but now greening over again and still lovely on the upper slopes.

Wales, being a country of relatively high rainfall and finding itself with more water than it needs, has come to a more or less amicable arrangement to export its surplus to England. Birmingham, for instance, draws the bulk of its water supply from the lovely Elan Valley, west of Rhayader in what used to be Radnorshire (now part of Powys). The first dams were built at the end of the 19th century and the latest after the Second World War. The enormous artificial lakes that now occupy the valleys have become a major tourist attraction in an area that was once one of the remotest in Wales. The poet Shelley brought his 16-year-old wife, Harriet Westbrook, to live in the valley. Cwmlan, their home for a few months, lies at the bottom of one of the reservoirs. One farmhouse, typical of those in the valley which were about to be submerged, was dismantled and rebuilt in the National Folk Museum at St Fagan's near Cardiff.

Further south, around the town of Brecon, the Brecon Beacons National Park spreads its largely unspoilt and well-cared-for countryside over 130,000 hectares (519 sq miles) of South Wales. Its scenery varies from the truly

Right: Llangorse lake lies 11 km (7 miles) north-east of the Brecon Beacons. It is the largest natural lake in South Wales and legends insist that its waters cover a buried community, in this case the town of Mara. It is a regular nesting place for great crested grebes, coots, goosanders and red-breasted mergansers.

Left: Where the river Wye marks the boundary between Wales and England at Monmouth, it is joined by a tributary, the Monow, and on the Monow bridge is this fortified gateway added to the Norman bridge in 1260 to form one of four gateways into the town.

Above: *Caerphilly Castle is over 700 years old and, after Windsor, the largest in Europe. During its early years it was repeatedly destroyed and rebuilt and, in the 17th century, Cromwell's troops blasted its famous leaning tower nearly three metres (nine feet) out of perpendicular.*

Top right: *The outer, castellated buildings of Cardiff Castle were created by William Burges in 1861 for the third Marquess of Bute; they include buildings in the Gothic, Arab and classical Greek styles and follow the outline of the walled enclosure of an earlier Roman fort. Within the grounds is a fine example of a Norman keep, built by Robert Fitz-Hamon, one of the nobles sent to Wales by William the Conqueror.*

Below right: *Remove the bell-tower from this little church at Capel-y-ffin and it becomes one of the little white-washed cottages that dot the hillsides of this thinly inhabited area where Gwent and Powys meet Hereford and Worcester. The churchyard is full of ancient yews and solemn gravestones.*

natural of the mountains – a landscape ladled out in generous, solidified helpings – to the carefully tailored fields of the farms in valleys below.

Many rivers rise in the National Park area, some joining the Wye or the Usk while others, less well-known, make their way to the Bristol Channel through the industrial valleys and towns. Because of industrial pollution to the lower reaches of the rivers, most of the South Wales towns now draw their water from the 16 reservoirs high up on the southern edge of the Park. Cardiff, for example, is served by a reservoir in the Taf Fawr valley and Swansea water comes from Talybont. These reservoir-lakes, like those in the Elan valley, add greatly to the scenic pleasures of the park area.

The Brecon Beacons themselves swell out of the landscape like breakers arching from the sea. The highest crest, Pen y Fan (883m/2906ft), drops a precipitous 182m (600ft) on its northern face.

Prehistoric man left his imprint on the Beacons. Four thousand-year-old stone circles on the moors between Llandovery and Trecastle indicate that Bronze Age men pioneered the track along the ridge, later used by Roman soldiers. At Carn Goch the hill-fort dates from the Iron Age and is large enough for a whole tribe to gather, complete with cattle, in case of attack.

The cliff-top where Carreg-Cennan Castle stands has probably been fortified for at least 2000 years but the existing castle, with precipices making it impregnable on three sides, is an excellent example of mediaeval military architecture. In the corner of the inner ward is the entrance to a 46m (150ft) passage, bored through solid rock, leading to a natural cave. To the south-east are the long grassy mounds called 'druids' graves', in reality man-made rabbit warrens, built to provide a supply of rabbit meat in mediaeval times.

In the remote Vale of Ewyas which runs through the Black Mountains in the east are the remains of Llanthony Priory, founded in the 12th century by William de Lacy, Earl of Hereford, who prayed that it might never be spoiled by growing rich. Within forty years the monks were complaining that there was little point in 'singing to the wolves' and the majority moved to more hospitable surroundings in Gloucestershire.

Right: *Three Cliffs Bay is a dreamy, idyllic spot on the spectacularly beautiful Gower Peninsula coastline. Though it is only a few miles from Swansea, Neath and Llanelli, the Peninsula manages to preserve its natural charm while enlarging its recreational attractions – a tribute to the firmness and foresight of the local authorities.*

Left: *The steeply dropping Wye valley road from Monmouth to the south passes Tintern Abbey about halfway to Chepstow. The beauty of the Abbey's setting in lush green meadows beside the river, with tree-covered hills rising beyond, was an inspiration not only to William Wordsworth to write poetry – 'These waters, rolling from their mountain springs with a soft inland murmur' – but also to many artists to paint the 13th and 14th century ruins.*

Right: *Tenby is an ancient town that began to grow in the middle of the 18th century when John Jones, a local physician, promoted the virtues of sea water baths which the Tenby town fathers had established. New houses were built to accommodate the visiting gentry and the advent of the railway in 1853 further helped expansion.*

Left: *It may be hard to believe, looking at this idyllic view of Swansea, that it is Wales' second largest town, being a major industrial area with coal and anthracite mines, and the Anglo-Iranian oil port of Great Britain. Despite this, Swansea is a beautiful holiday resort, and merits the name given to it by local boy Dylan Thomas of the 'ugly lovely' town.*

Below: *Resembling the snake the Normans named it after the Worm's head near Rhosili winds out to sea. The beautiful, unspoiled headland from which it starts is now a nature reserve. The nearby coastline has seen many a shipwreck. The gaunt ribs of one still appear at low tide and vast quantities of silver coins from another found there in 1833 started a silver rush by the locals.*

The chief towns of the area are Brecon, a peaceful place dominated by its cathedral, and Abergavenny, known as the 'gateway to Wales', set on the Usk and flanked by hills. Abergavenny Castle has seen scenes of savagery: in 1177 the most important chieftains of Powys, invited to a banquet by William de Braose, were massacred as they feasted and in revenge their followers attacked and burned the castle. The town was sacked by Owain Glyndwr in 1404 and again by Parliament in 1646.

In this area craftsmen still produce traditional wood furniture, from milking stools to the renowned Welsh dressers and the folk tradition of carved wooden love-spoons – the more ornate the carving, the greater the love – has been revived for the tourist market.

The canal which flows past Abergavenny was built in the late 18th century, running for 51km (32ml) to link the Brecon area with the industrial towns of South Wales. Once it was heavily used by barges laden with coal, coke and iron, now it is a place for pleasure boats and a peaceful walk along to Llangattock, where the church still has its old stocks and a whipping post with two pairs of loops at differing heights for adults and children. Across the river Usk is Crickhowell, with the remains of a 13th century castle, finally destroyed by Owain Glyndwr.

To the south the Brecon Beacons slope down to the Glamorgan coalfields. These coalfields, in their heyday, made Cardiff the greatest coal-exporting port in the world, but the years of depression in the 1920s taught her not to rely on heavy industries alone and today the city, which has been the capital of Wales since 20th December 1955, has varied industrial and commercial interests and is the cultural centre for the whole country. It has a city centre castle with a magnificent Norman keep and amazing Victorian Gothic decoration, a new £12 million concert hall and a museum with an important collection of paintings by Welsh artists.

In the South Wales valleys, for so long synonymous with the coal industry, visitors can come to understand what life was like for miners in the past at the workings of Big Pit, Blaenavon and the Afan Argoed Country Park Welsh Miners' Museum, near Port Talbot and the industrial history of the area is imaginatively interpreted at the Valleys Inheritance Centre in Pontypool.

South Wales is particularly proud of – and particularly concerned about – the Gower Peninsula. It is remarkable that this delectable stretch of headlands, sandy bays and open downs so close to Swansea and Llanelli, was not

Above: *Paxton's Tower is a romantic folly, triangular in plan with turrets and a central tower, standing in splendid isolation in the valley of the Tywi in Dyfed. It was built by Sir William Paxton, a wealthy banker and Mayor of Carmarthen, in honour of Lord Nelson. Designed by Samuel Pepys Cockerell, it is often called Nelson's Tower and it has an inscription to the great man in Welsh, Latin and English, one on each of its three doors.*

overrun by its industrialized neighbours in the inconsiderate past. But thanks to the combined efforts of the Welsh Tourist Board, the National Trust (who have acquired or been given some 1800 hectares/4465 acres in the peninsula) and the local preservation societies, its wild charm and beauty have been saved. However, this does mean that what was once an inaccessible and unknown beauty spot is now attracting people in their thousands. The dilemma is how much human pressure can a beautiful but limited area take without losing its beauty.

Gower really begins with Mumbles Head and several pretty bays before the caves of Pwll-du Head, where evidence of prehistoric occupation has been found, besides the bones of elephant, bison and hyena. In the caves at Paviland a headless human skeleton from the Old Stone Age was discovered. At the bottom of the sea-bed beyond the cliffs at Rhossili lies a wreck known as 'The Dollar Ship' because of the gold doubloons washed up on the beach from time to time. No one knows her history, though the local story says she was carrying a Spanish lady's dowry to her British husband. Inland Rhosili Down rises to the highest point on Gower and the Neolithic burial chamber supposed to be the grave of a Viking chief named Sweyne, who gave his name to Swansea. The northern coast of Gower is a place of marshland and saltings but the mudflats of the estuary at Penclawdd support millions of cockles, so cockle-picking, cooking and selling is a cottage industry.

Further to the west the equally beautiful Pembroke coast has been declared a national park, which takes in the upper waters of Milford Haven and the islands of Caldy, Skokholm, Skomer, Grassholm and Ramsey. The 273km (170 mile) coastal path, which is the main artery of the park, runs from St Dogmaels, near Cardigan, to Amroth beyond Saundersfoot Bay. Walkers can enjoy a succession of splendid views, towering headlands, hidden inlets, cliffs dotted with wild flowers. The cliffs and offshore islands are busy with birds – among them razor-bills, kittiwakes, shags, gannets and puffins – and grey seals bask on the rocks below.

Tenby, an old walled town of colour-washed stone houses, is a useful exploring base near the southern end of the coast path. It stands on a rocky peninsula with a wide sandy beach on either side and a picturesque harbour. Boats take visitors to Caldy, the 'island of the saints' which has been a religious centre since the 6th century. The present Cistercian community was founded in 1929 and the monks raise barley and make the famous Caldy perfume which is sold on the island. The abbey is the main building but there is also the church, which houses the Ogham Stone, inscribed with ancient Celtic script 1400 years ago, and the remains of the old monastic buildings on the site of the first priory, near the island's only water supply.

Manorbier Castle, with its park, mill and ruined dovecote, is best known as the birthplace of Giraldus Cambrensis, Archdeacon of Brecon, who travelled through Wales on a recruiting campaign for the Third Crusade and wrote a vivid description of the country in the 12th century in *Itinerary Through Wales*. The red sandstone cliffs running westwards give way to limestone at Stackpole Quay and Broad Haven where a narrow neck of dunes, built up gradually since the late 18th century, separates the beach from Bosherston ponds. Thousands of white water-lilies bloom on the freshwater pools in June and graceful herons, kingfishers and swans complete the picture. The cliff path from Broad Haven leads to the 700-year-old chapel of St Govan's, built deep in a rocky cliff, on the site of a hermit's cell. The superstition is that if you count the steps going down then coming up, the total will always differ. Another ravine nearby is known as Huntsman's Leap after the rider who cleared the chasm, only to die of fright when he realised what he had done. The path ends with a view of the Elegug Stacks, lofty columns of limestone crowded with sea-birds, and the natural rock arch, which is known as 'the green bridge of Wales'.

The Normans chose Pembroke as their base against the Irish and the Welsh, its great rock a natural fortress, reinforced by the sea. The great keep is nearly 30m (100ft) high, the walls 6m (20ft) thick at the base. Henry VII was born in the castle and in the Civil War it was held by the Mayor of Pembroke

Left: *Walkers along the Dyfed coast between Tenby and the quieter resort of Saundersfoot can find magnificent seascapes, sandy beaches without a single footmark – and peace, as this scene at Monkstone beach shows.*

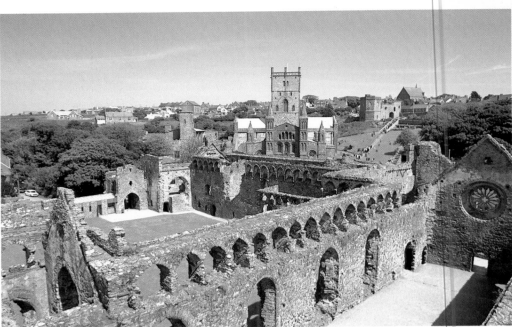

Right: *The mediaeval Bishop's Palace of St David's is magnificent even in ruin. When the roof was removed, at the Reformation, the lead is said to have raised enough money for the dowries of the five daughters of Bishop Barlow. This view looks over the ruins to the Cathedral, once part of an important religious settlement on the western tip of Wales, and probably its finest church.*

for Parliament but when he later changed sides, Cromwell led the siege against it in person.

In mediaeval times, two pilgrimages to the remote shrine of St David's were equal to one pilgrimage to Rome. Now, because St David's has its cathedral, it is a city rather than a village. It was built in a hollow, hidden from raiders, and from a distance only the top of the tower, added in the 16th century when danger was over, can be seen. The outside is austere, the inside rich in colour and interest. The top of St David's Head, which stretches out into the Atlantic, was used as an Iron Age fort and the massive 'Warrior's Dyke' is the remains of the wall which sealed it off in safety.

Just beyond the northern boundary of the National Park is the little market town of Cardigan, its bridge the scene of a Welsh victory against Norman forces in 1136, its castle the scene of a 12th century Eisteddfod organised by Rhys, Prince of South Wales. Even before the Romans came to Britain, the Welsh were using little boats called coracles, made from laths of willow and hazel intertwined; now their use is confined to the areas near Cardigan and Carmathen. They can be seen fishing for salmon along the Teifi river at Cenarth, within sound of its splendid waterfalls. Along the river at Newcastle Emlyn the only remaining water-powered flour mill in Wales demonstrates all stages of production and visitors can take home bags of wholemeal flour to bake their own bread. Lampeter is a market centre for the area and in 1822 Bishop Burgess founded St David's College there, for training students to holy orders. It was once linked with Oxford and Cambridge, on whose colleges it was modelled and, with its river background, it is reminiscent of the Cambridge 'backs'.

In the 18th century South Wales had its own centres for 'taking the waters' and, though many of the baths are no longer in operation, the little towns near the Irfon river keep the indefinable character of spa towns. One of the loveliest watering places in Wales was Llanwrtyd Wells where the Rev. Theophilus Evans discovered the medicinal properties of the sulphur and chalybeate springs after, it is said, seeing the energy of the frogs living around them. Now that the waters are no longer fashionable, it is a fishing and pony-trekking centre. Visitors were once lured to Llandrindod Wells by the pumproom with its salons and ballrooms, set up to popularize the thirty wells in the area, and found it a scenic healthy spot 213m (700ft) above sea leavel. Builth Wells, too, has a beautiful situation on the bank of the Wye, just below its meeting with the Irfon, and it became fashionable in international circles at the beginning of the last century, when Lady Hester Stanhope, niece of Prime Minister William Pitt, made her home there. It now makes an excellent centre for the discovery of South Wales in its many moods, from level farming country to rolling uplands and craggy mountains.

Above: *In spite of its popularity with tourists and yachtsmen, the harbour village of Lower Fishguard in Dyfed has remained remarkably unspoiled. It stands at the point where the Gwan river meets the sea and the narrow Gwan valley is a joy to naturalists, carpeted with wild flowers and home to a wealth of wild birds: kestrels, dippers, buzzards and owls.*

Right: *The white waters of River Teifi, the 85 km long river of South Wales, make exciting canoeing territory. For over 3,000 years, however, the river has known the very different, less streamlined craft of the coracle, a round boat of hide or calico stretched over a wooden frame. It is still in use on the river today for salmon fishing.*

NORTHERN IRELAND

The radiant beauty of the Northern Irish countryside contrasts strongly with the strife that the province has so long endured. Enmity seems out of place in so welcoming a countryside. Away from the cities of Belfast or Londonderry the physical scars are relatively few.

This north-east corner of Ireland has had close ties with Scotland and England since James VI of Scotland 'planted' thousands of settlers, the majority Scottish Presbyterians, in Ulster in the early 17th century. Determined attempts to spread Anglicanism followed, fuelling rivalries which left their bitter legacy. When the Irish Free State came into existence, with the Anglo-Irish treaty of 1921, the six northern counties of Londonderry, Tyrone, Fermanagh, Armagh, Down and Antrim remained part of the United Kingdom.

The north had already outstripped the south industrially and 100 years ago three-quarters of Ireland's industrial wealth was concentrated in the Belfast area, its prosperity founded on linen, washed and bleached in the Lagan valley above Belfast Lough, at a time when no-one calling himself a gentleman wore shirts of anything but linen and every lady carried a linen handkerchief. Yet through times of prosperity and recession alike agriculture has remained the largest industry and it is not in the cities that visitors find the appeal of Northern Ireland.

The scenery is soothing rather than breathtaking. The Sperrin mountains and glens of Antrim have a haunting beauty and under dark Mourne there lies a soft country sprinkled with clean farmsteads and well-tamed sands. The shores of the loughs are homes for many types of waterbirds and wild ducks, the bogs and peatlands shelter many rare plants and the Atlantic shores are rich in seashells. The restful nature of the Irish scene has long been recognized. The leafy roads have a rural tranquillity, with trees touching their branches overhead, walls and hedges bright with flowers, and fishermen sitting patiently under creeper-covered bridges. There is a special quality of light which tinges the landscape a unique green, softens the outline of mountains, clarifies water and whitens the long, uncrowded beaches.

For lovers of the outdoors, Northern Ireland has endless riches to offer. Anglers can find good sport almost anywhere, spoiled for choice among the rivers and loughs. Many of the forests have fishing stands, nature trails and pony tracks. Golf was first played in Ireland at Newtownards, County Down, in the 17th century and there are over 60 courses.

Ancient monuments dot the countryside and most farmers can boast a standing stone or cairn on their land. The earthen ramparts known as raths or *lis* were once defensive enclosures for groups of dwellings, the stone circles were probably surrounds for places of religious significance (the earliest date from about 1500 BC). The dolmens, made from a large flat capstone on several upright stones, were probably erected as sepulchres.

Northern Ireland is justly proud of its ecclesiastical heritage for it was there that St Patrick, originally a slave boy kidnapped from England by Irish raiders in the 5th century, concentrated his missionary activities, though he spread Christianity throughout the country, bringing people 'by the net of the Gospel to the harbour of life'. Historians argue over most of the facts of his life but there are claims that he lived to be 100, that one of his many miracles was banishing snakes from Irish soil and that he used the shamrock, since adopted as an emblem of Ireland, to explain the concept of the Trinity.

Northern Ireland people are by and large gentle, friendly, hospitable, relaxed men and women whose indifference to punctuality can sometimes be so infuriating to those who have appointments to keep.

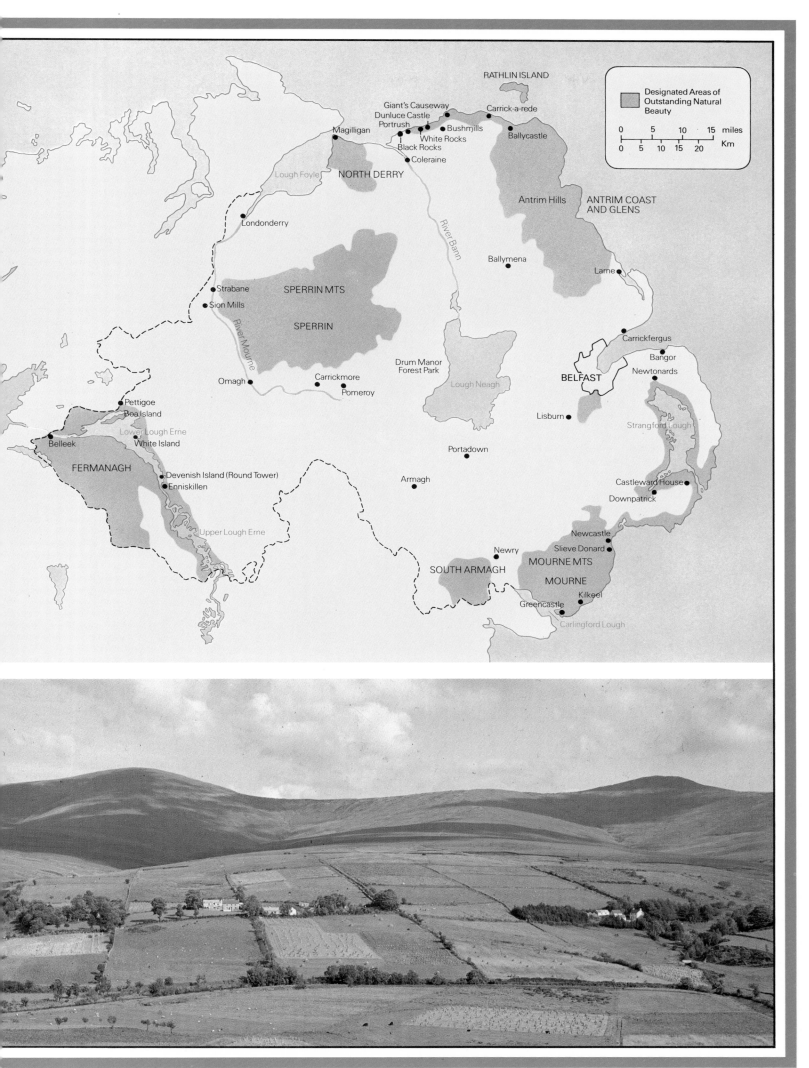

RATHLIN ISLAND

Giant's Causeway
Dunluce Castle
Portrush
Magilligan
White Rocks
Black Rocks
Coleraine
Bushmills
Carrick-a-rede
Ballycastle

NORTH DERRY

Lough Foyle

Antrim Hills

ANTRIM COAST
AND GLENS

Designated Areas of
Outstanding Natural
Beauty

0   5   10   15 miles
0   5   10   15   20   Km

Londonderry

River Bann

Ballymena

Larne

Strabane
Sion Mills

SPERRIN MTS

SPERRIN

River Mourne

Carrickfergus

Bangor
Newtonards

Drum Manor
Forest Park

BELFAST

Omagh

Carrickmore
Pomeroy

Lough Neagh

Strangford Lough

Pettigoe
Boa Island
Lower Lough Erne
White Island

Lisburn

Belleek

FERMANAGH

Devenish Island (Round Tower)
Enniskillen

Portadown

Castleward House

Upper Lough Erne

Armagh

Downpatrick

Newcastle
Slieve Donard

Newry

MOURNE MTS

SOUTH ARMAGH

MOURNE

Kilkeel

Greencastle

Carlingford Lough

NORTHERN IRELAND

Few capital cities can have easy access to so much beautiful countryside as Belfast. To the north are the mountains and glens of Antrim with the coast road just a stone's throw from the sea all the way from Larne to Cushendall. To the west is Lough Neagh, the largest lake in the British Isles and almost as full of legends as it is of water. To the south are the Mountains of Mourne which, as everyone knows and every Irishman sings, sweep down to the sea. To the east Belfast Lough itself opens like a great horn of plenty to the sea with the seaside resorts of Bangor and Carrickfergus on its shores.

The city is mainly a creation of the industrial revolution and its public buildings are somewhat undistinguished. The most interesting are the City Hall and St Anne's Cathedral, both dating from the early 1900s, and the Parliament building, a triumphant essay in 1930s 'government classical' style. Belfast Castle is much visited, not for its history (it was built in 1867) but for the city park, pleasure gardens, zoo and hill of caves which surround it. On the south side of the city is the large Queen's University, which holds a major Arts' Festival every autumn. Adjoining the university is the artistically planted Botanic Gardens, including in its grounds the Ulster Museum, with exhibitions on the development of local industry and a collection of work by local artists.

Above: *Belfast, growing fast from almost nothing in late Victorian times, is not known for its architecture but Belfast Castle is among its more impressive buildings. Built in the Scottish baronial style by the Marquis of Donegall in 1867, it was given to the city in 1934 and its large park is one of the favourite recreation areas for the citizens.*

Right: *The haunting beauty of Tyrone and Londonderry's Sperrin mountains is little known to the tourist and they remain largely unvisited. As their wild grandeur descends to moorland and fields enclosed by stone walls, sheep graze on the lush grass that the soft Irish climate provides. Four fifths of Northern Ireland's many farms deal in livestock*

Only a few miles from the city, to the south of Belfast Lough, the Ulster Folk and Transport Museum at Cultra brings the past to life with old buildings transported from their original settings, including a 19th century school, a terrace of industrial workers' cottages and a 200 year old church. There is a blacksmith's forge, a water-powered spade mill, a linen scutch mill and several styles of farmhouse.

Along the coast, the Ards peninsula, Strangford Lough (almost land-locked now except for a narrow entrance with Strangford on one side and Portaferry on the other), the south Down coast and Carlingford Lough, are a ribbon of seaside places, golf courses and yachting centres. Bangor, County Down, is now known as Belfast-by-the-sea; before the Vikings ravaged this coast in the 9th century, Bernard of Clairvaux named it Nursery of the Saints. Many of Ireland's saints and scholars were trained at Saint Comgall's abbey, founded in about 555, on the site where Bangor Abbey now stands.

Below: *The Giant's Causeway, one of the great sights of County Antrim, was formed when a huge sheet of molten basalt cooled several million years ago. The strange shapes and varying heights of the columns have given rise to names like the Giants' Pot Lid, My Lady's Fan, and the Wishing Chair.*

St Patrick, we are told, was a shepherd boy on the Slemish mountains, which overlook the ferry port of Larne. After his holy visions he studied in France, returning to Ulster to preach the gospel. He was buried, so the story goes, under the church he founded at Downpatrick. The church is now the Protestant cathedral and the headstone inscribed PATRIC is a Victorian embellishment.

Newcastle and Kilkeel are the smart resorts of the south Down shore. Between them runs Slieve Donard (852m/2796ft), a viewpoint for six 'kingdoms' – England, Ireland, Scotland, Wales, Isle of Man and heaven itself. Donard or Domangard was another Ulster saint, son of the last pagan king and guardian of the mountain, who lived in about AD 500. The coast between Newcastle and Greencastle was once notorious for smuggling and still has many coastal lookout points. Contraband was taken inland to Hilltown over Brandy Pad, now a popular walk, and 'Hilltown measure' still means a measure that brims over.

Only a valley away, and on the southern limits of the province, the Mourne country begins: hilltracks, heathery pastures, up-hill-and-down-dale-lanes. Though the province is only 100km (60 miles) wide, walkers feel they are striding across vast open spaces. 'Where the Mountains of Mourne sweep down to the sea' is from one of the songs of Percy French, who was born in the marsh country of Cavan. A humble inspector of drains, he had no ambition to be a millionaire songwriter and he sold outright, for modest fees, the copyrights of his lyrics for this and other songs like 'Phil the Fluter's Ball', 'Come Back Paddy Riley', 'The Pride of Petravore' and dozens more, which made fortunes for other people.

Down and Antrim are two of the five counties bordering Northern Ireland's 'inland sea', Lough Neagh, famed for its eels, salmon and pollan trout. According to legend the giant Finn McCool, the Fingal of Pictish mythology, scooped up a handful of earth to throw, in a fight with other ogres. It landed in the sea and became the Isle of Man; the hole it left behind became Lough Neagh. Other stories say that the underworld exists beneath its waters and fishermen on the lake report many strange phenomena: sudden unexplained currents which drag at their nets and sudden booming noises known by the locals as 'waterguns'.

The Giant's Causeway, Northern Ireland's most famous sight, is an amazing geological phenomemon with some 37,000 basalt columns, formed by the cooling and shrinking of lava from an ancient volcano. Celtic imagination saw them as stepping stones used by Finn McCool to reach Scotland, which at this point is only 48km (30 miles) away. Midway between here and Portrush, a resort with a splendid situation and long sweeping beaches, is the romantic ruin of Dunluce Castle, perched on a craggy rock, a narrow bridge linking it to the mainland, replacing the former drawbridge.

East of Portrush are the White Rocks, and their curious formations: the giant's head, the elephant arch, the lion's paw and the cathedral cave, 60m (196ft) long and 15m (49ft) wide, the roof supported by massive limestone columns. To the west are the Black Rocks , where in the distant past molten lava baked the original clay as hard as flint and preserved the fossils of sea creatures that lived 150 million years ago.

Most places in Northern Ireland have their share of folk tales and legends. Above the glen is Dun-clana-mourna, a mound where Finn McCool and his son, the poet Ossian, lived in the 1st century. Ossian, like Orpheus, is supposed to have visited the underworld and returned and the late Stone Age tomb and stone circle near Cushendall is said to be his burial place. Robert the Bruce is known to have sought refuge on Rathlin Island, Antrim, while fleeing from the English in 1306. In one of the cliff caves, they say, he watched a spider repeatedly trying to get to the roof of the cave on its fragile thread. It inspired him to return to Scotland to 'try, try and try again', triumphing at Bannockburn. In 1617 there was a long legal dispute over whether Rathlin belonged to Ireland or Scotland. It was decided in favour of Ireland because Rathlin had no snakes, and everyone knows that St Patrick banished all snakes from Ireland.

Below: *Perched on an isolated crag off the coast east of Portrush and connected with the mainland by the narrowest of bridges, Dunluce Castle is now a romantic ruin. Dating back to the 14th century, it was built on the site of an early fort and became the favourite residence of the Earls of Antrim. The family moved away after a great storm in 1639 when part of the kitchen fell into the sea, taking most of the servants with it. A tinker mending pans in a window-seat survived and the 'tinker's window' is still there.*

Real history is threaded on to fiction at Carrickfergus, on the north side of Belfast Lough, supposedly the site of the death by drowning of Prince Fergus, ancestor of the early kings of Scotland. The castle, subject of many paintings and picture-postcards, dates back to the 12th century and is well preserved. Watchers on its towers in 1778 saw the warship *Ranger*, Captain John Paul Jones in command, fight the first action and secure the first victory of American arms in European waters.

The second city of Northern Ireland is Londonderry (locally known simply as Derry), which received its name when James I of England granted the area to the citizens of London in 1613. Londonderry today is fundamentally the planned city enclosed in massive walls (the most complete set of walls in the British Isles) which expatriate Londoners built in the 17th century. The most memorable event in Londonderry's history occurred towards the end of the same century, when townsfolk successfully withstood a six-month siege by Jacobite forces attempting a Stuart restoration.

Within recent memory, its strategic position at the head of the long, deep and sheltered Lough Foyle has made it an important base for the British Navy and Air Force. The town still has its seaborne trade, and a concentration of shirt and pyjama manufacturers.

On the shores and waters of Lough Foyle is a scenic holiday spot which seems remote from any industrial town. Near Glenagivny, local sub-aqua divers raised from the wreck of a Spanish galleon of 1588 the finest known collection of cannon of that era. Some of the artifacts from the wreck can be seen at Magee University College in Londonderry. On the County Londonderry shore, the silver strand of Magilligan, 9½km (6 miles) long, stretches to the mouth of Limavady's river. On a clifftop near Magilligan is Mussenden Temple, a palatial little rotunda from the 18th century, inspired by the temples of Vesta in Rome, which once housed Bishop Harvey's library. It was near Limavady, 'on the road to Derry town one day' that the composer of the world's well-loved song picked up the melody of 'The Londonderry Air' from a wandering musician.

Strabane, 24km (15 miles) from Londonderry on the river Mourne, has several interesting American associations. John Dunlop and James Wilson were both apprentices at Gray's 18th century printing shop in the main street and both emigrated to Philadelphia. Dunlop founded America's first daily newspaper *The Pennsylvania Packet* and he printed the American Declaration of Independence from Jefferson's manuscript in 1776. James Wilson, who also became a newspaper editor, was the grandfather of President Woodrow Wilson. His birthplace can be seen at nearby Dergalt and his wife, Anne Adams, came from Sion Mills, a 'model' village built for workers at the linen mills by their owners, the Herdman family.

The Sperrin Mountains spill over from County Londonderry to County Tyrone, offering scenic drives, forest parks and rivers renowned for trout, salmon and roach. Outside Omagh, at Camp Hill, is the Ulster-American Folk Park with a recreated Tyrone village of 200 years ago and a log stockade to show what life was like for American pioneers in the same period. Carrickmore, between Omagh and Pomeroy, has the remains of a monastery reputedly founded by St Columba and Dromore has a ruined 14th century church with a holy well said to cure eye complaints. Near Cookstown are the remains of a 5000 year old civilisation and, in Drum Manor Forest Park, a butterfly garden where all their favourite flowers and weeds are grown and rare species can be seen in summer.

County Fermanagh has so many lakes, it might well be called the county of 1000 islands. It is a place for peaceful cruising and angling is a way of life. Fish breed ever more prolifically under banks of disintegrated limestone in the maze of slow-flowing rivers and stagnant backwaters.

Romantically sited on an island at the neck of water linking Upper and Lower Lough Erne is the town and star-shaped fort of Enniskillen. It was the key to the military dispositions of the region and its history through the turbulent 17th century was of continual capture and recapture by the Irish Maguires and the English troops. Descendants of the warring factions

Left: *The Carrick-a-rede rope bridge crosses the chasm separating an isolated rock from the coast of Antrim. The name means 'road in the rock' and the bridge is intended for the use of salmon fishermen though it is, of course, a popular tourist attraction.*

Below: *Rathlin Island, off the Antrim coast, is a peaceful home to farmers and fishermen. Once Rathlin was the haunt of pirates and smugglers; now it is a paradise for bird-watchers, anglers and botanists. Rathlin Sound, between the island and the mainland, is so rough that it is known as the* Brochan, *or 'boiling porridge pot'.*

Above: *While Upper Lough Erne is a slender maze of bays and inlets, Lower Lough Erne, as this picture shows, broadens out into a splendid sheet of water, which can become quite choppy on a windy day. Hugging the shores of the lough, which extends to the northern border of County Fermanagh, are 97 islands, including Boa and White Island.*

Previous pages: *This view, from the Slieve Donard Hotel, is a Northern Ireland classic: the resort of Newcastle, whose castle was new four centuries ago, nestling in a hollow below the mountains. Newcastle stretches for nearly 4 km (2 miles) along the curve of Dundrum bay and is famous for its sandy beaches and dunes, the yachting harbour and the Royal County Down golf course.*

eventually combined to form two renowned British regiments, the Iniskilling Dragoon Guards and the Royal Inniskilling Fusiliers.

Devenish Island has the sculpted Round Tower 25m (81ft) high, acknowledged to be the handsomest in Ireland, and alongside it is St Molaise's Oratory, a little 12th century church. The Abbey of St Mary, begun in the same period, has beautifully carved doorways and a 15th century cross. These reminders of a cultivated past seem almost commonplace against the mysterious and grotesque carved stones on White Island, also in the lough. They are reminiscent of the figures on Easter Island and are known to date from the 9th century AD. They were found at various times during repair work, built into the walls of the church. The old cemetery on Boa Island has two strange stone figures with a face on each side, called Janus statues. One has a hollow which might have been used for the blood of animal or human sacrifice.

Monks once inhabited Pettigoe, a market village which belongs to both Northern Ireland and the Republic, as the county boundary between Fermanagh and Donegal follows the village stream down the main street. Here on a barren rock in Lough Derg pilgrims to a cave associated with St Patrick's 'purgatory' submit to severe disciplines: bare feet, all-night vigils, daily meal of dry bread and 'Lough Derg soup' (water). The pilgrim season is from early June to mid-August and only those who accept the routine are allowed to land on the island.

Northern Ireland's smallest county is Armagh, often called 'the garden of Ireland' because of its apple orchards and soft fruit farms. Small though it is, its city is the ecclesiastical capital of Ireland, where St Patrick is said to have founded his main church in the 5th century. Both its cathedrals are dedicated to St Patrick. The Catholic cathedral, which took over 70 years to build, is decorated with coloured mosaic and has several dozen angels and saints depicted in its statues, pictures and carvings. The Church of Ireland cathedral has a splendid array of carved mediaeval heads high on the outside walls.

The ancient game of An Bol Chumann, or road bowls, is still played in Armagh on Sundays, when a stretch of winding country road is chosen as a course and players compete in throwing an iron ball to cover the course in the fewest number of shots. Another old custom, its origins lost in antiquity, is the Ould Lammas Fair, held on the last Monday and Tuesday in August in Ballycastle, County Antrim. Visitors can sample a special toffee called 'yellow man' and 'dulse', a dried seaweed. Pictures made from dried seaweed are also a local speciality.

Further north of Lough Neagh are the nine glens of Antrim with their fascinating names like Glencorp, 'glen of the slaughter', Glenarm, 'glen of the army' and Glentaisie, 'glen of Taisie', who was a princess fought over by a Viking and an Irish chief. Among the interesting places to visit, set in beautiful countryside, are the pretty village of Glenarm, where the castle, first built in the 17th century, looks surprisingly like the Tower of London with its four solid corner turrets; nearby Madman's Window, a great hole torn in a chalk boulder by wind and rain; and Nanny's Cave at Red Bay, which used to be the home of Ann Murray, who supported herself by weaving and selling 'poteen' and lived to be 100. Thackeray called the gorge-like Glenariff, with its steep waterfalls, a 'Switzerland in miniature'.

Long ago in Ireland, useful meant beautiful and some craftsmen have maintained the connection down the ages. Irish linen is world famous and its birthplace was Lisburn, in County Antrim, where it was started in 1698 by Louis Crommelin with Huguenots who fled from France in Louis XIV's reign. Tyrone is known for its crystal and Belleek, in County Fermanagh, is the most celebrated name in Irish pottery, begun in 1857 when local clay deposits were found. Its creamy lustre 'baskets' look as though woven from lace.

No chapter on Ireland would be complete without a mention of the world's oldest whiskey distillery at Bushmills, County Antrim. The first licence to distil whiskey at Bushmills was granted in 1609, though the 'water of life' had already been drunk for hundreds of years and in 1612 the lord mayor of London, Sir William Cockayne, had to sell some of his property to pay for his Bushmills whiskey.

Right: *The Antrim mountains form a rampart along the coast of the county, intersected by a series of beautiful valleys, the 'nine glens of Antrim'. This photograph was taken near Glenariff, described by Thackeray as 'Switzerland in miniature' and visited for its cascades and waterfalls. In spring and early summer the glen is carpeted with primroses, bluebells and other wild flowers.*

Below: *The rocket-like Round Tower of Devenish (Ox Island), County Fermanagh, 25 m (81 ft) high, is part of a 6th century monastery founded by St Molaise. The well-preserved tower is notable for its richly decorated cornice with four carved heads. Nearby were discovered the foundations of another tower, thought to have been a 'false start' for the existing tower.*

LONDON

No one can satisfactorily explain what personal magnetism is. As the famous author Sir James Barrie said of charm 'It's a sort of bloom on a woman. If you have it you don't need to have anything else; and if you don't have it, it doesn't matter what else you have'.

Anyone who doubts the personal magnetism of London should join the thousands who make the morning pilgrimage to Buckingham Palace to watch the Changing of the Guard or who queue at the Tower of London to get a glimpse of the Crown Jewels. Where royalty and pageantry combine, London's magnetism can be seen at its most powerful.

But the attractions of London in more specialized ways are just as strong. London's shops draw in their customers not only from the most distant parts of Britain but also from half the countries of the world. The London theatre has an unchallenged reputation. Though London is reticent about its treasures, its art galleries and museums house more of the world's great artistic masterpieces than Paris or Rome. Palaces, cathedrals, churches, historic buildings, parks, concert halls: London provides a richness of choice which leaves the receptive visitor – and even the grateful resident – gasping. In addition there are in London, for those who seek them, haunts 'where the busy world is hushed': an alley off some city street leading to a secret garden; a square cool with plane trees, those uncomplaining providers of London shade; a deck chair beside a park lake where the only sound is the quacking of bright-eyed ducks; the heart-lifting glow of a London sunset seen from a boat on the Serpentine. No wonder that Londoners, however far from home, look to this city with all its varied attractions as the centre of their world.

London's magnetism is nothing new. More than two thousand years ago the Early Britons were

attracted to the site and established a settlement on the north bank of the Thames, where Cannon Street station stands today.

The site's advantages were self-evident: it was above the level of the nearby marshes, was defended on the west by the river Fleet and to the south by the broad natural moat of the Thames. It lay in the centre of the island's most populous and fertile region and a fine broad tideway gave the rapidly developing trade of the country easy access to the continent of Europe. Upstream the sinuous Thames wound its way through the expanding heart of England. As the site for the country's principal city it seemed then, as it seems today, the inevitable choice.

When the Romans colonized the country and established London as their administrative base one of their first actions was to build a wall around the city to defend it against land attack. By building a 6m (20ft) high wall of Kentish ragstone and Roman tiles they set the limits of the city for the next thousand years. Parts of the wall can be seen near the Tower of London, by the Barbican, and in St Martin's-le-Grand. The Romans finally withdrew from Britain in AD 423. Saxon invaders then captured London, destroying everything except the wall, which they used to mark the limits of their own city.

Until 1066, when William was crowned king of England, the advantages of living within the safety of the city walls were so great that the population of London had exploded. Development had spread westward beyond the walls, along what is now Queen Victoria Street, Holborn and Fleet Street. Further west, and quite separate from the City of London, the City of Westminster had grown up around the abbey founded in the dark ages and rebuilt by Edward the Confessor. Thus the London of today has grown out of the union of two separate cities.

HARROW
w School

Kenwood House

HIGHGATE

Hackney Marshes

Wembley Stadium

WEMBLEY

HAMPSTEAD

Zoo

St. Pancras

Mosque

Regents Park

PADDINGTON

British Museum

Barbican

MARYLEBONE

St. Paul's Cathedral

Guildhall

THE CITY

Oxford Street

Bank of England

Kensington Gardens

Marble Arch

Covent

Dickens' House

Hyde Park

Trafalgar Square

Garden

Tower of London

Kensington Palace

St. James' Palace

St. Catherine's Dock

River Thames

Gunnersbury Park

Albert Hall

Buckingham Palace

Royal Festival Hall

Tower Bridge

ey Park

KENSINGTON

Westminster Abbey

HMS Belfast

Victoria and Albert

Houses of Parliament

SOUTHWARK

Museum

Westminster

Lambeth Palace

CHELSEA

Cathedral

Chiswick House

Royal Hospital

Cutty Sark

Royal Naval College

FULHAM

Battersea Park

GREENWICH

Syon House

BATTERSEA

Greenwich Park

Kew Gardens

Hurlingham Club

CLAPHAM

RICHMOND

PUTNEY

Clapham Common

River Thames

Dulwich Park

Richmond Park

Dulwich College

Wimbledon Park

Eltham Palace

All England Tennis Club

shy Park

WIMBLEDON

Crystal Palace

Hampton Court Palace

Wimbledon Common

| 0 | | 1 | | 2 | miles |
| 0 | 1 | 2 | 3 | | Km |

THE CITY

ommercial and financial London – 'The City' – is little more than a village in terms of population. About six thousand people are permanent residents; but another half million flood into its offices, markets, shops and warehouses each morning and retreat to their homes outside the City each night. This twice-daily migration puts a daunting strain on the railways, underground and buses and, particularly, on the barely adequate roads.

Viewed from the air the City's road system within its roughly semicircular perimeter resembles a child's early efforts at drawing. There are plenty of roads, many of them narrow, and they dart off in every direction, merging, forking, bending and doubling back on themselves – a traffic planner's nightmare. If there seems to be little logic in the layout it has to be remembered that these are streets that have grown out of Roman, Saxon and Danish streets – all streets within the walled City that was the beginning of London, streets that had nowhere to go outside the walls. Though the seven City gates that pierced the walls in mediaeval times are now gone, the streets that led to them still exist and are named after them: Cripplegate, Ludgate, Newgate, Aldersgate, Moorgate, Bishopsgate and Aldgate.

In mediaeval times there was so little wheeled traffic that the narrow streets, though filthy, were more or less adequate. Even in the late 17th century the quickest and cheapest way to travel to Westminster or Greenwich (as Samuel Pepys so often records) was not to go by coach but to walk down one of the many lanes leading to the Thames and there hire a waterman to row you. The Thames was the great east-west highway.

There have been two occasions when it would have been possible to replan the City's streets: the first after the Great Fire of London in 1666 and the second after the devastation of the *Blitz* during World War II. Curiously the area of damage in these two catastrophes was similar and in both cases the imaginative plans for rebuilding were watered down and opportunities lost.

Sir Christopher Wren was early on the scene after the Great Fire. Almost before the embers had cooled he presented a plan which envisaged a new Royal Exchange as the centre of the City, surrounded by an extensive piazza from which wide streets radiated in all directions, two of them forming main east-west thoroughfares. Unfortunately this plan was rejected on the grounds that it involved too much redistribution of property. The only parts of his plan to survive were the rebuilding of St Paul's Cathedral and a broad quay between the Tower and the Temple (sadly built over in the 19th century). He also rebuilt many of the 87 city churches destroyed in the fire, turning London into a treasure house of ecclesiastical architecture. In addition, some streets were widened (though not to the extent that Wren advised) and many of the extremely advanced building standards he recommended to prevent future fires were adopted.

One of the major attractions in the City, for visitors and Londoners, is the Barbican Centre for Arts and Conferences. Office buildings and flats came first and the Museum of London, with exhibitions and tableaux of London's history and development, opened in 1976. The Arts and Conference Centre (opened in 1982) has become the permanent home of the London Symphony Orchestra and the London home of the Royal Shakespeare Company.

Since World War II, certain areas of the City have been redeveloped with great courage and imagination – notably the Barbican scheme and the improvement in traffic flow as a result of the widening of London Wall – but there is little outward sign of any long-term plan for the City. Happily its post-war buildings, many of them tower blocks which dwarf the 110m (365ft) high dome of St Paul's, make no attempt to ape the past and so encourage closer attention to the ancient treasures that remain: St Paul's Cathedral,

Above: *St Paul's Cathedral has had a history stretching over nearly 14 centuries. The first cathedral founded in AD 604 was burnt; the second vandalized by the Vikings; a third was burnt to the ground in 1087; the fourth succumbed to the great fire of 1666. The present cathedral – built by Sir Christopher Wren – has a dome climbing to a height of 111m (365ft), 34m (112ft) in diameter. Many of Britain's national heroes are buried within the cathedral, including Nelson and Wellington. Sir Christopher Wren's own tomb is in the crypt and bears the often quoted inscription 'Lector, si monumentum requiris, circumspice. 'Reader, if you seek his monument, look around you.'*

Left: *London's Barbican Centre for Arts and Conferences – to give it its full name – is a veritable treasure house for those keen on the arts; under the biggest flat roof in London, in a bewildering array of levels and floors, are housed 3 cinemas, one of the largest art galleries in London, a concert hall (home of the London Symphony Orchestra) and a theatre seating 1,160, as well as cafés and bookstalls. Initial complaints of impenetrability have ceased as visitors have learnt their way around the complex centre.*

Below: *In their ceremonial red and gold uniforms the Yeoman Warders are easily confused with the Yeoman of the Guard, the Queen's bodyguard known as 'Beefeaters'. The Yeoman Warders are the guardians and guides at the Tower of London.*

the Tower of London, the Guildhall, St Bartholomew-the-Great and the many city churches designed by Wren, the Inns of Court, the Royal Exchange, the Mansion House and several of the halls of the City Livery Companies.

The Bank of England is the City's centre of gravity and integrity, with six busy streets meeting at its door. The phrase 'safe as the Bank of England' still has meaning although there was the occasion when the directors of the bank received an anonymous letter stating that the writer knew a way into the bullion room. This they ignored until a second letter offered to meet them in the bullion room on any day and at any time they cared to name. The appointment was made and the directors locked themselves in to await the anonymous correspondent's arrival. He appeared, right on time, forcing up some boards in the floor of the vault to make his entry. Fortunately, he turned out to be an honest man employed on repairing sewers beneath the bank and he was awarded £800 for his integrity. There need be no concern for the safety of Britain's gold reserves : the incident is said to have happened in 1836 and the bank vaults have been totally rebuilt since then. In fact the whole of the bank was rebuilt between 1921 and the outbreak of World War II. All that remains of Sir John Soane's early 19th century building is the windowless curtain wall on the south and west sides.

Much that goes on in the City of London must look like idle ceremony to the outsider: the Lord Mayor's Show when the Lord Mayor rides to the Courts of Justice in a ceremonial 18th century coach to take office publicly, the mediaeval clothing of City officials and the nightly Ceremony of the Keys at the Tower of London are all quaint in the modern context in which they are seen, but they represent a thread of continuity in the life of the great City of London which would certainly make London the poorer for their passing.

The Livery Companies of the City, of which there are nearly 90 today, evolved out of the craft guilds of the late Middle Ages. Even in those days there were industrial disputes and in London the 'masters' split away from the craftsmen members of the guilds and formed their own city companies. Over the years these companies, many of which evolved their own ceremonial dress or 'livery', devoted themselves less to the daily problems of the craft and more to charitable and educational work. The school founded by the Merchant Taylors' Company is well known, and Sir John Gresham, a member of the Mercers' Company, founded Gresham's Schools in his home county of Norfolk. He became a member of the Fishmongers' Company who are still the school's trustees. Many of these city companies accumulated

Far right: *The City of London is administered from its historic Guildhall. Here, every year in November, the Lord Mayor's banquet is held, and here, every other Thursday, the Court of Common Council – the City's governing body – holds its meetings which are open to the public.*

Below: *These picturesquely uniformed pikemen are members of the Honourable Artillery Company, the oldest volunteer regiment in Britain. Founded as a body of archers known as the Guild of St George, it was granted a royal charter by Henry VIII in 1537 with the title of the Fraternity of Longbows, Crossbows and Handguns. Though the HAC is an active, modern army unit, it provides the Company of Pikemen and Musketeers who do duty on ceremonial occasions.*

Right: *Each November the new Lord Mayor rides in a traditional procession to the Royal Courts of Justice to make his statutory declaration of office before continuing along the Strand and the Victoria Embankment through cheering crowds back to the Mansion House. The magnificent coach used in the Lord Mayor's Show was built in 1757 and is normally to be seen in the Guildhall Museum. For its one day of glory in the outside world its two and a half tonnes of elaborately gilded, carved and painted coachwork are hauled by six shire horses from the stables of Whitbread's brewery. Beside it march the Pikemen of the Honourable Artillery Company in their 17th century uniforms with plumed helmets and crimson sashes. Within the coach the Lord Mayor is dressed in the fur-trimmed scarlet robe, the Cap of Dignity and the 16th century chain of office known as the Lord Mayor's Collar of 'SS'. For him it is the beginning of an exhausting year.*

Right: *Lincoln's Inn, one of London's four Inns of Court – the university of the legal profession – is an oasis of calm just out of earshot of the thundering traffic of Fleet Street and Chancery Lane. To wander through its Tudor brick gatehouse is to discover an unexpected world of manicured lawns and echoing courtyards full of narrow doorways and staircases, reminiscent of Oxford or Cambridge.*

great wealth and were able to build handsome and luxurious Livery Halls, several of which still exist. The Fishmongers' Hall is a prominent building at the north end of London Bridge and the Fishmongers still inspect all fish sold to Billingsgate. The Goldsmiths' Hall is harder to find – in Foster Lane, off Gresham Street. Here the annual Trial of the Pyx is held – a picturesque ceremony with a serious purpose: to check the accuracy of composition and weight of newly minted coinage.

About half of the daily influx of workers into the City must cross one of the four road bridges and two rail bridges that link it with South London across the Thames. The most easily recognized of these is Tower Bridge, whose profile is almost a London trade mark. But the most used is its upstream neighbour, London Bridge. There has been a bridge here since at least the 10th century and until 1749, old London Bridge was the only river crossing for traffic in London. The first permanent bridge was begun here in 1176, at the instigation of the rector of St Mary Colechurch, a church which was destroyed in the Great Fire and never rebuilt. The bridge, 33 years in the building, ultimately had 19 pointed stone arches, two waterwheels operated by the tide, a drawbridge at its northern end, tall blocks of shops and houses, and a chapel dedicated to Thomas à Becket. As time went by the narrow roadway became quite inadequate for the traffic wanting to cross, and the narrow arches, becoming blocked by ice, caused the Thames to freeze over in the arctic winters of 1515, 1564, 1620, 1683 and 1814. Londoners made the best of it, holding fairs, ox-roastings and even a fox hunt on the frozen surface. By the end of the 18th century Old London Bridge had become such an anachronism that the *Quarterly Review* was prompted to write: 'The pernicious structure has wasted more money in perpetual repairs than would have sufficed to build a dozen safe and commodious bridges'. A new London Bridge, designed by John Rennie, was built by his son in 1831, 46m (50yds) upstream from the old, and this bridge stood for a further 140 years, by which time it, too, had become over-congested. As the present bridge was being built, Rennie's bridge was being dismantled stone by stone and shipped to Lake Havasu City, Arizona, where it has become a popular tourist attraction, with a red London bus making hourly crossings.

WESTMINSTER
& ROYAL LONDON

Westminster, though only one of London's thirty-two boroughs, stoutly preserves its traditional entity as a city in its own right – a city which, until building development seeped along the north bank of the Thames in the Middle Ages, was quite separate from the City of London, three km (two miles) to the east.

Today, unless you happen to be the Queen, you can pass freely between Westminster and the City 'without let or hindrance'. But the Queen is obliged to stop at the City's western boundary where Temple Bar used to stand and indicate her intention to enter the City. The Lord Mayor of London immediately surrenders the Pearl Sword presented to the City by Queen Elizabeth I in 1571 which the Queen equally immediately returns, and Her Majesty continues on her way. This picturesque ceremony is, of course, merely a formality but it underlines the City's traditional independence without disrespect to the Crown.

Within the City of Westminster the Queen suffers no restrictions. She and her ancestors have made it their home for more than a thousand years. Ever since the early English kings dragged themselves away from their ancient capital at Winchester (it was the excellent hunting in the New Forest that kept them there so long) Westminster has enjoyed a special relationship with the Crown. Every monarch since William the Conqueror (except Edward V and Edward VIII who were never crowned) has been crowned in Westminster Abbey. Parliament has gathered there (at one time in the Abbey's chapter house) since the 10th century. Most of London's royal pageantry takes place within Westminster's boundaries. The history of these islands and its monarchy is embedded in its stones. Though Westminster in recent years has spread and absorbed the London boroughs of Marylebone and Paddington, making it in terms of rateable value richer than the City of London itself, most people think of it as the relatively compact area between the Thames and Buckingham Palace and between the Houses of Parliament and Trafalgar Square. Within this readily explorable area the imaginative visitor can enjoy two Westminsters: the imposing present day city of parks and Parliament and palaces and the Westminster of history whose many streets and buildings link the disappearing past with the fast changing present.

The Houses of Parliament are Westminster's most prominent present day feature but adjoining them is Westminster Hall, built by William Rufus, son of the Conqueror, and reroofed (1377-99) by Richard II with one of the most splendid hammerbeam roofs in Europe. It is the sole surviving building of the fascinating jumble that was once the extensive Palace of Westminster, destroyed in the fire of 1834. Fortunately for our imagination both Turner and Constable rushed to the scene with their sketch pads and made vivid pictorial records of the biggest conflagration that London had seen since the Great Fire of 1666.

Halfway up Whitehall, opposite the Horse Guards, the Banqueting House reminds modern London that here, stretching from the banks of the Thames to St James's Park, stood the no longer seen Palace of Whitehall, the favourite Royal residence from 1530 to 1698. Originally known as York Place, it was the London residence of the Archbishops of York. In the reign of Henry VIII, Cardinal Wolsey lived here in far greater luxury than the King, so when Wolsey fell from grace in 1530, Henry was not slow to take over what he had long regarded as a very desirable property. As he annexed Hampton Court at the same time he was clearly the winner in an outsize game of real-life 'Monopoly'. The Banqueting House is, in fact, a Stuart replacement for an earlier Tudor hall and it must have dwarfed and outshone the comparatively modest Tudor buildings that surrounded it. It was designed by Inigo Jones, the son of a London cloth-worker who rose to become the first English

Right: *George III bought Buckingham House, now the Palace, in 1761. William IV disliked it and offered it to the Government when the Houses of Parliament were burnt down and it was little used as a Royal residence until the 19th century when Queen Victoria first took residence there. It is now the principal London home of the Sovereign. The Queen was not at home when the photograph was taken: no Royal standard is flying over the Palace.*

Below: *Almost within sight of Buckingham Palace The Two Chairmen, an old pub near St James's Park, perpetuates the memory of two of the ruffians who used to elbow their way through the crowds of 18th century London carrying the 'quality' in sedan chairs. Chairs were built with opening roofs to allow room for the lofty wigs of the period.*

architect in the modern sense of the word. He first came into contact with James I as a designer of scenery for court masques, an art form which he raised to such heights that Ben Jonson, the poet and dramatist, refused to collaborate with him on the grounds that his words were being overshadowed by the scenery.

The Banqueting House was completed in 1622 except for the magnificent Rubens ceiling which was commissioned by Charles I in 1629 when the painter-diplomat was on a visit to London. The painting took a further five years and the ceiling was not installed until 1635. It is ironical to realize that 14 years later Charles I must have walked beneath this very ceiling on his way to execution: the scaffold was erected outside the north front of the Banqueting House and a passage from it was knocked through the wall. Charles I had planned to rebuild the whole of the Palace of Whitehall in this new style by Inigo Jones but, sadly for London, he did not have the opportunity. Inigo Jones himself died three years after the King's execution.

The remainder of Whitehall today is mainly Government offices of Victorian origin and permanence. Exceptions include the Admiralty (1725), the Horse Guards (1760) and parts of the Treasury building, designed by Sir John Soane, which are hidden behind its Victorian façade. Sir John Soane's own

Below: *The Royal Salutes that loudly thump the air of Hyde Park make immensely exciting spectacles as well as audible reminders of state occasions, and people are sometimes curious to know why those taking part should be known as the King's Troop of the Royal Horse Artillery when Britain has a Queen on the throne. It was King George VI who suggested the name for the troop when it was revived after the War and Queen Elizabeth decided that the title should be retained in memory of her father.*

Above: *Once every regiment had its own regimental band but economies in recent years have reduced their numbers very considerably. As a result the services of those that remain are very much in demand. Until 1988 all army bandsmen will get their training at the Royal Military School of Music at Kneller Hall, Twickenham, once the home of the famous 17th century portrait painter, Sir Godfrey Kneller.*

Above: *Westminster Cathedral is near Victoria Station on a site where the Westminster Bridewell prison stood until the late 19th century. It was bought by Cardinal Manning but it was his successor, Cardinal Vaughan, who commissioned John Bentley to prepare plans in the Italian or Byzantine style in 1894. His cathedral has been described as 'the nearest thing to Byzantium in London'. As the photograph shows, the exterior is of red brick with stripes, arches and domes of stone. Inside, although there is still some brickwork exposed, most of it has been encased in glittering marble and mosaics.*

Right: *Despite the impression they give of great antiquity the Houses of Parliament, seen from across the Thames here, are amongst London's younger public buildings. On the other side of the Square from them is Westminster Abbey, genuinely old, being founded in 1055 and rebuilt in the 13th century. It is the primary church of the Church of England but not a Cathedral.*

Left: *In contrast to the opulent architecture of much of Whitehall, No. 10 Downing Street, the official home of Britain's Prime Ministers, presents a very modest façade to the world. But behind that famous and much photographed front door there is a much larger and more elegant house than the outside would suggest. It has, too, quite an extensive garden which is well hidden from the public gaze.*

Many Prime Ministers, including Lord Melbourne and Sir Robert Peel and, in recent years, Mr Callaghan, have used No. 10 mainly as an office, preferring to have their homes elsewhere.

designs for improvements to the Houses of Parliament – done long before the 1834 fire – may be seen in his house, which is now a museum, situated in Lincoln's Inn Fields.

Off the north side of Whitehall is a house that attracts much public attention: No.10 Downing Street. This, the official residence of Britain's Prime Ministers, is much larger than the modest front would suggest. It inter-connects with nos. 11 and 12 to form a rabbit warren of rooms, added to and altered over three centuries. The street is named after Sir George Downing who built the houses in it at the end of the 17th century. It was at No.14, then part of the Colonial Office, that Wellington and Nelson are said to have met for the first and only time in their lives. The Duke recognized Nelson from his pictures, but Nelson was so impressed by this unknown man's conversation that he briefly left the room to inquire who he was.

The building of the present Houses of Parliament began in 1840. The House of Lords was first used in 1847 and the House of Commons in 1852. The House of Commons was destroyed during World War II and rebuilt in 1950. The most famous feature is the clock tower popularly known as 'Big Ben' which is strictly the nickname of the bell on which the hours are struck.

Above: *The magnificent interior of the House of Lords' debating chamber was designed by Augustus Pugin in the rich reds and browns he loved. His concern for gothic detail extended to the minutest particular; doorknobs, inkwells and umbrella stands were all especially designed. The centre-piece is the Queen's throne from which she speaks when opening Parliament. In* *front of the throne is the Woolsack, seat of the Lord High Chancellor in the House, a reminder of the days when the wool trade was the chief cause of England's prosperity. In the niches above the throne and between the windows are statues of the 18 barons who persuaded King John to sign the Magna Carta in 1215, a reminder of the traditional power of the aristocracy.*

The bell weighs 13½ tons and was cast in Mears' foundry in Whitechapel in 1858. An earlier bell, cast at Norton near Stockton-on-Tees and nearly lost at sea on its journey to London, proved to be faulty. After only a few months in the tower it developed a crack and had to be broken up. 'Big Ben' was so named after Sir Benjamin Hall who was Commissioner of Works at the time.

The opening of each annual session of Parliament is a great ceremonial occasion, when the Queen drives to Parliament in the Irish State Coach and walks in procession to the House of Lords, where she ascends the throne and delivers a speech, outlining the government's programme for the coming session. The ceremony has changed little since the 16th century and the ritual of the monarch's speech can be traced back to the mid-13th century. Thousands of spectators line the processional route.

Whitehall, running from Trafalgar Square to Parliament Square, is certainly the grandest street in a city which is not noted for its civic planning, and it is one which millions hold in special reverence because of the Cenotaph, the non-denominational memorial to the dead of two World Wars. Now the Cenotaph emerges into prominence on the second Sunday in November when a vast Remembrance Day ceremony is held around it.

Whitehall may be the grandest street but the most regal is the Mall. This broad avenue, flanked by double rows of plane trees, leads from the fore-court of Buckingham Palace to Trafalgar Square. Along its broad surface every Royal procession sets out on its triumphant way.

To the south of the Mall lies St James's Park, one of many for which London is noted and envied. First laid out for Henry VIII as a deer park adjoining Whitehall Palace, it was remodelled on more formal pleasure garden lines for Charles II and, finally, laid out once more very much in its present form for George IV by John Nash. From the delicate modern bridge which crosses the lake there is a most surprising view of London giving, towards Whitehall, the impression of an almost oriental city.

Standing on Westminster Bridge 170 years ago, William Wordsworth composed that often-quoted line: 'Earth has not anything to show more fair'. One wonders whether he would have written it today though he might well have retained that later line: 'A sight so touching in its majesty'.

Right: *Each year on Remembrance Sunday in November the Cenotaph in Whitehall becomes, for two silent minutes, the heart of the Commonwealth when the Queen attends the short but moving ceremony to commemorate the dead of two world wars. The Cenotaph, designed by Sir Edwin Lutyens, was unveiled by King George V in 1920.*

Left: *The members of the Household Cavalry, known as the Life Guards because of their duty protecting the life of the Sovereign, make a colourful display with their distinctive plumed helmets, gleaming armour and magnificently groomed horses as they ride up Constitution Hill. In a more practical uniform they also go overseas on active service.*

Right: *There is some magic ingredient in the evening light that enriches London and transforms her buildings into romantic silhouettes. As seen here, lighting up time brings to Big Ben an impressive dignity.*

Below: *The scale of Constitution Arch at Hyde Park corner is so massive that the sculptor of the horses on top, Adrian Jones, gave a dinner party for eight people inside one of them shortly before finishing them. One of London's smallest police stations is situated inside the arch.*

THE WEST END

alf the world goes shopping in London's 'West End'. Actors and actresses dream about having their names in lights in the 'West End'. People complain when out-of-town restaurants charge 'West End' prices. What exactly is the 'West End' and where is it found?

The Concise Oxford Dictionary is indeed concise about it. 'West End', it says, 'is the richer and more fashionable district of London'. All right in Victorian or Edwardian days, perhaps, when Mayfair, Marylebone and Belgravia housed the rich and fashion was their occupation. But in the more egalitarian days since two World Wars, is one part of London notably richer or more fashionable than another? The two don't necessarily go together any more. Today, 'West End' is more of a feeling and less of a fact. 'West End' is where the shops are. 'West End' is where the theatres are. 'West End' is where the pleasure is. And none of it is very far from Piccadilly Circus, London's traditional centre of gaiety. In the evening, when the theatres open, crowds throng the area.

Traditionally, it is presided over by a cupid-like figure with bow and arrow popularly known as 'Eros'. Visitors to London find it appropriate that Aphrodite's son should symbolize the city's pleasure-seeking centre, so it comes as a suprise to many to learn that 'Eros' is, in fact, part of a memorial fountain erected in 1892 by earnest Victorian admirers of Lord Shaftesbury, a noted philanthropist and social reformer, and that the figure was intended to be not the embodiment of physical love but the Angel of Christian Charity. The remodelling of the Circus gave the opportunity to remove and renovate the famous statue.

Westward from the Circus, Piccadilly stretches as far as Hyde Park Corner where a spacious, grassy but coldly impersonal roundabout, threaded with subways and underpasses, has successfully uncorked one of London's most persistent bottlenecks. Between the two points there is architectural variation that few London streets can outdo: St. James's Church - Christopher Wren's own favourite – tucked away in its cool courtyard; Simpson's store, designed by Joseph Emberton back in 1935; Fortnum and Mason's grown-up grocer's shop with Mr Fortnum and Mr Mason personally striking the hours

Right: *When Inigo Jones built Covent Garden after an Italian tour, residents briefly named their daughters 'Piazza' after the exciting new style. After 300 years of market trading, it has regained continental elegance with its open air cafés, street performers and cosmopolitan crowds.*

Below: *John Nash's Regent Street disappeared for ever in the 1920s, but the Quadrant – the curve that diverts the street into Piccadilly Circus – was part of his plan to give it what a visiting German admirer called its 'peculiar beauty'. This famous street is lined with some of London's finest shops – less strident than Oxford Street, less pricey than Bond Street.*

Left: *Names change but the lights shine
perennially in Shaftesbury Avenue, the central
thoroughfare of London's eating and
entertainment district of Soho. The name Soho
derives from a hunting call, adopted by the Duke
of Monmouth as his rallying cry at the battle of
Sedgemoor in 1685, when Soho Square was
being built where Monmouth House once stood.*

on a Disneyesque clock; Burlington House, home of the Royal Academy of
Arts and many other learned societies, hiding some real charm behind a
pretentious Victorian front; Burlington Arcade, a superior shopping precinct
which, if the shops were not so eminently respectable, might be known as
the 'Top Tourist Trap'; Hatchard's, the famous bookshop, with a façade that
must be virtually unchanged since early Georgian times; the Ritz Hotel, a
piece of Paris in Piccadilly designed by Mewes and Davis whose French
inclination can be seen in many London buildings of the first half of this
century.

Beyond the Ritz, on the south side of Piccadilly, all building ends. Here,
suddenly, is verdant treescape – the Green Park undulating towards Constitution Hill and Buckingham Palace. In this park on 27 April 1749 'an exhibition
of fireworks which in grandeur could not have been surpassed' was held to
celebrate the Peace of Aix-la-Chapelle, and Handel's *Music for the Royal
Fireworks* received its first performance. A contemporary print shows that
what are now the gardens of Buckingham Palace were then part of the park.

From the desert island of Hyde Park Corner, round which the traffic tides
constantly flow, the Duke of Wellington on his favourite charger,
Copenhagen, gazes across Piccadilly towards the building which used to be
known as No.1 London – Apsley House, the Duke's home from 1817 onwards
when he bought it from his brother after his victory at Waterloo. In 1947, the
7th Duke returned Apsley House to the nation and in 1952 it was opened as
the Wellington Museum. Here can be seen many of the exquisite and
fantastic gifts that a relieved Europe showered on its saviour after the defeat
of Napoleon.

Some of the finest pictures in the museum – works by Goya, Velázquez,
Correggio, Rubens, Brueghel, Jan Steen and Jan van der Heyden – were
acquired when Joseph Napoleon's baggage train was captured during the
Spanish campaign. Wellington – very correctly – offered to return the pictures
to Spain, but a grateful Spanish government pointed out that they had come
into Wellington's possession 'by means that are as just as they are honourable' and that he was to keep them.

Park Lane runs north from Hyde Park Corner along the edge of the park.
Today it is a vast carriageway of almost motorway proportions, but in Queen
Anne's reign 'the lane leading from Piccadilly to Tyburn' was described as 'a
desolate by-road'. At Tyburn, close to where the Marble Arch now stands,
Londoners could, until 1783, watch public hangings. Dr Johnson's biog-
rapher, James Boswell, was a regular spectator.

Some of London's most luxurious hotels look out across Park Lane to the
inviting green acres of Hyde Park. After the execution of Charles I, it was
auctioned off to the highest bidder, and realized just over £17,000. John
Evelyn wrote in his diary for 11 April 1653: 'I went to take the aire in Hide Park,
when every coach was made to pay a shilling and horse sixpence by the
sordid fellow who had purchased it of the State'. At the Restoration of the
Monarchy in 1660, all such sales were declared null and void. Hyde Park
again became a Royal park (as it is today) and it was reopened to the public
freely though the king retained the right to 'one half of the pippins or
red-streaks, either in apples or cider, as His Majesty may prefer'.

That famous landmark the Marble Arch effectively signals the western limit
of London's West End. It was designed by John Nash and originally erected,
at a cost of £80,000, at the entrance to Buckingham Palace. The equestrian
statue of George IV, which now stands in Trafalgar Square, was intended to
surmount it. The arch was moved to its present position in 1851.

Above Right: *In 1705 a William Fortnum became footman in Queen Anne's household. A born entrepreneur, one of his jobs was to refill the candelabra and he used to sell off the candle ends to ladies at court. From such a humble beginning, he set up a shop with his friend Mr Mason, selling groceries, and excelled in supplying exotic and high-quality foods and specially packed hampers, something Fortnum's does to this day.*

Left: *In Berwick Street, almost within sight of Piccadilly Circus, is the sort of street market you would expect to find in any country town – stalls lit by naked swinging bulbs, heaped high with every sort and variety of fruit and vegetable. As fascinating as the multi-coloured displays is the cockney banter of the stallholders. Salty epithets are served and returned across the street with the speed and precision of world-class tennis players. The prevailing mood is good humoured but the competition is fierce.*

Right: *Off the north side of Piccadilly, alongside Burlington House, a covered arcade of single storey shops leads through to Burlington Gardens. This is the Burlington Arcade, the most exclusive shopping precinct in London. During shopping hours (it closes after dark) it is full from end to end with tourists, a United Nations of shoppers, magnetized by the opulent displays of cashmeres and cameras, silver, shirts, pewter, ivory, tweeds, linen – 'infinite riches in a little room'. The arcade was built as a bazaar by Lord George Cavendish, afterwards Earl of Burlington, in 1819. It was unworthily refronted in 1911.*

Oxford Street, running east from Marble Arch for close on three km (two miles) is London's most concentrated shopping area, with stores that are household names side by side with newer, specialist shops anxious to get a foot in the door of this golden treasure house. Many of the stores have been in Oxford Street for well over a hundred years. Peter Robinson came down from Yorkshire to open his draper's shop in 1833. William Debenham, from Suffolk, was in business in nearby Wigmore Street even earlier. Marshall went into partnership with Snelgrove in 1848. John Lewis left Peter Robinson's to set up his own in 1864. And Dan H. Evans, a comparative newcomer from Llanelli in Wales, started up in Oxford Street in 1879. But it was in 1909 that Oxford Street first became the nation's – rather than fashionable London's – shopping mecca when Gordon Selfridge came over from Chicago to open his spectacular popular-price store. Not until 1930 did Marks and Spencer, surely the most successful merchandisers of all time, invade Oxford Street, though they had stores in the suburbs as early as 1903.

In Charles II's reign, 'He who then rambled to what is now (1650) the gayest and most crowded part of Regent Street, found himself in solitude, and was so fortunate sometimes as to have a shot at a woodcock.' Regent Street was designed by John Nash to be a triumphal way joining Carlton House, the Prince Regent's palatial Westminster home, with Marylebone Park in the northerly village of Marylebone, now Regent's Park. The building began in 1813 and as Nash had control of the design of all the buildings in the street, there was a continuity of design which made Regent Street one of the most admired architectural developments in Europe. The line of the street remains but all Nash's buildings are gone except at the north end of Portland Place where Park Crescent demonstrates the original Nash style.

These four streets – Piccadilly, Park Lane, Oxford Street and Regent Street – form the periphery of the area known as Mayfair. Though Mayfair is no longer exclusively the home of the wealthy (there is only one private house left in Berkeley Square) it retains an air of affluence – especially in Bond Street, the High Street of Mayfair – 'high' referring to quality and price.

By contrast – and much of London's charm stems from its many contrasts – the area east of Regent Street, on the far side of Golden Square (once a burial pit for the plague victims of 1665), is affluent in a different manner. Soho, as it is called, is one of the most cosmopolitan areas of any city in the world. Members of every race and nationality live and work here, making money mainly out of restaurants and other more dubious establishments. The restaurants are mostly first-class; the bookshops and strip clubs distinctly sleazy. On one side of Soho's main artery – Shaftesbury Avenue – theatres stand almost arm in arm. South of Shaftesbury Avenue, large plush cinemas overlook Leicester Square.

BLOOMSBURY & MARYLEBONE

To many visitors and, indeed, to many Londoners, the district north of Oxford Street – Bloomsbury and Marylebone – is *terra incognita*. A visitor may cross it on his way to Euston Station, or a Londoner may penetrate it minimally on his way to keep an appointment with a specialist in Harley Street but, by and large, the area is left to its own devices, to the satisfaction of its many residents. The Euston Road roars across it from west to east but on either side there is relative calm. Not that the area is without tourist attractions. Within its bounds are Regent's Park, the Zoo, Lord's Cricket Ground, Madame Tussaud's and the Planetarium, the Courtauld Institute Galleries, the Jewish Museum, the Wallace Collection, and – crown jewel of them all – the British Museum. What has given the area its character is the fact that it was a guinea-pig for the ideas of the early town planners and the planning took place in a period during which English architecture experienced its finest flowering – the 18th century.

Bloomsbury, bounded by Euston Road, Gray's Inn Road, High Holborn and New Oxford Street, and Tottenham Court Road, was earlier known as Lomesbury. It was merely a village on the outskirts of London where the King's horses were stabled and his hunting hawks were kept. Writing (in the 19th century) of the neighbourhood in the year 1685, Lord Macaulay, in his *History of England*, says: 'A little way north from Holborn and on the verge of pastures and cornfields, rose two celebrated palaces, each with an ample garden. One of them, then called Southampton House and, subsequently, Bedford House, was removed early in the present century to make room for a new city which now covers with its squares, streets and churches a vast area renowned in the seventeenth century for peaches and snipes. The other, known as Montagu House, celebrated for its furniture and frescoes, was, a few months after the death of Charles II, burned to the ground and was

Above: *Great pacifist Mahatma Gandhi gazes over the regimental ranks of scarlet tulips in Tavistock Square in spring. It is a square rich in associations with the famous; President Nehru planted the copper beech; Dickens lived in Tavistock House (rebuilt by Lutyens in 1953) and Virginia and Leonard Woolf lived at number 52.*

Left: *The Prince Regent's ambitious plans in collaboration with his favourite architect, John Nash, to build a triumphal route from Carlton House to Regent's Park, were never fully consummated. But indications of what might have been achieved are to be seen in Park Crescent, just south of the park, at the top of Portland Place. The plainness of the upper storeys is cleverly contradicted by the ground floor colonnades of twin Ionic columns. Portland Place itself has suffered architectural vandalism over the years, but Park Crescent is a worthy prelude to the park.*

Right: *In Woburn Walk, a short way up the road from Euston station, the Georgian shop fronts with elegant, slim wrought iron balustrades are straight out of the 18th century. They look out on to a paved pedestrian walk full of tubs of flowers. These glimpses of Bloomsbury's Georgian past serve to emphasize what a handsome area it must have been and – in parts – still is.*

Above: *Although midsummer nights are unpredictable in London, the Open-Air Theatre in Regents Park, founded in 1933, has managed to survive and even prosper. It specializes in Shakespeare's more light-hearted plays.*

Below: *London's Moslem population has risen greatly in the past 30 years and although the Moslem, provided he turns towards Mecca, can perform his act of worship wherever he happens to be, he is required to attend a mosque on Fridays to recite prayers in public and hear a sermon. This mosque, adjacent to the Islamic Cultural Centre in Regent's Park, has been built to meet the needs of London's many followers of Mohammed.*

Right: *Do not be misled by this very modern aviary, designed by Lord Snowdon: the London Zoo has been in Regent's Park since 1828, two years after the founding of the Zoological Society of London by Sir Stamford Raffles (of Singapore fame) 'for the advancement of zoology, and the introduction and exhibition of subjects of the animal kingdom, alive or in a state of preservation.' Since then literally millions of people have visited the Zoo or its country branch at Whipsnade, north of London.*

succeeded by a more magnificent Montagu House.

Macaulay's 'new city' was, of course, Bloomsbury and 'the edifice more magnificent still' the newly built British Museum. The architectural style of Bloomsbury blossoms fully in Bedford Square, developed in 1775 by the Duke of Bedford who owned most of the land in the district. The square was designed as an entity by Thomas Leverton, later an unsuccessful contestant for the rebuilding of Regent Street. As is sometimes the way with architects, he reserved the best of the houses – No. 1 Bedford Square – for his own.

Bedford Square is happily so little altered that its present appearance gives a good idea of what much of Bloomsbury must have looked like in its heyday. Signs of the area's architectural good manners can also be seen in Blooms-bury Square, Gordon Square, Tavistock Square and Bedford Row, but much that gave Bloomsbury its town-planned appearance has been pulled down, and when juggernauts like the Senate House of London University, with its 64m (210 ft) tower, are dropped into the heart of a Georgian town, balance is inevitably lost.

The British Museum is vast. Its treasures have been accumulating steadily since 1753 when Sir Hans Sloane, the physician, bequeathed his valuable collection of books and manuscripts to the nation for a payment of £20,000 to his executors. People have been known to spend their lives there; others to 'do' it in a couple of hours. What a boon it must be to the 42,000 students of London University. University College – the heart of the University – was founded in 1826 to provide 'literary and scientific education at a moderate expense'. The architect of the college, which is in Gower Street, was William Wilkins, who also designed the National Gallery. It was opened in 1828, just 18 months after the laying of the foundation stone.

Just as Bloomsbury developed around Bedford Square, so Marylebone's growth may be said to have stemmed from Cavendish Square. The project was begun in 1715 when Lady Henrietta Harley, daughter of the Duke of Newcastle, inherited her father's Marylebone estate. Her husband, Lord Harley (later to become 2nd Earl of Oxford and Mortimer) was a wealthy man and able to enlist the help of the very best architects and builders. For his architect he chose James Gibbs who later designed the church of St Martin-in-the-Fields. Building began in 1717 but three years later the South Sea Bubble, the notorious financial scandal, hit Lord Harley very severely and the development of Cavendish Square came almost to a halt. An even stronger influence on the development of Marylebone was that of the Prince Regent (later George IV) and his favourite architect, John Nash. The Prince dreamed of a triumphal way linking his home in the Mall with a new palace that Nash would build for him in Regent's Park. The palace never materialized and though Nash did build Regent Street, it was not on the grand scale originally planned. He pressed on with the Regent's Park project, transforming the featureless heath of Marylebone into the handsome park we know today, studding its surroundings with opulent terraces and villas.

Far right: *The supreme example of Victorian self-confidence and conviction that the railway age would last for ever is St Pancras, the cathedral of all railway termini, and the subject of continuing architectural controversy. The saint himself – St Pancras – is rarely discussed but he was a young Phrygian nobleman who suffered martyrdom at Rome under the Emperor Diocletian for his adherence to the Christian faith. Because he was only 14 when he died he is generally known as the patron saint of children. The railway station named after him was built between 1868 and 1874 by Sir George Gilbert Scott. The front on to Euston Road was the 600-room Midland Grand Hotel adapted from Sir George's rejected plan for a new Foreign Office. As the railway dream faded the hotel reverted to the purpose of the original design as offices.*

Right: *Many people are discouraged from visiting the British Museum by the* embarras de choix *that confronts them. Shall they make for the Elgin Marbles? The Assyrian and Babylonian collections or the two surviving copies of Magna Carta? As at all banquets it is necessary to be abstemious or suffer the penalty of indigestion. The British Museum's treasures have been accumulating steadily since 1753 when Sir Hans Sloane, the physician, bequeathed his valuable collection of books and manuscripts to the nation. The British Museum was established in Montagu House, to be replaced a hundred years later by the present formidable building.*

KENSINGTON & CHELSEA

Kensington and Chelsea add up to the smallest of the inner London boroughs, though it is clearly one of the wealthier and more fashionable, and the Greater London Council blue plaques, marking the former homes of the famous, are thick on the walls.

Up to the middle of the 19th century, Kensington was little more than an overgrown village in the county of Middlesex. In 1899 it became a London borough and the council presented an address to Queen Victoria asking her to confer some special distinction on the newly created borough to perpetuate the memory of her birth in Kensington Palace. At that time Kensington Palace was technically within the London boundary, but an adjustment was hastily made to transfer it from Westminster to Kensington. Before Kensington's request could be granted, the Queen had died, but her wishes in the matter were well known and King Edward VII conferred the title 'Royal' on the borough in 1901, making it England's third royal borough – the other two being Kingston-upon-Thames and Windsor.

Though officially recognized in 1901, Kensington's ascent to royal status had been going on for many years. In 1698, William III, whose asthma was exacerbated by the fogs and fumes of Whitehall, bought Nottingham House, one of the finest properties in the village, for £18,000. Sir Christopher Wren was given the task of converting it into Kensington Palace, which he did under the watchful and often critical eye of Queen Mary who, during the alterations, stayed at Holland House, much of which is still to be seen in Holland Park.

Five years after the royal couple had moved into Kensington Palace, Queen Mary died of smallpox and, eight years later, William III fell from his horse while riding at Hampton Court, developed pneumonia and died at the early age of 51, to be succeeded by his sister-in-law Anne. Queen Anne, with the aid of 100 gardeners, had the grounds laid out in a less formal, more English style and commissioned Nicholas Hawksmoor (though some say it was Wren) to build the orangery, a delightful feature of the gardens. Twelve years later, Queen Anne was dead and George I hastened from Hanover to claim the throne. He made extensive alterations to the palace and once again the gardens were re-designed more to the Hanoverian taste. At this time they covered more than 120 hectares (300 acres) of what is today Kensington Gardens, including the Round Pond. George II allowed selected members of Society to use the gardens but, at the beginning of the 19th century, George III opened the gardens to 'respectably dressed' members of the public and they have remained open ever since.

Kensington Palace has an astonishingly rural outlook towards the Long Water, as the upper part of the Serpentine is called. The horse ride known as Rotten Row began life as an 'infamously bad' coach road from Kensington Palace to Whitehall – the *route du roi*. Englishmen always have managed to massacre the French language!

The southern fringe of Kensington Gardens, curtained with blossom and carpeted with daffodils in the spring, borders the busy part of the Kensington Road known as Kensington Gore which separates the Albert Memorial from the Albert Hall – a part of London dedicated to the memory of Queen Victoria's much mourned husband, Albert, the Prince Consort who died in 1861. The site of the Albert Memorial is a few hundred yards west of the scene of the Great Exhibition of 1851 in which Albert had played such an outstanding part. The Royal Albert Hall, which had a shaky start (there was a financial panic in 1866) was ultimately paid for by the sale of 999-year leases of seats and boxes. It was opened by Queen Victoria on 29 March 1871 and is probably best known today as the home of the BBC's annual season of promenade concerts.

Right: *As big businesses and rich foreigners move into London's large houses, the families they were built for vie for the secluded yet central charms of the 600 mews streets. Where, in the past, horses were stabled and grooms slept overhead, flower baskets and statuary now embellish the street. Kynance Mews, shown here, is a typical example with its cobbles, arch, and lack of pavements.*

Below: *When Harrods burnt down in 1883, Charles Harrod apologised to customers that deliveries would be delayed for 'a day or two'. It is this punctilious service, and the massive range of products, that make Harrods one of the top department stores in the world. With 210 departments including kennels, a funeral service, library and portrait gallery, it can literally cater for your every need.*

Just behind the Albert Hall, the Royal Horticultural Society had a 9 hectare (22 acre) garden until 1882. Their present gardens are at Wisley in Surrey, but they continue to hold their main annual flower show in the Borough – in the grounds of the Royal Hospital, Chelsea. This handsome range of buildings, designed by Wren, was commissioned by Charles II as a home for veteran and invalid soldiers. It still houses more than 500 'Chelsea pensioners' and their scarlet dress uniform heavy with medals and years is a familiar sight. The army's own splendid new museum is only a stone's throw away.

King's Road, running west from Sloane Square, was originally a private track crossing the orchards and market gardens of Chelsea and Fulham and reserved for the convenience of Charles II on his amorous outings to Sandford Manor House, where Nell Gwyn lived, and to Hampton Court, where several other of his mistresses were likely to be found. Today it is one of the most cosmopolitan streets in London and a show place for all that is new, eccentric and non-conformist.

A most prominent feature of Kensington is the museums – the Victoria and Albert, the Science Museum, the Natural History Museum and the Geological Museum. Their solid Victorian exteriors give no hint of the excitement and stimulation within.

Above: *London's squares provide quiet areas for busy workers to sit, eat lunch and enjoy the sunshine, or for tourists to rest their aching feet. Sloane Square is an unusual example with its paved surface, fully matured plane trees, and fountain, all somewhat rare in the smaller London squares. Around the bronze nude in the centre of the fountain are carved reliefs of Charles II dallying with Nell Gwynn. The glass modernity of the Peter Jones store dominates one side, appropriate for a square that marks the beginning of the King's road.*

Left: *For nearly 300 years the Chelsea Pensioners have been residents of Chelsea, and recognized all over London by the scarlet (in summer) and blue (in winter) uniforms which they have inherited from those worn by the Duke of Marlborough's troops in the 18th century. The grounds of their home – the Royal Hospital – are generally open for one week in the year (in May), when they are the scene of one of the most colourful events of the London season: the Royal Horticultural Society's Chelsea Flower Show.*

213

Left: *Between them Hyde Park and Kensington Gardens make up 250 hectares (616 acres) of precious land right in the heart of London – land which no-one since Cromwell has ever tried to dispose of. Kings and Queens from time to time annexed portions of Kensington Gardens for their private enjoyment, but for nearly 200 years Londoners have had free access to both parks. Queen Caroline, wife of George II, ordered the damming of the Westbourne stream to form the Serpentine – the distinctive elongated stretch of water that is shared between the two parks. Above the Serpentine Bridge it is known as the Long Water. From it the Round Pond in Kensington Gardens is fed.*

Below: *Anyone may ride in Rotten Row – the anglicized 'route du roi' – but 'Galloping is not allowed'. By utilizing every yard of horseride in the Park and then crossing over Hyde Park Corner to the horse tracks in Constitution Hill and the Mall, it is possible to trot for about 6 km (nearly 4 miles) right in the heart of London without covering the same ground twice.*

Below: *Any similarity between the Albert Memorial and St Pancras station is not coincidental: Sir George Gilbert Scott was the architect of both. The Albert Memorial he regarded as his 'most prominent work'. Its prominence is undeniable – a 53 m (175 ft) pinnacle of Victorian exuberance and genuine respect for Prince Albert, contributed to by the outstanding sculptors of the day. The memorial was erected out of public subscriptions and with the surplus a start was made on the Albert Hall on the other side of Kensington Gore. It is a vast amphitheatre, seating 8,000 people in three tiers of boxes and a balcony. Its acoustic properties were something of a joke for many years (the Albert Hall echo was very persistent) but modern technology seems to have overcome the problem satisfactorily.*

THE THAMES

The Thames may not rate a place in the list of the world's greatest rivers, but it is often one of England's loveliest, and for many centuries, its busiest.

To many people today the Thames seems to be sadly under-used. The London docks are in decline, trade having moved towards the estuary, to Tilbury and beyond. The wide water highway still cuts through the centre of the City but a passing boat is now something to stop and stare at. The ships that are moored in central London are now mostly museums. However, all is far from lost. Just over a century ago the Thames was an open sewer, fish were driven from its putrid waters, cholera and typhoid were rampant. Today its waters are relatively pure. Nearly 100 different species of fish have returned to the river. It is firmly expected that salmon will once again thrive in it as they did in the 19th century when more than 400 fishermen between Westminster and Deptford made a living from the Thames. Then, the noblemen who occupied the great houses along what is now the Strand, regularly swam for pleasure in the river, and Lord Byron refers in a letter to the occasion on which he swam the five kilometres (three miles) from Lambeth to London Bridge.

In the 19th century, the great growth of London's population and its spreading industrialization became too much for the Thames: sewage and pollution swamped it, and drastic action had to be taken. A huge sewage system for London was incorporated in the Victoria Embankment, completed in 1865 and involving the reclamation of 15 hectares (37 acres) from the river. Today London's sewage system depends on Thames water to maintain its flow, and almost half of London's fresh water requirements – about 400 million gallons a day – are met from the Thames.

Between the magnificent Tudor palace of Hampton Court, where it enters Greater London, and Kingston, the Thames is still an up-country river, alive in summer with small craft, bordered with houseboats that rock gently to the swell of Oxford-bound launches. Kingston-upon-Thames (to give it its full title) is a royal borough, the crowning place of Saxon kings – and the town has a coronation stone to prove it. Until 1730, Kingston Bridge was the first road crossing above London Bridge.

At Teddington, with its lock, the river dives over its last down-stream weir - an average flow of 1,000 million gallons a day – and the tidal river begins, its twice daily rise and fall providing a gentle reminder that the cruel sea is not far away. Past Strawberry Hill and Twickenham, the river flows through the elegant arches of Richmond's humpback bridge, the oldest still spanning the river in London. It was built in 1774 but widened in 1937.

Adjoining Richmond's Old Deer Park (once part of Richmond Palace where Elizabeth I died in 1603) Kew Gardens welcome anyone who cares to take the poet's advice to 'Go down to Kew in lilac time'.

By Chiswick bridge there are acres of sports grounds followed, appropriately, by the famous Mortlake brewery which dominates the finish of one of the thirstiest events in the sporting calendar: the Oxford and Cambridge boat race. From here to Putney Bridge, where the race begins, the winding 6.8km (4¼ miles) of river is lined with landmarks that are familiar to those who follow this annual event: Barnes Bridge, Harrods Repository, Chiswick Eyot, Hammersmith Bridge, Fulham Football Ground, the Mile Post and Putney Bridge itself.

Up to 1884, when the present bridge was built, Putney Bridge was a constant object of criticism and complaint, forcing one visitor to write: 'The decayed and apparently dangerous state of Putney Bridge, an ugly, black structure of timber with no feature to recommend it, cannot fail to disgust the observer'. The scene is very different today.

Above: *So much of the Thames in London has been embanked or industrially developed that it is cheering to come across a stretch that must look much as it has done for the past 200 years – a stretch of the north bank below Kew Bridge known as Strand-on-the-Green. Here, a collection of smallish houses of mixed styles and periods face boldly on to the river, separated from what would seem to be inevitable flooding by nothing more defensive than a narrow, willow-bordered footpath.*

Left: *Richmond, the only borough with land on both sides of the river, is a peaceful place to come for a pint on a summer's evening. It is well supplied with pubs, many being built to supply the needs of the Thames's watermen, thirsty after the prodigious pull up the river from London.*

Beyond the Hurlingham Club, where polo was played until the last war, both banks of the Thames have become industrialized but, hidden away near the chimneys of Lots Road on the north bank, it is said to be possible to find the remains of Sandford Manor House, where Nell Gwyn lived.

At Chelsea, the elegant terrace houses of Cheyne Walk face the river. Around here the Greater London Council's blue plaques that mark the former homes of the famous are numerous: Mark Twain, Leigh Hunt, Oscar Wilde, Captain Scott, Mrs Gaskell, the Brunels, George Eliot and Thomas Carlyle among them.

The Thames is now approaching the heart of London and once through Lambeth Bridge the full panorama of the city comes into view, from the dominating Victoria Tower of the House of Lords, down river to St Paul's, now dwarfed by the hectic, vertical architecture that has fractured the old city skyline, round past the concrete complex of the South Bank, past County Hall, the headquarters of the Greater London Council. The high block of St Thomas's Hospital still gives its patients one of the finest views of London and a front row seat for Big Ben's hourly concerts. The great sweep ends at one of London's least appreciated treasures: Lambeth Palace, the mediaeval home of the Archbishop of Canterbury.

This is the Thames that did duty as the main street of London for 1,000 years. This was the scene of constant processions and pageantry, but in recent years, apart from the funeral of Sir Winston Churchill and the Queen's Silver Jubilee River Pageant and celebrations to mark the opening of the Thames Barrier in 1984, the Thames has not taken much part in the nation's ceremonial events. Ever since the middle of the 17th century, water traffic dwindled as road transport improved. Yet, as late as 1820, when George IV came to the throne, there were still 3,000 wherries plying for hire on the Thames, while the highroad alternative – the Hackney carriage – numbered only 1,200 throughout the whole of London. Back in the 16th century there were said to be 40,000 watermen on the river between Windsor and Gravesend.

From the Tower to Hampton Court, 23 road, rail and foot bridges span the Thames, many of them within a few hundred yards of each other. Until 1730, London Bridge was the only route across the river below Kingston-upon-Thames, and there was intense opposition from the City of London when it was suggested that a further bridge should be built at Putney. However, one was finally built there in 1730.

Some 10,000 tons of relatively modern history is firmly anchored offshore between London Bridge and Tower Bridge – H.M.S. *Belfast*, the only major British warship of World War II that is still afloat – and it is a sobering thought

Below: *In accordance with a 600 year old tradition, all the swans on the Thames belong either to the Sovereign or to the Vintners or the Dyers, two of the City's livery companies. Each July, teams under three Swan Herdsmen set off on a week's trip up as far as Henley to catch, identify and mark their respective birds, except for those of the Sovereign, which are left unmarked. The expedition is known as Swan Upping.*

Above: *The Thames barrier which lies between Greenwich and Woolwich, 12 miles out of London. Built in 1983 at the cost of £600 million, it was designed to protect London from the flood tides which frequently cause serious damage and could kill thousands. The gates lie in sills on the bottom of the river, to be raised by the machinery shown if a flood occurs.*

Right: *For one Saturday in early April, members of Oxford and Cambridge become fiercely partisan as the Boat Race is rowed between Putney and Mortlake bridges. Others watch more impartially, hoping for excitements like the 1912 race when both boats sank. Here, an increasingly familiar scene as Oxford pull ahead to win.*

to realize that a warship less than 40 years old is now only useful as a museum. She is, in fact, as important a representative of her times as H.M.S. *Victory* is of the Napoleonic wars.

Below Tower Bridge, beyond the Pool of London, dockland, once the busiest port in the world, became sadly inactive as shipping found more seaward ports more convenient. The scenery is flattish, enlivened here and there by an ancient pub like the Prospect of Whitby, or a handsome riverside church. A major redevelopment is planned, including factories, housing, an airport, museum and sports centre. Like all good theatrical impresarios, Father Thames keeps his big number for the grand finale – the magnificent spectacle of Greenwich. A combined operation by several architects – Christopher Wren, Nicholas Hawksmoor, John Webb, James Stewart and John Vanbrugh – built the Greenwich Hospital, now the Royal Naval College, over a number of years. Inigo Jones designed the delightful Queen's House, built in 1616 for Anne of Denmark, James I's queen. She died three years later and the house was finally completed for Henrietta Maria by Charles I. It was added to by John Webb in 1662. The College, the Queen's House, the

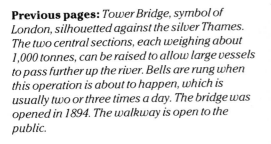

Previous pages: *Tower Bridge, symbol of London, silhouetted against the silver Thames. The two central sections, each weighing about 1,000 tonnes, can be raised to allow large vessels to pass further up the river. Bells are rung when this operation is about to happen, which is usually two or three times a day. The bridge was opened in 1894. The walkway is open to the public.*

Right: *In 1870, it was estimated, London contained 100,000 tramps, 30,000 paupers, 16,000 criminals and 20,000 public houses – one for every 150 men, women and children in the city. Right through Queen Victoria's reign, widely regarded as a period of prosperity and propriety, poverty and drunkenness were the twin cankers of working-class society. The London pubs, disparagingly known as gin palaces, had a most unwholesome reputation, not only for drunken debauchery but also as the haunts of criminals and every kind of vice. In the Thames-side area of Wapping High Street alone there were 36 public houses and taverns with names such as North American Sailor, Ship and Punchbowl and Prospect of Whitby. Smuggling was their undercover trade and most of them were forced to close, but the Prospect of Whitby has survived and become eminently respectable.*

National Maritime Museum, the *Cutty Sark* and *Gypsy Moth*, all of which front the Thames at Greenwich, add up to an enthralling down-Thames expedition from London.

But for the Thames, there would be no London: a fact of life that outsiders have quickly had to learn. When King James I, fresh from Scotland, demanded that the City of London should lend him £20,000, the then Lord Mayor told him that they could not. 'Then I will compel you to', said the king. 'Sire,' said the mayor firmly, 'neither you nor anyone can compel us.' To which the king retorted angrily, 'Then I'll ruin you and your city for ever. I'll remove my courts of law, my court itself and my parliament to Winchester or Oxford and make a desert of Westminster; and then what will become of you?' The Lord Mayor replied quietly, 'May it please Your Majesty, you are at liberty to remove yourself and your courts wherever you please; but, sire, there will always be one consolation to the merchants of London: your majesty cannot take the Thames with you.'

Above: *Two Thames sailing barges, once busy coastal traders, now mainly privately owned pleasure boats, pass Greenwich in the annual barge race.*

Right: *Moored opposite the Tower of London, just upstream from Tower Bridge, is the only surviving major warship of World War II – HMS Belfast, built in 1939 at the famous Harland & Wolff yard in Belfast, due to be scrapped after 30 years active service, but saved by the HMS Belfast Trust which stepped in to buy her for the nation. Today she is a floating museum, preserving as far as possible the working atmosphere of a ship that took part in the sinking of the* Scharnhorst *off the North Cape of Norway, bombarded the D-Day beaches of Normandy, served in Korean waters and was finally the flagship of Britain's Far Eastern fleet.*

THE SOUTH BANK

C entral London south of the Thames, the strip lying between Vauxhall Bridge and Tower Bridge, has come to be known as the South Bank. Tourists observe it from the opposite side of the river but do not often visit it except when they cross to the Festival Hall or the National Theatre. In addition to its known attractions it contains some evocative glimpses of old London – streets of Dickensian gloom alternating with rows of squat, friendly homes, though development will soon transform the area for the better.

The South Bank isn't a place in the accepted sense of the word yet it has a strong sense of community. Hundreds of years of being on the 'wrong side of the river' has bred in its people a cheerful pugnacity that is the mark of the south Londoner. They know that Lambeth and Camberwell have little in common with Mayfair and Marylebone, but they know to which they would rather belong.

Moving upstream, just before Waterloo Bridge, one is confronted by the all too solid concrete hull of the new National Theatre. This monument to persistence had its foundation stone laid in Kensington more than 50 years ago. Like the Flying Dutchman it seemed doomed to sail in limbo until, largely thanks to the Greater London Council who donated the site, it finally made harbour beside the Thames. And what a splendid ship it has turned out to be with its three auditoriums and its totally new attitude to theatre-going. Instead of merely coming to the theatre, watching the performance and going home again, the National Theatre audience is invited to come early and stay late; wander around the lushly-carpeted complex; eat and drink on the terraces or in the foyers; enter into discussions with the actors; be entertained by strolling musicians and pop groups; and generally become part of the show. It seems to be an attitude that is working well and one that should greatly contribute to the South Bank resurgence in spite of the theatre's lofty, tower-block neighbour, London Weekend Television, whose aim must surely be to keep the folks at home.

The South Bank resurgence really dates back to the decision to hold the 1951 Festival of Britain (celebrating the centenary of the famous 1851 Exhibition) on what was virtually derelict land between Waterloo Bridge and County Hall. As its contribution to the Festival, the then London County Council (now Greater London Council) built the Royal Festival Hall, an object of much controversy in its day, but now acknowledged as a landmark in London's postwar architecture and a triumph of internal planning and acoustic engineering. In nearly 30 years since its opening, the Royal Festival Hall has provided Londoners – and millions of London visitors – with a rich musical diet. At lunch-time visitors can enjoy free music and exhibitions.

Between the Royal Festival Hall and Waterloo Bridge a further concrete complex has taken what some people might describe as shape: the Queen Elizabeth Hall for smaller concerts (the Royal Festival Hall seats 3,000), the Purcell Room for recitals and the Hayward Gallery where a series of exhibitions is arranged by the Arts Council of Great Britain. In spite of their austere exteriors, all these buildings are warm and comfortable within, and offer the visitor a variety of performances and exhibitions.

To celebrate Queen Elizabeth II's 1977 Silver Jubilee, most of the vacant land between the Royal Festival Hall and County Hall has been transformed into an imaginative garden with play space for children.

County Hall, the dominant headquarters of the Greater London Council, is relatively modern. It was designed by Ralph Knott who died four years before the main block was completed in 1933. More blocks have been added since to cope with the increasing size of London and the growing responsibilities of a council whose annual budget amounts to some £2,000 million. To the

Right: *London's South Bank shuffles every card in the architectural pack from the aggressive concrete parapets of the Festival Hall complex to the faded Victorian brickwork façades of deserted riverside warehouses. The Thames, in the centre of London, turns through a complete right-angle totally confusing most people's sense of direction. St Paul's Cathedral which here seems to be so much part of the picture, is in fact on the north bank of the river.*

Below: *In 20 years the National Theatre has amply justified its name: it has successfully revived neglected classics, commissioned new works, tackled masked Greek tragic trilogies and medieval mystery cycles, among others, and adapted for the stage works as diverse as 'Hiawatha' and 'Lark Rise'. Its three theatres allow it both the razzamatazz of a Hollywood musical and the intimacy of a one-man show.*

Above: *There is a move afoot to release Southwark Cathedral from its dwarfing surroundings and let in light and air to a building whose exterior is worthy of an uncluttered view. Southwark developed around the southern end of the first ever bridge across the Thames and there was a church on the cathedral site in the first years of the 12th century. This Norman church was burned in 1212 and the church built in its stead was one of the first in England to be designed in the new Gothic style.*

Far right: *Preserved with care, as befits the last of its kind, the George Inn, Southwark is one of the most popular stopping places for organized tours of London; there are not many monuments that serve a pint of beer to the onlooker. The inn's uniqueness is its galleried courtyard where the coaches from Dover and Canterbury would stop to set down their passengers and change horses. Built in 1676 after a great fire had destroyed much of Southwark, a large part of the original inn was demolished in 1889.*

Right: *The fine Tudor gateway, built by Cardinal Morton in 1490 is, apart from a glimpse of the Lollards' Tower, about as much of Lambeth Palace as most Londoners ever see; it is the residence and office of the Archbishop of Canterbury. The gardens through the gate are part of the Museum of Garden History, administered by the Tradescant Trust, a name recalling the family of early botanists and zoologists who lived here in the 17th century.*

visitor, the interior of County Hall presents miles of highly polished corridors flanked by regiments of doors. Outside, at the southern approach to Westminster Bridge, stands the Coade stone lion that had to be evacuated from the Festival of Britain site in 1951. It is not an aggressive beast but it does, perhaps, serve to remind the people of London on the other side of the bridge that much of their welfare is determined by the Greater London Council here on the southern bank.

Near the eastern end of Lambeth Bridge the brick gateway built by Archbishop Morton in 1495 marks the entrance to Lambeth Palace, the London home of Archbishops of Canterbury for close on 800 years. The extent of the Palace and its grounds indicate the almost regal splendour in which earlier archbishops lived, with their private armies and shoals of retainers – in marked contrast to the comparative austerity of the present archbishop's household.

Southwark, which surrounds the southern approach to London Bridge, was the first area of development south of the river. Beyond it were scattered villages, mere country cousins, some with an excellent view of the growing city across the water.

Playhouses were not permitted in the City of London so Bankside saw the establishment of some of London's first theatres and here Shakespeare lived and worked. He had a ten per cent interest in the Globe Playhouse which was burnt to the ground in 1613, but by then Shakespeare had returned to Stratford-upon-Avon and was not financially involved in the loss.

There is a tradition that Sir Christopher Wren lived in a house on Bankside when St Paul's Cathedral was being built after its destruction in the fire of 1666. If the tradition is true, Cardinal's Wharf, a house that is claimed to have been his, was in an ideal position as it would have given Wren a wide and uninterrupted view of his work. It is a pleasant 17th century house next door to that of the Provost of Southwark Cathedral.

Southwark Cathedral's square, pinnacled tower is a famous landmark in south-east London. It began life as the Priory of St Mary Overie – meaning 'over the river'. After the dissolution of the monasteries it served as Southwark's parish church and was renamed St Saviour's. It was made a cathedral with the double dedication of St Saviour and St Mary Overie only in 1905. Though architecturally very mixed, it is a building of considerable charm and character. There is the inevitable memorial to William Shakespeare (he was buried, of course, at Stratford-upon-Avon) and also to his lesser known brother Edmund, an actor who died at the early age of 27 and is buried beneath the choir. The Harvard Chapel, rebuilt in 1907, commemorates John Harvard, the founder of Harvard University.

COCKNEY LONDON & THE EAST END

The church of St Mary-le-Bow in Cheapside is one of Sir Christopher Wren's most splendid churches – especially the pinnacled square tower supporting the pillared rotunda with its slender spire. Within this tower hangs a chime of 12 bells including one – the Great Bell of Bow – whose sonorous boom is said to have recalled the young Dick Whittington from Highgate, ultimately to become London's most celebrated Lord Mayor. But there is another legend connected with these bells (they crashed to the floor of the tower during the *Blitz* and have been re-cast from the original metal) and that is the belief that to be a true Cockney you must have been born within their sound. The derivation of the word Cockney is obscure, but it has come to be applied to the people of London living mainly to the east of the city – a special kind of person, born and bred of a long line of cheerful, quick witted, gregarious, independent people who have lived hard and laboured hard in an often inhospitable environment.

London's East End (in contrast to its fashionable counterpart the West End) does not feature much in the guide books though, to the sociologist, it teems with interest. In around 40 years since the end of World War II it has experienced probably more – and certainly more fundamental – changes than any other part of London.

Sadly the London costermongers are a dying race, for it is they who have always been the core of Cockney London. In the 19th century this irrepressible band of highly independent, mobile traders was said to number nearly 40,000. Nothing but their tough, cynical good humour and grim determination (as the *Blitz* was later to prove) could have kept them going in the face of the grinding poverty and discouragement of life in the East End of those times. They lived – or, rather existed – as close as they could to the great London markets and dockland merchants who supplied their stock-in-trade. Their day began with the opening of Smithfield or Billingsgate or Covent Garden long before dawn when they would load up their barrows for the day's trading. From then on, probably without a proper meal and often until nearly midnight, they would tramp the streets calling their wares and selling in pennyworths to people often poorer than themselves. Sometimes, by the day's end, the coster would find that his takings did not cover the cost of his often perishable stock which he had to dump at a loss. Before he could stock up for the next day he would have to borrow from the moneylender and pay an exorbitant rate of interest. The pawnbrokers did a roaring trade and, to the mortification of the reformers, so did the pubs.

But Cockney optimism persisted – as their taste in amusements demonstrated: the singing in the pubs; the robust music halls (there were 400 in London alone at the end of the 19th century); the boisterous bank holiday outings to Hampstead Heath, Epping Forest or the Crystal Palace; the occasional day trip to the seaside; the rare working holiday hop-picking in Kent.

Cockneys are a gregarious people and, as such, they were extremely tolerant of the immigrants from the north of England, from Ireland and from Europe at a time when London was expanding at a dizzy pace. The construction of the London docks, the railway termini, roads, houses, waterworks and sewage systems brought unskilled labourers and the unemployed flooding into the eastern suburbs in their thousands. Writing of the docks in the 1850s, Henry Mayhew, whose book *London Labour and the London Poor* is a classic of its kind, said:

'Those persons who are unable to live by the occupation to which they have been educated can obtain a living there without any previous training. Hence we find men of every calling labouring at the docks. There are decayed and bankrupt master butchers, master bakers, publicans, grocers, old soldiers,

229

Right: *When St Katharine's Dock was built in 1828 by Thomas Telford, to make room for it, 11,000 people were evicted without compensation. Now, after years of disuse, it is the first of London's docks to be given a facelift. The Ivory House, a former warehouse, has been converted into a row of tourist-attracting shops with offices and apartments above. The old dock basin which used to house salt-caked cargo ships is now the mooring place for smart yachts and cruisers.*

Below: *A relic of a bygone age still lingers on in the East End. The rag and bone man, who may equally be an 'any-old-iron' man, spreads his net wide, working the inner suburbs or, as here, 'up west'. He performs a useful service for the London housewife, taking away old mangles or worn out gas fires that are otherwise hard to dispose of. He is a shrewd buyer and there are few objects that he can't find a market for.*

Above: *Wapping, thanks to authors like Charles Dickens, Sax Rohmer and Edgar Wallace, has a sinister sound. Here in their novels you find bodies floating in the Thames, heroes trapped in flooded basements, and opium dens and smugglers' hideouts in every deserted warehouse.*

old sailors, Polish refugees, broken-down gentlemen, discharged lawyers' clerks, suspended government clerks, almsmen, pensioners, servants, thieves – indeed everyone who wants a loaf and is prepared to work for it.'

'Working for it' brought them in perhaps fourpence an hour and even that depended upon the wind being in the right quarter to enable shipping to sail up the estuary.

Their homes were mostly rudimentary hovels, but the demand produced a supply of cheap, simple terraced houses spreading over the flat and sometimes marshy landscape of Stepney, Poplar, Mile End, Stratford and Bow. Living was inevitably a communal affair but that suited the Cockney temperament. Everyone knew his neighbour. Help was always close at hand.

Out of these close-knit communities grew an organization that is known perhaps more widely overseas than it is in the rest of Britain – the Pearlies who epitomize the generous Cockney spirit. It was begun by a small band of public-spirited costermongers anxious to alleviate the tragic poverty they saw around them but who realized that they could expect help from no-one but themselves.

The familiar all-over pearly dress is said to have been first worn by a roadsweeper named Henry Croft who used to help a group of costermongers in their charitable work. Pearl buttons were the fashionable dress accessory of the period and Croft created something of a sensation when he appeared in the ultimate all-button outfit in one of the charity carnival processions. The fashion spread to other parts of London and it became the custom to select a 'pearly' leader in each borough. The leadership became an hereditary office handed down from father to son – the Pearly Kings and Queens of London. To see them in their splendour, visit the church of St Martin-in-the-Fields on the first Sunday in October for the annual Pearly Harvest Festival. It is unique.

Great changes came to the East End in the aftermath of World War II. Whole streets had been wiped out by enemy bombing and, in an effort to economize on land, tower blocks of flats were built to rehouse the very overcrowded population. Cockneys soon discovered that this new vertical living had none of the advantages of the horizontal system they were accustomed to before: no sitting at the door and chatting on a summer's evening; no friends to call to across the street; no opportunity to observe the comings and goings of the day; no way of keeping an eye on the children at play; no meeting and nattering in the corner shop. All these had been the small change of living that made up for some of the hardships of life. Now they were all gone and only a distant view of London from a fourteenth-floor balcony was offered instead. The warmth and humanity of Cockney street life was something the planners had overlooked.

It is difficult for the tourist to acquire the flavour of the East End. Emerging from the underground at Whitechapel or taking a bus to Wapping, he will find little to attract his eye other than the picturesque riverside pubs like the Prospect of Whitby, a smartened-up smugglers' inn, or the unexpectedly avant-garde exhibitions at the Whitechapel Art Gallery. In Stepney there are some splendid, outsize churches by that master-architect, Nicholas Hawksmoor – St Anne, Limehouse, Christ Church, Spitalfields and St George-in-the-East, Cannon Street Road.

The area around St Katharine's Dock gives perhaps the best and most hopeful picture of what the future of the East End could be. Here, just east of the Tower of London, the run-down dock area has been imaginatively transformed in a joint operation by the Greater London Council and the Taylor Woodrow Property Company. The disused dock is now a yacht haven with sleek and expensive cruisers moored close to brown-sailed Thames barges and the retired Trinity House lightship from the Nore. A large and luxurious hotel looks out towards Tower Bridge while behind the yacht haven is the rather grandiosely named World Trade Centre which turns out to be a block of modern office suites with centralized communication and secretarial services. Around the yacht haven are a restaurant, pub and shop and, on the river bank, a well planned housing-estate of some 700 dwellings.

Left: *The deep charitable instincts of London's Cockneys express themselves in an organization that flourishes more strongly south of the Thames than north – the Pearlies. The Pearly Kings and Queens – the royal families of Cockneydom – usually inherit their titles from their fathers and mothers, but the obligation that goes with the title is to engage in charitable activities, raising money for good causes and seeing that no fellow Cockney is in need. Mindful of their blessings, the Pearlies hold an annual Costermongers' Harvest Festival. Before the war this service took place in the church of St Mary Magdalene in Congreve Street off the Old Kent Road, but the church was destroyed in an air raid and the service has been transferred to St Martin-in-the-Fields, the famous church on the corner of Trafalgar Square. The scene outside St Martin's after the service shows to what lengths the Pearlies go to elaborate their outfits. Coats, skirts and trousers are emblazoned with hundreds of pearl buttons, and hats are adorned with gaily coloured ostrich plumes – sartorial extroversion at its most pungent.*

Below: *One of the landmarks of East London is Tubby Isaacs jellied eel stall in Goulston Street off Aldgate High Street. To visit London without sampling Tubby's jellied eels is like failing to try clam chowder in New England or curry in India. In Victorian times there were more than five hundred such stalls scattered over East London. Casual labourers, many of them unmarried and without homes of their own, had nowhere else to eat. Tastes may change but Tubby is unlikely to go out of business while Cockneys are still around.*

233

OUTER LONDON

The Romans were right if they judged that the wall they built around London would fix its boundaries for a thousand years, for it was not until early mediaeval times that sheer pressure from within forced the growth of settlements outside the wall, and with the bridging of the Thames in the 10th century, London's remaining boundary to the south was breached if not abolished.

As students of Parkinson's Law well know, where there is room for expansion, expansion takes place. So, in the next thousand years of its life, London expanded, slowly at first, but at what we now see was an accelerating pace. The one square mile known as The City has grown into the more than 600 square miles known as Greater London. Six hundred square miles – four hundred thousand acres – one hundred and sixty thousand hectares - however it is expressed, London covers an immense amount of land. From Charing Cross it is possible to travel more than 20km (12 miles) in any direction and still be within the confines of Greater London. In recent years parts of Kent, Surrey, Hertfordshire and Essex and the whole of Middlesex have been sucked into 'the great wen of all' as William Cobbett contemptuously called London in his lifelong crusade against the outward spread of the city. Recent growth has created obvious absurdities: the transfer of Kingston-upon-Thames into Greater London, for instance, means that Surrey's county hall is no longer in Surrey.

Even 15 years ago it would have been unthinkable to speak of someone living in, say, Northwood or Coulsdon as a Londoner, but that's what they are today, as are the people of Bromley, Barnet, Croydon and Harrow. But William Cobbett can rest in peace: the limits of London have now been fixed: the so-called 'green belt' that surrounds it is (so the politicians assure us) inviolable. Even those who hold that big is beautiful now agree that London is big enough. During its lifelong foraging expeditions London has devoured dozens of separate small towns and villages. Most of those near the heart of London have been under the city's domination for so long that they have become suburbanized and lost their individuality. Two notable exceptions to this generalization are Hampstead and Dulwich, one a few kilometres north of the City, the other a similar distance south.

Long before Hampstead became a part of London, wealthy Londoners took to its breezy uplands for the sake of their families' health. In the early part of the 19th century, when Sir Thomas Wilson was Lord of the Manor of Hampstead, a public inquiry revealed that he regarded the heath as his private property and that he was negotiating to sell it as building land for £2½ million. Fortunately the law concerned with common land rights prevented him from doing so and, in 1872, his successor was quite glad to dispose of it for £55,045 to the Metropolitian Board of Works, forerunner to the Greater London Council, who guaranteed public access for all time.

Dulwich owes its preservation to Edward Alleyn, an actor-manager and contemporary of Shakespeare who, in 1605, bought the Manor of Dulwich for £10,000. It was a lot of money for even a successful actor-manager to put his hand on in those days, but as some 600 hectares (1,500 acres) of land went with the manorial rights, it was something of a bargain. Fortunately for

Right: *Kenwood House, surrounded by its lake and 80 hectares (200 acres) of landscaped grounds, was rebuilt for the first Earl of Mansfield in 1767 by Robert Adam. A later owner, Lord Iveagh, who died in 1927, bequeathed it to the nation together with the furniture and his fabulous collection of pictures including works by Rembrandt, Gainsborough, Vermeer, Frans Hals, Reynolds, Raeburn and Van Dyck. Its extensive grounds adjoin Hampstead Heath.*

Right: *When medicinal waters were discovered in Hampstead in the eighteenth century, an obscure out-of-town village quickly grew into a fashionable spa. Holly Hill is one of several steep, tree-lined streets of elegant Georgian houses leading off the busy High Street. Near here, at Grove Lodge, was the home of John Galsworthy, author of 'The Forsyte Saga'. Romney and Keats also lived nearby as did John Constable, whose famous painting of Hampstead Heath may be seen in the Tate Gallery.*

Below: *High Beach in Epping Forest, a beautiful woodland area of ancient hornbeams, sunny glades and rough heath, 26 km north east of London. It is a remnant of the ancient forest of Waltham which once covered all Essex, part of the vast hunting reserves of the Saxon and Norman kings. Loved by the poets John Clare and Tennyson, it has remained ever popular with Londoners for a day out.*

Dulwich, most of the land is still intact. In 1616 Alleyn founded the College of God's Gift from which sprang Dulwich College, Alleyn's School, the almshouses and chapel and the Dulwich College Picture Gallery, one of the finest collections of pictures outside central London. Dulwich Park (now the responsibility of the Greater London Council) was 'presented to the people of London' and opened by Lord Rosebery in 1890. An observer writing about Dulwich over 100 years ago wrote that 'the craving of merchants for suburban residences has done much to alter the aspect of the place, but compared with neighbouring suburbs, it has died hard and not until William Cowper's "opulent, enlarged and still-increasing London" had laid its hands upon it, will Dulwich surrender its individuality'. Dulwich has evidently continued to die very hard for its individuality remains unsurrendered.

Close to Dulwich is another of London's lungs – the Crystal Palace, a name which must puzzle those who do not know its historical significance. When the Great Exhibition of 1851 closed, its main exhibition hall, a unique structure of cast iron and glass designed by Sir Joseph Paxton, was moved from Hyde Park to the slopes of Sydenham and re-erected in a newly created park. It was opened by Queen Victoria in 1854 and became a highly popular centre for entertainment throughout south London and universally known as the Crystal Palace. The building was severely damaged by fire in 1866 and totally destroyed 70 years later in the most spectacular blaze London had seen since the Palace of Westminster fire in 1834. The Crystal Palace park now contains a children's zoo, a concert bowl for outdoor concerts and, beside the lake, a collection of life-size, prehistoric monsters carved in 1853. Part of the park has been given over to the National Sports Centre, one of the best equipped sports stadiums and training centres in Europe.

Thirteen km (eight miles) to the south-east, beyond Bromley, there is a large area of totally rural countryside unaffected by its allegiance to London. In its centre is the village of Downe where Charles Darwin, the scientist, came to live after his marriage to his cousin, Emma Wedgwood, and where he died in 1882. Wild life is to be expected in such unspoilt surroundings, but it is surprising how much and how varied is the wild life much closer to London's centre. The parks are natural habitats for many varieties of birds, but less common breeds, like owls, kestrels and peregrine falcons have been observed in central London, and a pair of black redstarts is known to have raised young in the precincts of Westminster Abbey. The outer suburbs with their stretches of heath and common, their sometimes overgrown cemeteries and their larger gardens attract birds that are familiar throughout southern England, while lakes, reservoirs and flooded gravel pits provide sanctuary for an astonishing variety of water-fowl – teal, wigeon, common pochard, tufted duck, goosander, great crested grebe and coot among them.

Both Bushey Park and Richmond Park have large herds of deer, but wild deer from Kent, Surrey and Hertfordshire often wander across the boundaries into London without asking the Lord Mayor's permission. But then the Lord Mayor has his own herd of deer in Epping Forest, most of which is not in London at all. In 1882 the City Corporation, with commendable foresight, bought 2,500 hectares (6,000 acres) of the forest for £250,000 for the benefit of the people of London. To give west Londoners equal opportunity to enjoy a day in the country, the Corporation also bought Burnham Beeches, the lovely wooded area near Slough.

Richmond Park, in addition to its herd of deer, has badgers, hares, foxes, rabbits and weasels living in the wild only ten km (six miles) from Westminster. It is also a popular area for horse-riding.

In several areas on the outskirts of London country parks are being developed for sport and recreation. Two are at Trent Park, Enfield and in Hainault Forest, adjoining the London boundary near Chigwell. To the west of London, the valley of the river Colne is to become a regional park where sailing, fishing and riding will be catered for.

Throughout London, there are excellent opportunities in parks and public gardens to study – or merely admire – plants and flowers of every kind. The Royal Botanic Gardens, Kew, is world-renowned for its collection but, on the opposite bank of the Thames, at Syon House, home of the Duke of Northumberland, plants can be both admired and bought. In the grounds of this historic house, with its superb rose-garden and collection of fuchsias, there is a garden centre where it is possible to buy everything the ardent gardener could desire. Not very far away, in Richmond Park, the Isabella Plantation puts on a dazzling show of dwarf azaleas and rhododendrons in springtime.

There is so much going on in outer London that its inhabitants do not find it essential to come into central London for their entertainment. Bromley, for example, had its new Churchill Theatre opened a few years back. Richmond and Greenwich have lively theatres of their own. The Fairfield Halls in Croydon's city-like centre welcome most of Europe's finest conductors and their orchestras. You can ice skate at Streatham, Richmond and East London, or roller skate at the Alexandra Palace. Wimbledon and tennis are synonymous. Wembley Stadium has staged both the Olympic games and the World Cup. Open-air concerts are held beside the lake at Kenwood House and at the Crystal Palace Concert Bowl. A quarter of a million people join adult education classes throughout Greater London.

One way and another the outer Londoner need never have a dull moment.

Below: *The Isabella plantation ablaze with rhododendrons in Spring. One of the largest (2,470 acres) of London's parks, Richmond has magnificent oak trees, sports pitches, golf courses and beautiful parkland. Originally the park of Richmond Palace where Henry VIII was born and Richard II feasted 10,000 guests every night, the only part of the old palace left now is the old gate.*

INDEX

Acknowledgements

The publishers thank the following organizations and individuals for their permission to reproduce the photographs in this book.
Malcolm Aird 16 above right and below, 105 above, 157 below, 236 right; K. M. Andrew 39; Peter Baker 18-19, 56, 130, 134, 145 below; Barnabys 168; 6th Marquess of Bath 4-5; John Bethell 69 above, 88 above, 98, 157 above, 194-5, 205; James Betts 48; British Tourist Authority 17, 74, 76, 104 left, 124 above, 148, 149 below, 150, 152-3, 162 below, 164 above, 203 below, 206 above, (Patrick Thurston) 86, 149 above, (A. Woolfit) 77, 104 left; J. Allan Cash 113, 147 below, 196 above; Colorsport 219 right; Michael Crockett 192-3, 195, 204 below, 223 below, 225, 230 left, 231; Daily Telegraph 8 above, (S. Burman) 8 below, (R. Hallman) 85, (John Sims) 9 below, 145 above, (S. Skelly) 126, (Patrick Thurston) 86; James Davis 176, 203, above, 221, 236 left; Elisabeth Photo Library 218; Robert Estall 6, 7 below, 9 above, 96-7, 135 above, 137, 179, 214 below, 217, 219 left; Greg Evans 178, 211, 226;

Derek Forss 84, 97, 122 left, 136; Susan Griggs 35 below, (A. Howarth) 116; Noel Habgood 16 above left, 34, 38, 40-41, 49, 50-51, 67, 78, 79, 118-9, 124-5; Noel Habgood/Derek Widdicombe 177 above; Robert Hallman 156; Robert Harding 204-5; Heart of England Tourist Board 95, 110 above; Neil Holmes 102, 106 left, 120-1, 199, 210; A. F. Kersting 89, 127 above right; Sarah King 188, 189, 202, 223, 226 below, 233; Andrew Lawson 186-7; Raymond Lea 115 below; National Portrait Gallery 24 below; National Trust (J. Bethell) 75, (Vernon Shaw) 93; Northern Ireland Tourist Board 168-9, 170, 171, 172, 172-3, 174-5, 177 below; Octopus Library (Mike Sheil), 29, 30, 35 above, 52, 58 above, 59, 60, 61, (George Wright) 64; The Photo Source/Colour Library International 1, 2-3, 22-23, 42-43, 54, 73, 80 below, 81, 85, 86-7, 92, 96 left, 103, 106 right, 107, 110 below, 112 below, 114 left, 121, 123, 127 left and below right, 128, 129, 132, 133, 138 below, 180 above, 181, 224, 230-1; Photos Horticultural 10, 140 centre; Picturepoint 86 below, 94 below, 99 and inset, 109, 114-5

above, 146, 158-9, 159, 196 below, 237; Pix Photos (G. F. Allen) 88 below; John Rigby 198; Malcolm Robertson 183, 197, 200-1, 209, 222, 227; Clive Sawyer 187, 191, 206 below, 206-7, 220-1, 229, 234-5; Scottish Tourist Board 12, 13, 14-15, 20-21, 24 above, 25, 26-7, 28, 31, 32-33, 36-37, 44-45, 46, 47, 53, 55, 58 below, 62-63; Brian Seed 182, 184-5, 190-1, 216-7, 232-3; John Sims 104 right; Spectrum Colour Library 51 inset, 108, 120, 142-3; Peter Stiles 7 above, 80 above; Patrick Thurston 82; John Timbers 212; Wales Tourist Board 142, 144, 147 above, 164, 158 above right, 161 above, 165; W. J. Webster 19 right; Weed Research Organization 166; West Country Tourist Board 135 below, 138 above, Derek Widdicombe 66, 94 above, 121, 119; Andy Williams 208; Harry Williams 150-1, 160, 160-1, 162 above, 165 below; Trevor Wood 69 below, 100, 101, 105 below, 122 right; Zefa Picture Library (UK) Ltd 68, 70, 71, 72, 90-1, 114-5 below, 131.